25 TOP ROCK CLASSICS

TAB+ = TAB + TONE + TECHNIQUE

This is not your typical guitar tab book. In the new *Tab+* series from Hal Leonard, we provide you guidance on how to capture the guitar tones for each song as well as tips and advice on the techniques used to play the songs.

Where possible, we've confirmed the gear used on the original recordings via new and previously published interviews with the guitarists, producers, and/or engineers. Then we make general recommendations on how to achieve a similar tone, based on that info. You'll note that we do not mention specific modeling or software amps, as those units will typically contain models for the original amps we do cite.

Some of the songs herein will be easy to play even for advanced beginner players, whereas others present a much greater challenge. In either case, we've identified key techniques in each song that should help you learn the song with greater ease.

ISBN 978-1-4803-5086-1

HAL•LEONARD®
CORPORATION
7777 W. BLUEMOUND RD. P.O. BOX 13819 MILWAUKEE, WI 53213

Visit Hal Leonard Online at
www.halleonard.com

25TOPROCK CLASSICS

Performance Notes 4

Bad Motor Scooter 18
MONTROSE

Black and Blue. 33
VAN HALEN

Black or White. 48
MICHAEL JACKSON

Can't You Hear Me Knocking. 57
THE ROLLING STONES

Cocaine 77
ERIC CLAPTON

Everybody Hurts. 87
R.E.M.

Fat Bottomed Girls. 94
QUEEN

Funk #49. 107
JAMES GANG

Hey You 110
PINK FLOYD

I Wanna Be Sedated 119
RAMONES

I'm Going Home 125
TEN YEARS AFTER

Jealous Again 137
THE BLACK CROWES

La Grange 153
ZZ TOP

Long Distance Runaround .162
YES

One Way to Rock 173
SAMMY HAGAR

Only Time Will Tell 188
ASIA

Paradise City 202
GUNS N' ROSES

Rebel Yell 227
BILLY IDOL

Renegade 236
STYX

Separate Ways (Worlds Apart). 245
JOURNEY

Ship of Fools. 258
ROBERT PLANT

Simple Man. 267
LYNYRD SKYNYRD

Spirit of Radio. 274
RUSH

Sultans of Swing 284
DIRE STRAITS

Sunday Bloody Sunday. 297
U2

Guitar Notation Legend 304

PERFORMANCE NOTES TAB. TONE. TECHNIQUE.

By Chad Johnson

"BAD MOTOR SCOOTER"

Montrose

Ronnie Montrose had already amassed an impressive résumé before forming his namesake band. In addition to working as a session guitarist on Van Morrison's *Tupelo Honey* and Herbie Hancock's *Mwandishi*, among others, he played with the Edgar Winter Group on their best-selling *They Only Come Out at Night* (featuring the hit instrumental "Frankenstein"). Although the band Montrose would feature a rotating cast of members through the years, the original lineup featured a young vocalist known at the time as "Sam Hagar." After years of battling cancer, Ronnie tragically committed suicide in 2012 at age 64.

TONE

Ronnie's tone, chops, and melodic sensibility have been praised throughout the years, and he certainly possessed an immediately recognizable tone. Though he wielded a standard Les Paul, his amp of choice was actually a tweed Fender Bandmaster combo with three 10-inch speakers. For the slide part that makes several appearances throughout the song, Montrose added a Big Muff pedal for extra girth.

If you can't spring for a "Lester," a similar humbucker-equipped guitar, such as an SG, should get you close. In the amp department, you can snag a Custom Series '57 Bandmaster reissue for $2,500 if you've got the funds and you're a stickler for authenticity, but most of the tweed reissues, such as the '59 Bassman, should get you very close.

TECHNIQUE

Doing his best Harley impression, Montrose kicks off the tune with Gtr. 1, which is tuned to an alternate version of open G. Strings 5–1 are tuned as they normally would be, but string 6 is tuned *way* down to G, instead of just down to D. With slide in hand, he revs up and down the low strings, waiting for the light to turn green and the band to hit the open road. Remember to center the slide directly over the fret wire for proper intonation.

Gtr. 2 carries the majority of the verses by alternating the 5th/6th boogie pattern on D (stretching to the ♭7th, as well) with a sustained, open Cadd9 voicing. Whereas the more punk-minded guitarist may play the boogie patterns exclusively with downstrokes, Montrose's style is a bit more refined, as he uses alternate picking to lend a smoother, more flowing sound to the track. The stretches get much less comfortable during the boogie patterns of the chorus, so be sure to keep your thumb on the back of the neck!

For the solo, Montrose works almost entirely out of D minor pentatonic in either the standard box form (10th position) or the extension box (13th position). Although his ideas flow smoothly from one to the next, there's nothing terribly difficult here, so it shouldn't pose too much of a problem. For the *overbends* (1-1/2 steps) on string 2 toward the end, be sure add support to your bending finger.

"BLACK AND BLUE"

Van Halen

Apparently based on a personal account, Sammy Hagar conceived the story of "Black and Blue" after a particularly … *ahem* … lively encounter during the 5150 tour. The song went on to become a fan favorite of Hagar-era Van Halen and was a regular part of the set list for live shows during the time. With regard to the music, as was often the case, Eddie Van Halen's clever re-working of more typical blues-rock elements resulted in a classic track that sounded both fresh and familiar.

TONE

Eddie's sound has been slowly evolving since *Fair Warning*, thanks largely to an Eventide Harmonizer, which provided a chorus-type effect by slightly detuning the signal and mixing it with the dry signal. The effect was hardly noticeable before *1984* because the effect was mixed so low compared to the dry signal, but by *5150*, it was clearly audible. The ever-widening trend continued on *OU812*. It's this device, along with his trademark Frankenstrat and Marshall Super Lead, that's responsible for the thick tones heard on the record. The delay heard in the latter half of the solo was most likely added during mixdown.

The Eventide H910 harmonizer (or the similar H3000) can fetch a pretty penny these days, but lucky for you, Eventide released the Pitchfactor pedal, which will do an amazing job at recreating the effect (not to mention the long delay during the solo) for only a few hundred dollars. To simulate Eddie's sound, you'll want to detune the signal by about 18 cents, with approximately 12ms of delay, and mix it with the dry signal to taste. A super-Strat-style guitar, such as an Ibanez or Kramer, and a high-gain British-voiced amp, such as a Marshall or the Peavey 5150, will round out the rig nicely.

TECHNIQUE

For the opening riff, the fret hand has the most demanding job, as it needs to employ some muting (for the fourth string during the octaves) while maintaining enough arch in the fingers for the higher open strings to ring out. When the band kicks in at measure 9, don't neglect the rests, as they're essential to the groove. And be sure to keep the fingers arched for the measure right before the chorus so the open B string is allowed to ring out. As is often his M.O., Eddie employs a few perfectly placed natural harmonic fills, which, again, require fret-hand precision for maximum ringing.

During the solo, you'll find his patented tapped harmonic move, which is also much more difficult than Eddie makes it sound. You really have to whack the string forcefully and precisely to generate a clean note. For the chromatically ascending tapped phrase on string 2, it's really counterproductive to worry about matching the notation exactly. Eddie certainly never plays this phrase the same way twice, as it's purely for effect. The most important thing is to get the general idea down and play it well.

"BLACK OR WHITE"
Michael Jackson

After feeling as though he'd taken the relationship with Quincy Jones as far as he could, Michael Jackson enlisted a new group of collaborators for his 1991 *Dangerous* album, including engineer/producer/multi-instrumentalist Bill Bottrell. Michael wanted to get a rawer sound for the album, and Bottrell, with a background consisting of primarily country and roots rock, was happy to oblige. With both the single and the album hitting #1, and the latter selling over seven million copies, it's safe to say the collaboration was a success.

TONE

After hearing Michael hum the guitar part, Bottrell quickly grabbed a Kramer American guitar, miked up a Mesa Boogie amp with a Beyerdynamic M 160 ribbon mic, and laid down the classic rhythm riff. Shortly thereafter, Bottrell grabbed his 1940s Gibson LG2 and added the acoustic part without Michael's direction. Apparently, the gloved one found no fault in it, because he never complained. For the song's hard-rocking bridge, Bottrell brought in session ace Tim Pierce (with a résumé too long to even begin to list) to rock out with a Les Paul and a 100-watt Marshall.

For all the electric parts, you can most likely get close enough with either a super-Strat-style guitar or a humbucker-equipped Gibson-style guitar. And a Mesa Boogie or similar hi-gain combo tube amp—such as a Peavey, Blackstar, or Marshall—will be able to generate a range of tones capable of emulating both sections convincingly. The tone for the main riff needs a bit more mids, whereas you can scoop them out a bit for the middle section. Gibson has reissued the LG-2 American Eagle, but if its $1,900 tag is too steep, you should be fine with a similar small-bodied folk-style guitar, such as a Seagull Coastline S6 or a Yamaha FS720S.

TECHNIQUE

For the main riff of the song, try to keep your wrist loose. You'll be playing this riff a lot during the song, so you don't want to tighten up. Also be mindful of fret-hand muting to make sure no extraneous strings ring out. Allow the tips of your fingers to touch the fifth string to deaden it, and use the underside of the fingers to keep string 1 quiet.

For the bridge, tackle the open-string pull-offs of Rhy. Fig. 2 in third position, using your first and third fingers for the G and A notes, respectively. For the syncopated chordal answers (E7#9 and A5, respectively), keep pairing downstrokes with downbeats in the strum hand, as this will aid in maintaining a solid groove. The same exact idea applies to the clean funk riff (Rhy. Fig. 3) and is imperative in nearly all funk styles.

"CAN'T YOU HEAR ME KNOCKING"
The Rolling Stones

The Stones kicked off the '70s with a bunch of firsts on *Sticky Fingers*. It was their first album with no contributions from Brian Jones, the first with Mick Taylor acting as a fulltime band member, and the first release on their newly formed label, Rolling Stones Records. Working mostly from Mick Jagger's manor home—known as Stargroves—in Hampshire County, England, the band recorded most of the album using their mobile studio unit. Including classic tracks like "Brown Sugar," "Wild Horses," and "Can't You Hear Me Knocking," *Sticky Fingers* has gone on to become one of the band's most acclaimed albums.

TONE

The Stones favored small(ish) amps in the studio, such as the Fender Twin or Ampeg VT-40/VT-22, and either one of these is a safe bet for Keith or Mick on this track. Mick noted in an interview that he used his brown Gibson ES-345 for the track, but the exact guitar Keith used isn't clear. However, it's more than likely one of three: a Gibson ES-355, a '50s Telecaster, or an Ampeg Dan Armstrong model.

A Gibson ES-345 or ES-355 will run you at least several grand on the used market, but Epiphone features reissues of both of these models. They should get you close enough without having to take out a second mortgage on your home. In the amp department, a blackfaced Fender such as a Twin Reverb, Deluxe Reverb, or Pro Reverb, all of which have been reissued, will certainly do the job. Keith's parts feature a more overdriven tone in general, which is likely the effect of simply cranking up the amp more.

TECHNIQUE

Keith kicks off the tune with his trademark, open G-tuned (minus string 6) guitar riff. The tone is thick and gritty, and it really makes a statement right from the front. Keith never plays this riff the same way twice, so don't kill yourself trying to learn every single variation (unless you're a perfectionist). Obviously, the seventh-position, barred D shape is your home base for this riff. Note that Keith has a tendency to pick very near the neck of the guitar, which helps produce the thick, throaty tone.

For the main "can't you hear me knocking" riff that begins the verse, Keith barres fret 7 with his third finger, but you could use your third and fourth finger if it feels better. Taylor spends most of his time during the song playing barre chords of various types, but his restraint is rewarded with an extended jam at the end. For the octave melodies, use a hybrid (pick and finger) approach. For the held-bend lick involving frets 12, 13, and 10 on strings 3, 2, and 1, respectively, try using fingers 1, 2, and 3 or 1, 3, and 4 to see which feels best. For the repetitive, syncopated chromatic lick in 10th position, barre your ring finger for the 12th-fret dyads and your index finger for the 10th-fret ones.

"COCAINE"
Eric Clapton

One of multiple hits for Clapton penned by J.J. Cale—the other most notable being "After Midnight"—"Cocaine" became a live staple for Slowhand throughout the '70s and '80s. A mid-tempo rocker similar in feel to Cream's "Sunshine of Your Love," the song features a slightly-obscured anti-drug message. The album, *Slowhand*, hit #2 on the charts in 1978, and a live version of "Cocaine," from *Just One Night,* reached #30 two years later. It remains one of Clapton's signature songs.

TONE

Clapton most likely wielded a Strat for the song, if not his trademark "Blackie," and you can hear several different types of Strat tones on the recording. It sounds as though he's using different positions of the pickup selector to vary things up. This was the period when he was making use of Music Man amps—mainly the solid-state/tube hybrid and master-volume-equipped HD-130—as they allowed him to simulate the sound of a cranked Marshall without the excessive volume, and this would be a safe bet. But Clapton was notorious for making use of several amps in the studio, so vintage Fenders would be a good bet, as well.

On some of the tracks (both lead and rhythm), there's a hint of chorus-type wavering. This is quite possibly a Leslie cabinet (set to slow speed) mixed in lightly, or it could possibly be a chorus pedal set to a very low mix.

A Strat and a blackfaced Fender amp, like a Twin, would no doubt be able to get you close. However, a Music Man HD-130 2x12 combo—which, keep in mind, was designed by Leo Fender—is much more affordable on the used market these days, with some selling for as low as $300 in good condition. Grab a chorus pedal, such as the Boss CH-1 or older CE-3, and set the rate and depth fairly low, adjusting until you achieve the appropriate thickening effect.

TECHNIQUE

This song is filled with simple, tasty, effective playing, but none of it should pose too much difficulty. For the funky Gtr. 4 parts, use a continuous, alternating picking motion, pairing downstrokes with downbeats and using the fret hand to control whether the notes speak out or not. For the entirety of the solo, Clapton parks himself in the 12th-position box and phrases almost exclusively from the E minor pentatonic scale. The main thing here is to just lay back and settle into the groove. The licks aren't very difficult; they're just in the pocket.

"EVERYBODY HURTS"

R.E.M.

Originally brought to the band by drummer Bill Berry in its toddler stage with only a verse, "Everybody Hurts"—perhaps the most direct in sentiment of any R.E.M. song—appeared on *Automatic for the People* (#2 on the *Billboard* Hot 100 in 1992), the band's most commercially successful album and a mainstay on many "Greatest Albums of the '90s" lists. Ironically, Berry didn't perform on the song; he was replaced by a Univox drum machine.

TONE

Peter Buck is most famous for Rickenbacker guitars (particularly a Jetglo 360 model), but he's also made consistent use of Telecasters throughout his career. The track certainly sounds like a Rickenbacker, however, so that's a good guess. In the amp department, a likely candidate is a Vox AC30.

If you can't swing a Rick 360 (they can get a bit pricey), you can probably get pretty close with a semi-hollow Tele, such as the Classic Series '69 Thinline, which will run you much less. Plug into a reissue Vox AC30 or AC15 and you'll be good to go.

TECHNIQUE

Peter Buck plays it straight and minimally on this song, maintaining rolling eighth-note arpeggios through almost the entire song. There are a few things he does to help the chord transitions. The first is at the end of measure 2, where he lifts off the D chord an eighth note early and plucks the open G string. Notice also, in the second half of the bridge, that he uses a different type of G chord when following the C chord; this G voicing is much easier to alternate with C.

This is the type of guitar playing that can be deceptively difficult. It doesn't look like much on paper, but picking everything clearly and, most importantly, *in time* is not as easy as it first appears. With regard to the F♯ and Bm barre chords in the bridge, remember that you don't need to fret the entire chord on the downbeat; you can just fret the bass note first and then lay the chord down on the second eighth note.

"FAT BOTTOMED GIRLS"

Queen

Guitarist Brian May penned this ode to wide women for the band's 1978 album *Jazz*. The song reached #11 in the U.K. and #24 across the pond. For Queen, the album was a bit lean on the hits, comparatively speaking, but it still managed to earn a Top 10 spot and platinum sales in both countries. Although Freddie Mercury would sing lead for the whole song in concert, May actually sang lead on the chorus for the album version.

TONE

May has one of the most identifiable tones in all of rock, and that's no doubt due, in part, to his unique choice of tools. His famous Red Special guitar, hand-built from the wood of a mantle (neck, mahogany) and old table (body, oak), is custom in just about every single way. Though he was a famous user of Vox AC30 amps, in the studio, he had an affinity for augmenting his tone with the "Deacy." This was a one-watt transistor amp built by Queen bassist John Deacon. May would often crank this amp and mic it in the studio, blending it with the sound of the AC30, especially for his lead tones. His use of a sixpence, instead of a plectrum, also adds a unique bite to his tone.

Brian May makes his own line of guitars now (Brian May Guitars), and the Brian May signature model, which is based on the Red Special, isn't outlandish in the price department (it sells new for around $800 and has received quite rave reviews). So that would be an obvious choice, although a Mahogany-bodied Telecaster with single coils, such as the Classic Series '69 Thinline, would be a safe bet, as well. In the amp department, a cranked reissue Vox AC30 or AC15 would get you "close enough for jazz."

TECHNIQUE

This is one of the rare instances in which Brian May uses drop D tuning. It's certainly appropriate here, as it helps him add that extra "bottom" to his sound. For the main riff, don't worry about replicating the notation exactly. Although different strings are notated at different times because that's what Brian played on the album, when all is said and done, he's strumming a D chord for the most part here, so don't get carried away! The G5 and F5 chords can be easily handled with a third- and first-finger barre, respectively.

"FUNK #49"
James Gang

Leading off the band's second album, *Rides Again*, "Funk #49" didn't do much damage on the charts in 1970, but it became the James Gang's signature song (along with "Walk Away") and one of the most enduring tracks on classic rock radio. Containing an instantly recognizable and seriously grooving riff, the song began as a jam during soundchecks on tour. It hadn't even been considered as a "song" until they added lyrics to it in order to record it.

TONE

Walsh is famous for his use of smaller Fender tweed amps in the studio, and the debate is still alive regarding this track. Although it's fairly clear that he used a Fender Telecaster for the track, he's changed his stories in interviews regarding the amp. At times, he's said it was a tweed Champ; other times, he's claimed it was a blackfaced Champ. At any rate, it was most likely a cranked Fender Champ of some sort.

Grab a Telecaster and a low-wattage, tweed-style tube amp for this one, crank it up, and go. Fender reissued the '57 Champ a while ago and, although they're no longer made, you can easily find them used for $500–$700. A true vintage model, assuming it's in good, playable condition, could run you double that. Another more current option would be the Bad Cat Cougar 5.

TECHNIQUE

No doubt one of the coolest guitar intros of classic rock, Walsh kicks off "Funk #49" with a chicken-pickin' lick that's turned many a player's head. There are a few different noises going on here, so let's look at it. After bending the D note on string 3 up a whole step, you simply plant your pick hand on the strings forcefully to sound a dead note. While maintaining the bend, pluck the G note on string 2 and then re-pluck the bent D note on string 3, this time releasing it. The open B string on beat 4 is most likely unintentional, but it sure sounds cool.

Then comes the chicken pickin'. After bending fret 5, string 3 up a whole step with your index finger, silently bend string 3 up a whole step at fret 7 with your third finger in preparation for the next move. Here's the tricky part: touch the string with your pick-hand's second finger to deaden it, plucking the string with the pick. You should get a deadened "click." Immediately after that, pluck the string with your second finger. Alternate these two moves in the indicated rhythm while gradually releasing the bend, and you've got it.

For the song's main riff (measures 5–6, for example), remain in fifth position and barre the third finger for the D/A chord on beat 2.5 of measure 5. At the end of the measure, however, shift up to seventh position with a first-finger barre for the hammer-on move. Remember to keep the pick-hand moving, using downstrokes for downbeats, for a solid groove.

"HEY YOU"
Pink Floyd

In one of the most memorable tracks on Pink Floyd's 1979 masterpiece *The Wall*, "Hey You" demonstrates the band's strengths in more ways than one. Sporting lead vocals from both David Gilmour and Roger Waters, the song encapsulates Floyd's eerie soundscape-generating M.O. and teases the ear non-stop with brilliant studio use and deceptively simple compositional devices. In regard to the latter, one can clearly hear its influence on bands like Radiohead, particularly the parallel minor tonalities of the song's intro.

TONE

Gilmour most likely plucked his alternately-strung Ovation acoustic for the intro and verse figures, adding his Martin D-12 or D-28 for the strumming sections later on. For the electric parts, Gilmour ran his Strat through a Big Muff pedal en route to his Hiwatt DR-103 amps. He also most likely made use of his Jedson lap steel for the slide melodies.

A Strat and a Big Muff pedal are easy to come by and are obvious choices, but Hiwatts can be pretty steep. You can easily cut the mustard with a similar British-voiced tube amp, such as an EVH 5150III, Marshall JVM210H, or an Orange TH30H, running through a 4x12 cabinet. In the acoustic department, a midline Martin dreadnought, such as the Custom D, should suffice.

TECHNIQUE

Gilmour used a Nashville-strung acoustic—basically, all the higher-octave gauges of a 12-string set—to create the beautiful arpeggio sequences for this song. The picking pattern is very specific here, so experiment with pick direction to see what feels best for you. A suggested starting point is down-down-down-down, up-up-up-up.

Regarding the lead lines, note that Gilmour often uses the bar for vibrato, which sounds a bit different than using fingers because it's dipping in pitch rather than rising. It's not critical, but if you have a vibrato bar, try it out to see if you can tell the difference. Gilmour's intonation on the numerous bends is spot on, so make sure you're doing the same.

"I WANNA BE SEDATED"
Ramones

Singer Joey Ramone wrote "I Wanna Be Sedated" while on the road circa 1977 during his first trip to London. The product of being bored while the city had all but fallen asleep during the Christmas holiday, the song eventually went on to become one of the band's most enduring songs, helping to push the 1978 album *Road to Ruin* to #32 on the U.K. charts, although it did not fare as well in America, failing to crack the Top 100. Since then, it's been covered by numerous artists, including Vince Neil, the Go-Go's, the Offspring, and Tyson Ritter (of All-American Rejects), among many others.

TONE

In keeping with the spirit of their music—and the punk ethos in general—guitarist Johnny Ramone played the bare essentials. For the majority of his career, he ran one of several Mosrite Venture-model guitars through a cranked Marshall stack. He's particularly known for a White Mosrite Ventures II, which he used extensively from 1977–96.

Vintage Mosrite guitars can command ridiculous prices on the used market, but you can get close enough with several other surf-type guitars, including a Jay Turser Venture Mach 1 on the more affordable end or a Fender Jaguar or Jazzmaster. Plug into a Marshall stack, dime the treble and mids, and crank it to no end!

TECHNIQUE

Downstrokes, folks—and lots of them! This is about as punk as guitar gets. It's fast, it's loud, and it's in your face!

"I'M GOING HOME"
Ten Years After

Although the band had developed a decent following in their English homeland throughout the early part of the '60s, it was their performance at Woodstock in 1969 that really introduced the band to America in a big way. In particular, their extended version of "I'm Going Home," which featured Alvin Lee's scorching guitar performance and dynamic lead vocal, won the crowd over. The bluesy shuffle "Hear Me Calling," from *Stonedhenge* (1969), became a minor hit, but the band headed in a more commercial direction for *A Space in Time* (1971). Although the album didn't feature as much fiery fretboard work from Lee, the songwriting had certainly grown more mature, and "I'd Love to Change the World" became the band's one and only serious hit, peaking at #40 on the Billboard Hot 100.

TONE

Alvin Lee, nicknamed "the fastest guitarist at Woodstock," used his trademark Gibson ES-335 ("Big Red") for the Woodstock performance, as well as for the alternate live performance (shown here) of "I'm Going Home." A 100-watt Marshall with a 4x12 Marshall cabinet handled the amplification duties.

Gibson issued a brief run of signature Alvin Lee "Big Red" ES-335's in 2007 or so, but they're quite difficult to come by. A standard Gibson ES-335 would do the trick nicely, but if you can't swing the $3,000 price tag, an Epiphone model or a similar semi-hollow Gibson-type, such as an Ibanez Artcore AS93, will get you in the ballpark for sure. Plug into a Marshall or any British-style tube amp and crank it up!

TECHNIQUE

To say this song is a vehicle for Alvin Lee's guitar playing is an understatement, and he doesn't disappoint. At a blistering 208 bpm, you'd better have the A blues scale under your fingers! Lee works almost exclusively out of the standard box form in fifth position and the upper extension box in eighth position, often moving fluidly between the two by way of a slide on the G string.

The double pull-off blues scale lick on strings 1–2 that he plays for an extended period during both solos is a barn burner for sure and will take a good bit of woodshedding if you don't already have it under your fingers. Although most of these licks aren't terribly difficult in and of themselves, the sheer velocity of the proceedings will certainly test your endurance, so your chops will need to be in top shape if you want to avoid your forearm turning to jelly!

"JEALOUS AGAIN"

The Black Crowes

The Black Crowes struck gold (or platinum) right out of the gates in 1990. *Shake Your Money Maker* became a big success for the band, reaching #4 on the Billboard 200 and selling more than five million copies to date—a feat the Atlanta-based band hasn't equaled since. With each successive album, the band continued to expand their sound, carving out their own unique niche within the retro-rock sub-genre. However, the Crowes wore their influences—the Rolling Stones, the Faces, etc.—loudly and proudly on their sleeve when they first hit the scene. Case in point is "Jealous Again," which would've sounded perfectly at home on *Sticky Fingers* or *Exile on Main St.*

TONE

Rich Robinson started off as a Tele man and, although he's since amassed a huge collection of guitars (both vintage and custom-made), it was his trademark blonde 1968 Tele that fueled most of the hits on the first few albums, including "Jealous Again." He ran through a Marshall Silver Jubilee, cranking it just to the point of some nice breakup. Jeff Cease complimented Robinson with the standard Les Paul/Marshall combo. Great tone is in no short supply on this song!

If you're the only guitar player in a band playing this song, either a Tele or a humbucker-equipped Gibson-style guitar will do. Plug it into a Marshall and crank it up just past the point of lightly breaking up. You don't want it saturated by any means, but you want it to growl when you dig in.

TECHNIQUE

Robinson is somewhat of a Keith Richards disciple and often plays in open G tuning, but he keeps the sixth string on instead of removing it (as "Keif" does). This allows him to play not only the Stones-type stuff but also generate the super powerful Zeppelin-type sound. For "Jealous Again," Robinson mines familiar Keif territory, banking the verse off of the barred D chord in seventh position and ornamenting it with notes from the G/D voicing. Cease thickens things up by playing a similar riff, using the familiar 5th/6th boogie pattern. For the chorus, both guitarists mostly outline the descending chord progression (a hint at what would become a Crowes trademark) with power chords.

For the bridge, Cease moves up the neck to play 5th/root dyads for each chord, while Robinson moves down to the open position and alternates the open G chord with the ornamental C/G voicing. Note that this is essentially the same move that he uses in the intro and verses, only transposed down a 4th. Be sure to arch your fingers to allow the open strings to ring out; this is especially true during the guitar break, in which Rich moves notes from the D major scale against the open first string (D) drone.

The outro solo essentially modulates to the key of G and Cease works with repetitive, Skynyrd-type G major pentatonic phrases. Try using a downstroke/hammer-on/upstroke approach for the three-against-four repeated patterns in the open and 12th positions.

"LA GRANGE"

ZZ Top

ZZ Top, that "little ol' band from Texas," has spent the last four-and-a-half decades earning their reputation as one of the most successful and well-respected blues-rock bands in history. Sure, they veered into synthesizer territory during the '80s and early '90s, disappointing some of their purist fans along the way with their pop-blues hybrid sound, but they've proven time and again that they're the real deal. In fact, in the past 15 years, the band has come nearly full circle, returning to a sound that resembles their earlier days. No doubt one of their signature songs, "La Grange" tells the story of a ... ahem ... whorehouse near the Texas town of the same name—also the subject of the famous 1982 Dolly Parton/Burt Reynolds film (and Broadway play) *The Best Little Whorehouse in Texas.* Reaching #41 on the *Billboard* charts, "La Grange" helped push the *Tres Hombres* album (their third) up to #8 and marked the beginning of the band's commercial breakthrough. The song has since gone on to become one of the most famous boogies of all.

TONE

Although Billy Gibbons has long been predominantly a Gibson player, famously wielding his '59 Les Paul Standard (known as "Pearly Gates") on countless tracks, he cut "La Grange" on a '55 Stratocaster with a stop tailpiece. For the intro, Gibbons wedged the pickup selector (only a three-position switch on those early Strats) in one of the in-between settings to achieve the famous "out of phase" Strat tone. (This is a common misnomer, actually. Even though the tone is thinner, it's still definitely "in phase.")

Gibbons plugged straight into a '69 Marshall Super Lead 100 with a 4x12 cabinet, with the varying amounts of grit the result of varying the guitar's pickup/volume setting and/or the amp's volume. All of the distortion comes from the amp.

Modern-day Strats make it easier to achieve the in-between sound, so that's a good thing. Since you won't have the ability to stop and adjust the amp settings for different parts of the song, as is common in the studio, you may want to run through an overdrive pedal, such as an Ibanez Tube Screamer, en route to the Marshall amp. This will allow you to kick up the dirt when it's time for the leads and dial it back down when necessary.

TECHNIQUE

There are two basic versions of the main hybrid (pick and fingers) riff that Gibbons uses: with and without vocals. At the intro, he maintains the A5 fingering on fret 2 of strings 4–3 and alternates a G note on string 4 and a C note on string 3—both on fret 5— occasionally banking against the open A string. Use the pick for string 5 and your second and third fingers for strings 4–3, respectively. Shortly after the vocals enter, Gibbons moves to a slightly different two-bar pattern that makes more use of the pick on string 5 (with the ascending C-to-D move). You needn't worry about trying to replicate the transcription here exactly, as Gibbons freely adds slight variations throughout—sometimes intentionally and many times unintentionally. "The Reverend" certainly would never play it exactly the same way twice anyway. Just get the basic idea down and then add your own variations if you'd like.

The first solo famously modulates up a minor 3rd to C, so be sure to anticipate that shift. Practically the entire solo takes place in the standard box form of C minor pentatonic (eighth position), the lower-extension box (sixth position), and the upper-extension box (11th position). For the famous turnaround (interlude), park your pinky on string 1 throughout. For the outro solo, which takes place in the key of A and uses A minor pentatonic, you'll get plenty of practice with pinch harmonics. For these, allow your thumb to brush the string while you pick them. Realize that the pitch will change, depending on where your thumb makes contact along the length of the string. Have fun with this song!

"LONG DISTANCE RUNAROUND"
Yes

Prog-rock champions Yes reached a new highpoint with *Fragile* (1971), cracking the Top 10 on both sides of the Atlantic and achieving eventual sales in excess of two million copies in the U.S. The first to feature keyboard wunderkind Rick Wakeman, the album spawned the hit single "Roundabout," with its B-side, "Long Distance Runaround," also performing admirably. The album began a fairly steady line of successful albums by the band that continued through most of the decade, although Wakeman would briefly leave the band to try his hand at a solo career.

TONE

Steve Howe crafted his parts on this tour de force with a hollowbody Gibson ES-175 (the guitar for which he is most famous) plugged into (most likely) a Fender Dual Showman amp with 15-inch speakers in the cabinet. Although he did make use of various fuzz pedals, including the Big Muff and Maestro Fuzz, everything on this track sounds like nothing more than slight tube distortion from a cranked Showman.

An ES-175 is not an inexpensive guitar, with few new models dipping below the $4,000 mark. However, most hollowbody guitars with humbucking pickups should get you in the ballpark, and there are more affordable ones out there, ranging from $1,500 (the Guild CE-100D Capri) to as little as $400 (Ibanez AF75). Pair it with a Fender blackface-style amp, such as a Twin Reverb, Deluxe Reverb, or, if you want to pony up several grand for a vintage blackface Dual Showman and cab, that's always an option as well! For the cadenza lick, you can make use of any delay pedal, but ones that are analog—or at least simulate an analog delay—will sound closest, as an analog delay was certainly used on the original recording.

TECHNIQUE

Although the song eventually settles into a B minor key center, it begins by running through various C9 arpeggios, with Howe and Wakeman harmonizing throughout. Left-hand fingering is a big deal here, as there are several ways to skin this cat, so experiment to see what feels best to you. If you want to see the way Howe himself plays this, he's posted several videos on YouTube demonstrating key parts of many songs, and this is one of them. At the end of the section, for the two sets of descending dyads, be sure to use hybrid picking to achieve the piano-like, simultaneous note attack. Although the ending cadenza looks pretty scary on paper, it's not as bad as it may seem due to the relatively slow tempo, 90 bpm. The delay makes it sound a little more intimidating.

"ONE WAY TO ROCK"

Sammy Hagar

After coming out of the gates running as lead vocalist for Montrose in the early '70s, Sammy Hagar quickly stepped out on his own with a solo career, beginning in 1976. The "Red Rocker" was incredibly prolific and consistent over the next eight years, releasing as many albums that steadily climbed the charts before snatching up the frontman spot with Van Halen in 1985. Along the way he scored several moderate hits, such as "One Way to Rock," as well as a few Top 40 singles, including "Your Love Is Driving Me Crazy" (#13) and "I Can't Drive 55" (#26). Of course, hit singles, not to mention #1 albums (four in a row!), began to pile up during the "Van Hagar" years (1986–95).

TONE

Sammy generally preferred Gibson guitars throughout his solo career, usually sporting either a Les Paul or an Explorer. It's the former, however, that's cranked "in your face" for this tune, as the Red Rocker himself declares during the bridge of "One Way to Rock." At the other end of the cable lay a Marshall half stack. Hagar's wingman at the time, Gary Phil, most likely ran his Jackson through either a Randall or a Marshall for his riffing duties.

There is a bit of whammy usage on the recording so, if you want to replicate that, you'll be best off with a super-Strat type of guitar, such as a Jackson or Kramer. Plug it into a Marshall or similar tube amp—probably a master-volume model, such as the JCM800—and let it rip.

TECHNIQUE

For the majority of the riffing, you'll be parked in second position. I suggest using your third and fourth fingers for the C#/F# dyad on strings 5–4, fret 4. Then you can barre your first finger on fret 2 for the dyads/triads and barre your third finger on fret 4. The fractional harmonics that begin to pop up after the first line of the verse aren't specific and precise, so don't kill yourself trying to replicate them exactly; they're just the product of slightly releasing fret-hand pressure while picking the strings.

Most of the lead lines are derived from the second-position F# minor pentatonic box form, although you will need to shift up through a few positions right before the bridge, so watch out for that. The Chuck Berry-style repetitive dyad lick at the end of the bridge is normally articulated with a partial barre of the first finger.

"ONLY TIME WILL TELL"

Asia

One of several supergroups of the '80s, Asia originally consisted of John Wetton (from King Crimson, Roxy Music, Uriah Heep, and others) on bass and vocals, Steve Howe (Yes) on guitars and backing vocals, Geoff Downes (Yes and the Buggles) on keyboards and backing vocals, and Carl Palmer (ELP) on drums. Although the fans of their former bands generally weren't too pleased with their new, more singles-driven direction, *Asia* (1982) became a bigger commercial success than any of the members had achieved before, topping the album charts, spawning the hit singles "Heat of the Moment" and "Only Time Will Tell," and selling over four million copies.

TONE

For his tenure in Asia, Howe spent much of his time with a Gibson Artist guitar. This was a unique semi-hollow guitar—aesthetically similar to an ES-335—with many interesting additions with regard to the electronics. A collaboration with Moog, the guitar featured active electronics and switches for a treble booster, a compressor, and an expander, along with low-output humbucking pickups and standard volume and tone knobs. Howe likely ran through a Fender Twin or Dual Showman for this track and most likely employed his Big Muff or Marshall Fuzz for the distortion.

You should be able to get reasonably close to the tone with a typical semi-hollow guitar, such as an ES-335 or something similar. Plug it into a blackface-style Fender and run through a distortion pedal, such as a Big Muff, for the leads.

TECHNIQUE

The trademark synth line is notated here if you'd like to play it on guitar. Although it's a little speedy it's not terribly difficult, but keep in mind that you should play it as straight as possible—no slides, bends, or vibrato—to convincingly mimic the synth. For the staccato triads that begin at measure 5, quickly bring your pick-hand palm down to mute the strings between each stroke.

During the chorus, the palm-muted triplets will most likely need to be alternate picked—unless you're really fast with the downstrokes or upstrokes—so strive for unity of sound. In other words, heavily mute the strings and make sure that you're strumming through all three strings on each downstroke and upstroke.

"PARADISE CITY"
Guns N' Roses

With one of the most successful debut albums in music history, Guns N' Roses simply took over the world in the late '80s. While it may have seemed like it happened overnight, *Appetite for Destruction* had actually been out for nearly a year before it topped the charts. The three Top 10 singles—"Sweet Child o' Mine" (#1), "Welcome to the Jungle" (#7), and "Paradise City" (#5)—kept the album on the charts for a total of 147 weeks, earning multi-platinum sales and cementing GN'R's status as the biggest band in the world. The album has gone on to become one of the best-selling albums in history, with over 18 million copies moved in the U.S. alone.

TONE

The stories of the *Appetite* sessions have become the stuff of legends over the years, as have the battles between various band members. After experimenting with several guitars, Slash settled on a custom-made Gibson Les Paul and ran it through a modified '60s Marshall 1959 head with a 4x12 cabinet. For the chorus in the intro, he most likely ran through an MXR stereo chorus. Izzy Stradlin most likely ran a semi-hollow (such as a Gibson ES-335) or a hollowbody (such as a Gibson ES-175 or ES-185) through a Mesa Boogie Mark III and into a 4x12 cabinet.

If you're the only guitar player in this song, a Les Paul and a Marshall would fit the bill nicely (when does it not?). However, if you've got another player, then you can really get close with a semi-hollow added in to the mix. A Gibson ES-335 would be a safe choice, but you could probably get close enough with an Epiphone model or something similar, such as a Peavey JF-1 or Ibanez Artcore AS73. You can snag a Boogie MK III combo for around $700 on the used market, which would do the trick nicely. Just about any chorus pedal will get you in the ballpark. Set it to a fairly high depth and a moderate rate.

TECHNIQUE

The hardest part of the intro riff will be getting the picking down, as it moves along fairly quickly, so try some different picking patterns until you find one that feels good to you. For the chromatic double-stop riff in the interlude, you'll probably find it easiest to use partial barres of your first, second, and third fingers on frets 3, 4, and 5, respectively. For Slash's nifty bridge lick, park your hand in 10th and eighth position for the D5 and C5 chords, respectively, shifting down a whole step, from C to B♭ (sixth position), at the end of the section. The fingering should be the same for the lick over each chord.

"REBEL YELL"
Billy Idol

An interesting synthesis of punk, pop, and heavy metal, Billy Idol's sound struck gold relatively quickly out of the gates. His self-titled debut suggested great promise, with his Elvis-esque baritone vocals taking center stage, and that promise was certainly fulfilled on his second outing, *Rebel Yell*, which shot to #6 on the Billboard 200 and produced his first Top 10 hit, "Eyes Without a Face," and the MTV staples "Rebel Yell" and "Flesh for Fantasy."

TONE

For "Rebel Yell," Steve Stevens ran his Kramer Pacer through a '70s metal-faced Marshall, using a vintage cabinet with 25-watt Celestion speakers. They miked the cab with both a Shure SM57 (dynamic mic) and a Neumann U87 (condenser), mixing them together for a composite tone. Stevens doubled the rhythm parts for the song, panning them left and right for a wide sound. Additionally, no digital reverbs were used on the track; only the reverb tank at Electric Lady Studios was used.

For the famous "ray gun" effect during the solo, Stevens & Co. used a PCM 41 digital delay. They set it for a very short delay time and cranked up the modulation all the way so that it was basically self-modulating (running away with infinite repeats).

A super-Strat type of guitar, such as a Kramer, Charvel, or Jackson, with a Floyd Rose-type whammy bar is essential for this song. Plug into a Marshall amp or a similar tube amp with a master volume, dial in some 'verb, and crank the gain. You'll also need a digital delay pedal, such as the Boss DD-3 or similar, for the verse after the solo. Set the delay time to a half note with several repeats.

TECHNIQUE

Stevens credits the intro to "Rebel Yell" to messing around with some fingerstyle blues patterns. He also wanted to emulate the keyboard concept of separate bass and treble parts. When he put the two ideas together, he came up with the patented intro riff. It's performed entirely fingerstyle, although you could do it hybrid-style (pick and fingers), as well. This will allow you to quickly move into the palm mutes that follow.

For the siren harmonic effect at the interlude, depress the bar until the strings are a good bit slackened, carefully pluck the harmonic, and return the bar to pitch, making sure to mute the other strings (string 1 and 3–6) with your fret hand so you get nothing but the harmonic sounding out.

"RENEGADE"

Styx

Although Styx's career—beginning in 1972 with their self-titled debut—had been flecked with occasional success, it was the arrival of Tommy Shaw that brought the band worldwide success. *The Grand Illusion* (1977) reached #6 on the charts, spawning two Top 40 singles, "Come Sail Away" and "Fooling Yourself." By the time *Pieces of Eight*—which contained "Renegade," "Blue Collar Man (Long Nights)," and "Sing for the Day"—was released in 1978, the band members were bona fide superstars. They would continued dominating the charts through *Kilroy Was Here* (1983), after which the band split due to mounting creative tensions.

TONE

For the rocking tones of "Renegade," the boys of Styx kept it pretty straightforward. Tommy Shaw ran his white '73 Gibson Les Paul into either a Mesa Boogie amp with a 4x12 Hiwatt cabinet or a Marshall head and cabinet. To compliment that tone, James Young plugged his vintage '65 Stratocaster (which most likely had modified pickups by then) into a Marshall head and cabinet. Another component in his signal chain was his "Yoshinarator" pedal, which was a preamp/distortion effect.

The Les Paul/Marshall or Les Paul/Boogie combination should get you where you need to be for this tune. Although, if you want to mimic Young's solo accurately, you'll need a guitar with a whammy bar, in which case a super-Strat-style Kramer or similar guitar would suffice. Crank up the mids a bit and back off the bass a tad. You may also want to employ a vintage-style overdrive pedal, such as an Ibanez Tube Screamer, Boss Blues Driver, or Maxon OD808 Overdrive, for the leads.

TECHNIQUE

To ensure maximum precision, you'll probably want to use fingers 3 and 4 for the fifth-fret dyads in the main chorus riff (as opposed to a barre), as this will prevent the accidental sounding of neighboring strings. There are a few fleet-fingered pull-off licks in the solos, but the vast majority of them are based off the G minor pentatonic box form, so it's just a matter of putting in the time to get the speed up to tempo.

"SEPARATE WAYS (WORLDS APART)"

Journey

Journey has certainly lived up to their namesake. Through numerous incarnations, they've ridden the crests and troughs of the success wave, including both world domination and complete disbandment. After an unlikely fusion-styled beginning in the '70s, the band continually steered their sound toward a more commercial direction with each release, eventually striking gold with the addition of lead singer Steve Perry for *Infinity* (1978). By the early '80s, they were one of the biggest bands in the world, with a #1 album, *Escape* (1981), and a #2 follow-up, *Frontiers* (1983). The first disbandment occurred in 1987, and the band has continued to resurface in various incarnations since, with varying degrees of success.

TONE

For "Separate Ways," Neal Schon followed the K.I.S.S. principle and plugged a Les Paul into a Marshall. The thickened tone during the rhythm riffs results from him doubling (or possibly tripling) the parts.

Most humbucker-equipped guitars, such as an SG, will get you close—if you don't want to spring for the Les Paul. In order to simulate the doubling effect, you could employ a digital delay pedal and set it for one repeat with a very short delay time (possibly 10ms or so) and a moderate level. Of course, as the music video demonstrates, you can get roughly the same sound by playing air guitar, as well.

TECHNIQUE

Schon works quite a nifty hook into the main rhythmic figure that supports the intro and verse, and it's deceptively hard to perform. The secret is to use fret-hand muting in the right spots, allowing only the notes that you want to sound to come out. For the octave E notes, allow the underside of your fret-hand fingers to mute strings 4–1 so you don't have to worry about avoiding them with the pick. For the harmonic at fret 5, string 3, try placing your hand in various positions to see which position allows you to get the harmonic to speak the clearest. I find it best to park my hand around third position and use my pinky for the harmonic. That way, I can deaden the strings by touching them with my other fingers and then quickly lift them up, leaving only the pinky touching, when I want the harmonic to speak.

As was often the case, Schon's solo begins with a sing-able melody from the E minor scale to make a memorable statement before closing with a climactic, fiery lick in the upper reaches of the neck. Though the lick looks a bit scary, it's actually more manageable than it seems at first glance, as it regularly alternates brief bursts of super speed with more modest 16th notes.

"SHIP OF FOOLS"
Robert Plant

Some singers make it a point to work with nothing but groundbreaking guitarists. Ozzy Osbourne, David Lee Roth, and David Coverdale certainly fit this mold, as does Robert Plant. After scaling the musical summit with Led Zeppelin in the '70s, Plant obviously had nothing to prove. Refusing to play Led Zeppelin songs in concert, he nevertheless carved out a successful solo career throughout the '80s, working first with Robbie Blunt and then Doug Boyle—both incredibly unique players that left an indelible sonic stamp on the songs from that period. Case in point is "Ship of Fools"—from the #6 album *Now and Zen* (1988)—which contains some spellbinding clean-tone work from Boyle.

TONE

Very little documentation exists on Boyle's studio equipment from this period, but he can be seen on stage playing an Ibanez RG-type guitar in numerous live videos from the time, and that's as good of a guess as any, as it doesn't have a typical Strat or Gibson tone. On the recording, it very much sounds like a direct tone (plugging directly into the mixing console via a DI box), with a very slight delay added for depth.

Ibanez still makes many RG models in affordable ranges of $400 and up. As long as you have a single-coil pickup in the neck position, most of them should be able to get you a similar sound. You may also want to try one of the in-between positions, if you have it available. As for an amp, you may have the best luck going with a super clean solid-state model, such as a Roland JC-120 or a red-knobbed Fender Eighty-Five, and add a decent touch of reverb for depth.

TECHNIQUE

A huge part of the sound in this track comes from Boyle's dynamic fingerstyle attack. Some notes leap out, while others are nearly swallowed completely. The song would simply not sound the same played with a pick. Boyle creates his own language in the intro by using mostly lead lines to convey the chord changes with subtlety and sophistication. Be sure to arch your fingers at the beginning of the phrase to allow the open high-E string to drone.

The solo is a brilliant display of motivic development, as he alludes to phrases from the intro and expands upon them in various instances of rhythmic and melodic imitation. Again, the fingerstyle attack is vital here, so keep the pick at bay!

"SIMPLE MAN"
Lynyrd Skynyrd

In their brief, initial four-year career, Skynyrd shined brightly with five highly successful albums, a string of hits, and a continually growing fan base. After the tragic death of lead singer Ronnie Van Zant, guitarist Steve Gaines, and backup vocalist Cassie Gaines (sister to Steve)—not to mention their assistant road manager, pilot, and co-pilot—in a plane crash, the band understandably collapsed from grief. With the likes of "Free Bird," "Simple Man," "Gimme Three Steps," and "Tuesday's Gone," their debut album, *Pronounced Leh-nerd Skin-nerd*, still ranks as a favorite among many fans.

TONE

Gary Rossington and Allen Collins handle guitar duties on "Simple Man." Collins most likely played his Gibson Explorer through a Marshall half stack, while Rossington most likely ran his Les Paul through a Fender Twin or Super Reverb. The tone during the verse arpeggio riffs is on the cleaner side, with only minor break up, whereas the overdubbed single-note interlude riff was likely performed with the amps cranked a bit more to achieve more overdrive.

Grab a Les Paul or similar humbucker-equipped guitar and run through a Marshall or a tweed Fender, and you should be good to go. In order to boost the gain a bit during the lead lines, you'll probably want to run through an overdrive pedal, such as an Ibanez Tube Screamer or something similar. Don't go overboard with the drive knob!

TECHNIQUE

The hardest part of the verse arpeggios is maintaining a strict rhythm and precision with the fret-hand fingers so that all of the open notes are allowed to ring out. The Skynyrd boys arranged the picking patterns so that the chord changes flow beautifully into one another with no clipped notes, which can sometimes happen when one static pattern is blindly applied to every chord. The guitar solo is a study in thematic development, as nearly every phrase is derived from the interlude riff!

"SPIRIT OF RADIO"
Rush

Rush has always been a unique band. After a brief flirtation with bluesier, Zeppelin-esque rock on their debut album, they quickly carved out their own special niche. Though they contained elements of each, they weren't quite metal, weren't quite prog, and certainly weren't pop-rock. You could call them "hard rock" and be safe, but that sells their sound short in numerous ways. Whatever you want to call it, they managed to make it their own, and millions have come along for the ride throughout the years. Among many fan favorites, "Spirit of Radio," from *Permanent Waves* (1980), ranks highly and is considered one of the band's signature songs.

TONE

Alex Lifeson cut "Spirit of Radio" on a modified Fender Stratocaster with a humbucker in the bridge position. He ran through either a Hiwatt or a Marshall amp and a 4x12 cabinet. The flanger heard on the song was an Electro-Harmonix Electric Mistress, and he used a Boss Chorus Ensemble pedal for the rhythm parts. He most likely added a Cry Baby for the wah chorus at the end of the song.

Since the song does contain a bit of whammy work—not to mention the fact that Lifeson occasionally applies vibrato via the whammy bar—a super-Strat-type guitar (with a humbucker in the bridge), such as a Kramer, Ibanez, or Charvel, will most likely be your best option. Fender also makes models that fit this bill, such as the Modern Player Stratocaster HSH or the Standard Stratocaster HSS. The Electric Mistress flanger is still around and is relatively affordable, while the current-production Boss CH-1 Super Chorus or CE-5 Chorus Ensemble would fit the bill in the chorus department. Add a Cry Baby or Vox wah, and you'll be able to cover it all.

TECHNIQUE

The trademark intro lick is not difficult to finger, but it does move along at a pretty good clip. You may want to experiment with different picking patterns to see what feels most natural and affords you the most effortless speed. With regard to rhythm guitar, there are a few tricky chordal hits that combine triplets, eighth notes, and 16th notes in close proximity, so be sure your beat subdivision is accurate during those spots. Lifeson often employs the open first and second strings as drones throughout the song, which requires your fingers to be arched. Keep your eyes out for the fluctuating tempo changes, as well!

"SULTANS OF SWING"
Dire Straits

After experiencing success with their self-titled debut, largely due to their #4 breakout hit, "Sultans of Swing," Dire Straits entered a bit of a holding pattern for the next four years. Though their albums continued to chart well, none of their singles performed as well as "Sultans," and they always seemed poised to make their next big move. Knopfler took a bit of a break after *Love Over Gold* (1982), writing and producing for other projects. The brief hiatus seemed to be just what the band needed, as *Brothers in Arms* (1985) caught fire in a huge way, turning out three Top 20 hits: "Money for Nothing" (#1), "So Far Away" (#19), and "Walk of Life" (#7). The album has gone on to sell over 30 million copies worldwide. Widely revered as one of the best guitarists and songwriters in the business, Mark Knopfler has maintained a diverse career since, working with such legends as Chet Atkins, Eric Clapton, Van Morrison, Sting, and Bob Dylan, to name but a few. For fans of early Dire Straits, "Sultans of Swing" still remains the band's signature song.

TONE

For "Sultans," Knopfler ran his '61 Strat into an early-'60s brownface Fender Vibrolux, which featured one 15-inch speaker. Famously, he jammed his three-position pickup switch in-between the bridge and middle position to generate the often-misnamed "out of phase" sound that remains to this day one of the prime examples of such a tone. The tone is relatively clean though, showing only the faintest hint of breakup when Knopfler digs in significantly.

Newer Strats all feature a five-position switch, so accessing that tone is a much easier affair these days. Fender hasn't reissued the Vibrolux amp, but a blackface amp such as a Twin Reverb, Super Reverb, or a Deluxe Reverb should get you well inside the ballpark.

TECHNIQUE

Obviously, a huge part of Knopfler's tone comes from the fact that he plucks with his fingers, often popping the strings against the fretboard to give them extra snap. In fact, I think if you try to play this song with a pick, your guitar's electronics will simply shut down until the pick is removed from the room. You'll get plenty of practice with 6th intervals and arpeggios with this track, as Knopfler tastefully scatters them about throughout the track.

For the faster playing in the outro solo, Knopfler most often resorts to alternating his thumb with his first finger and, of course, employing pull-offs and hammer-ons. For the lick, barre your fret-hand index finger on strings 1–2 at fret 10. Pluck fret 13, string 1 with your thumb, pull off to fret 10, pluck fret 10, string 2 with your thumb, and then pluck fret 10, string 1 with your first finger (or second, if you prefer). Repeat this same plucking pattern throughout.

"SUNDAY BLOODY SUNDAY"
U2

Few bands have had a career as charmed as U2 with regard to longevity, relevance, and commercial success. With a history spanning nearly 35 years, they've had over ten Top 10 albums, including seven #1 albums in the U.S. (more in the U.K.), more Top 40 hits than you can shake a stick at, and have won 22 Grammy Awards, which is the most by any band. In addition to having written many of the band's hits, guitarist The Edge (a.k.a. Dave Evans) has forged one of the most identifiable guitar sounds in rock history through the thoughtful use of effects, technique, and note choice.

TONE
After establishing his affinity for echo-laden guitar tones on the band's first two albums, the Edge & Co. decided to leave the delays at home for most of *War*. As such, the guitars sound much more present and more "rock 'n' roll" in general. For "Sunday Bloody Sunday," Edge most likely ran his '73 black Fender Strat through a tweed Fender amp. The tone contains a good amount of breakup, so the amp was most likely cranked or possibly dimed.

Grab a Strat and set it on the bridge pickup. Plug into a tweed-style Fender, such as a '59 Bassman reissue or a Blues Deluxe reissue, and crank it to at least 7 or so. You want a decent amount of breakup when you dig in.

TECHNIQUE
For the main arpeggio riff in the intro, barre your index finger across fret 2, strings 3–1. You can keep it there for the Bm and D chords. For G6, you simply lift your first finger. This is the way Edge plays it. It's very economical and results in smooth transitions between the chords. There's a good deal of *scratch rhythm* playing (X's in the music) once things pick up in the song. To execute the scratch rhythms, simply touch the strings with your fret hand without pushing them down to the fretboard. When you strum the strings, you should get a dead, scratchy sound. Your fret hand controls when you want to sound the chord and when you want the dead scratch-rhythm sound.

from Montrose - *Montrose*

Bad Motor Scooter

Words and Music by Sammy Hagar

Gtr. 1: Tuning:
(low to high) G♭-G-D-G-B-D

Intro
Free time

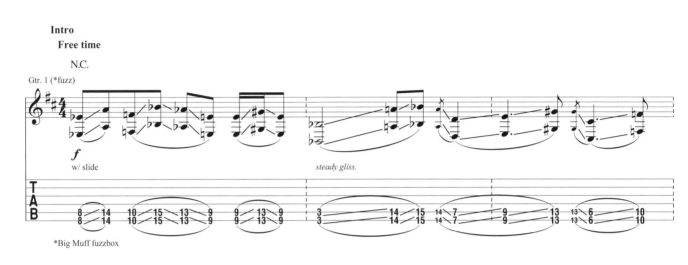

*Big Muff fuzzbox

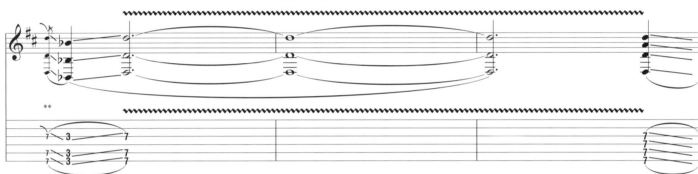

**G string sounds from slide.

Half-time feel

Gtr. 1 tacet

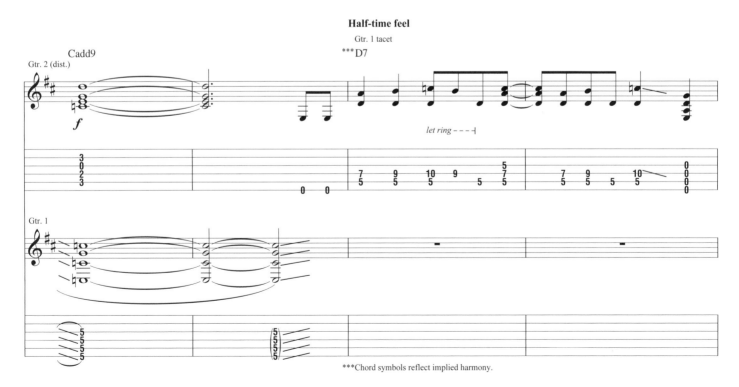

***Chord symbols reflect implied harmony.

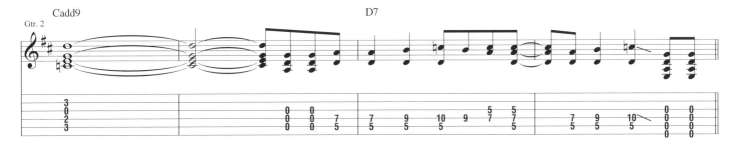

Verse

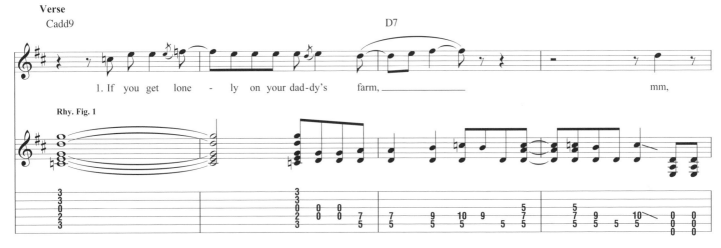

1. If you get lone - ly on your dad-dy's farm, _____ mm,

uh, just re-mem - ber I don't live too far, _____

End Rhy. Fig. 1

Gtr. 2: w/ Rhy. Fig. 1

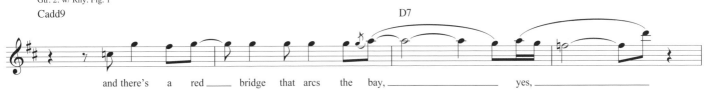

and there's a red _____ bridge that arcs the bay, _____ yes, _____

End half-time feel

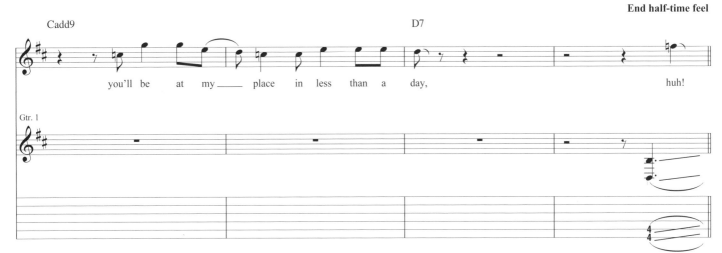

you'll be at my _____ place in less than a day, _____ huh!

Gtr. 1

Chorus

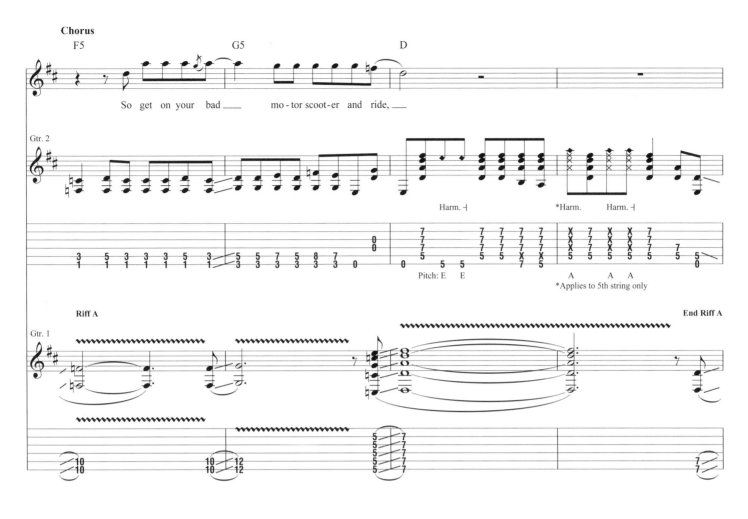

So get on your bad ___ mo-tor scoot-er and ride, ___

Harm. — / *Harm.* — *Harm.* — /

Pitch: E E   A A A
*Applies to 5th string only

Riff A   **End Riff A**

Gtr. 1: w/ Riff A (2 times)

up o-ver at my ___ place and stay all night, _____ hmm, ___ yeah.

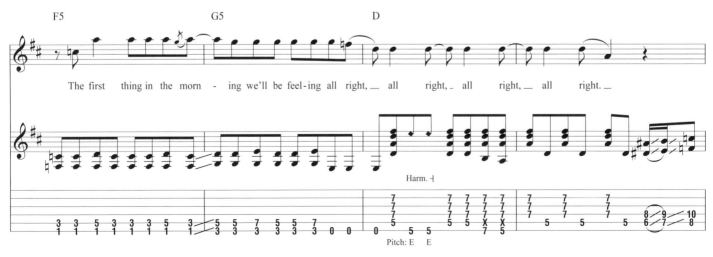

The first thing in the morn - ing we'll be feel-ing all right, __ all right, __ all right, __ all right. __

Harm. — /

Pitch: E E

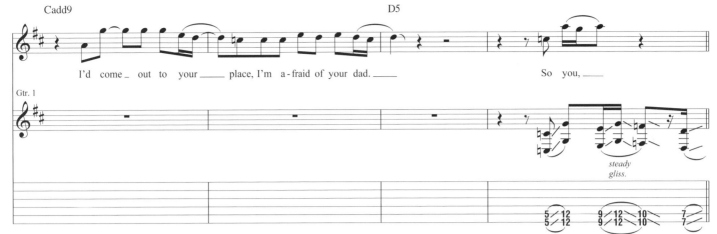

Chorus

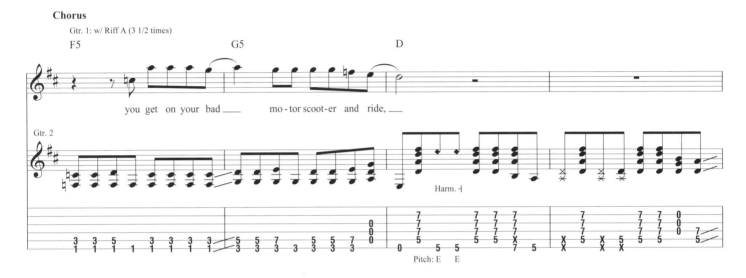

Get on your bad ____ mo - tor scoot-er and ride, _____ yeah.

Ride, ____ ride, ____ ride. _____ Come on, ba -

steady gliss.

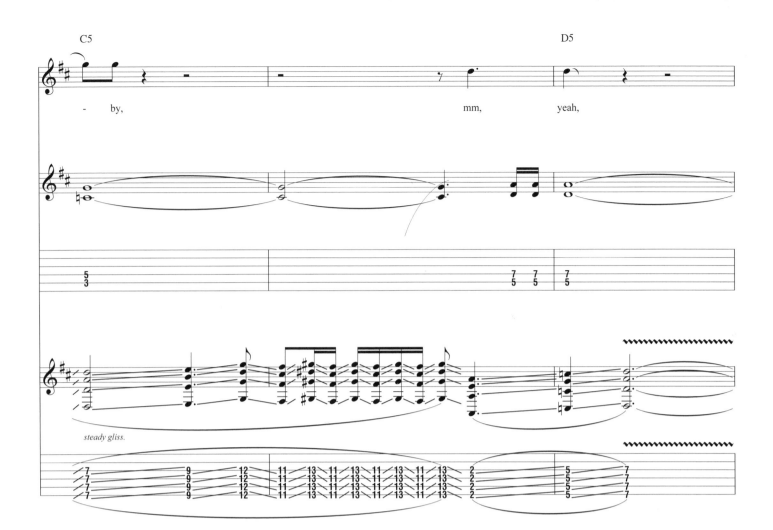

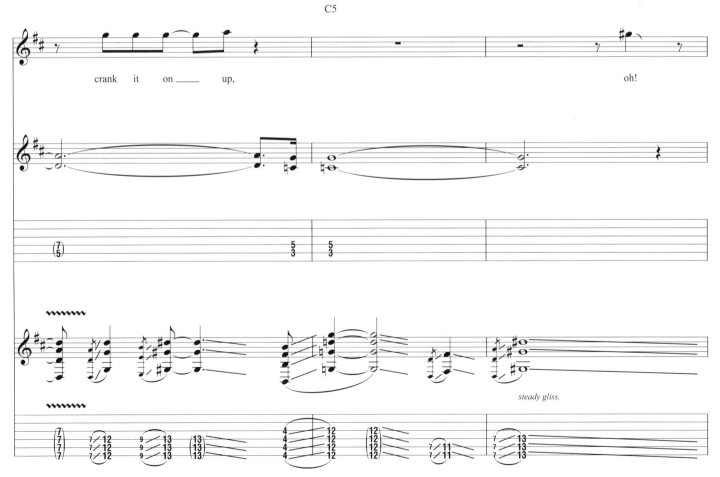

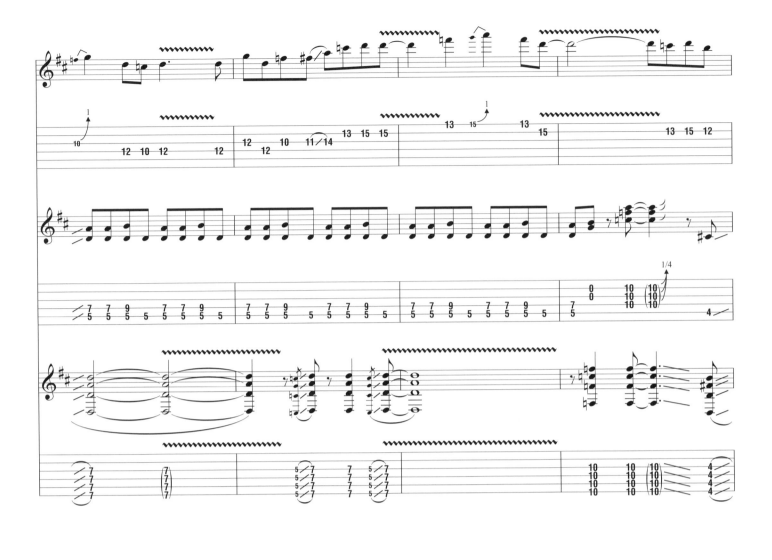

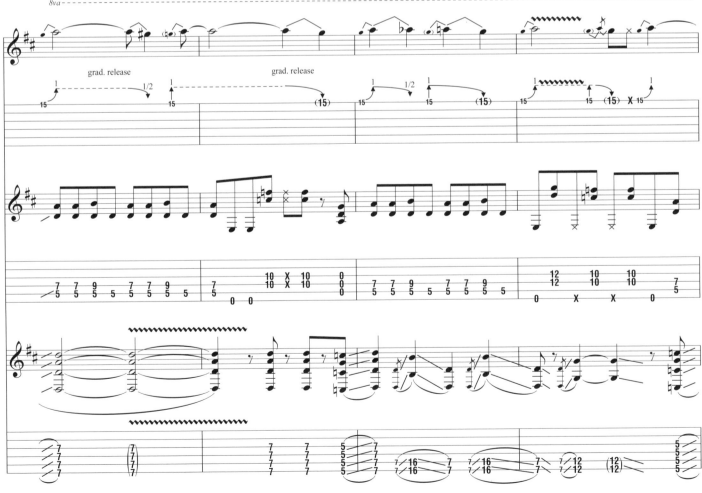

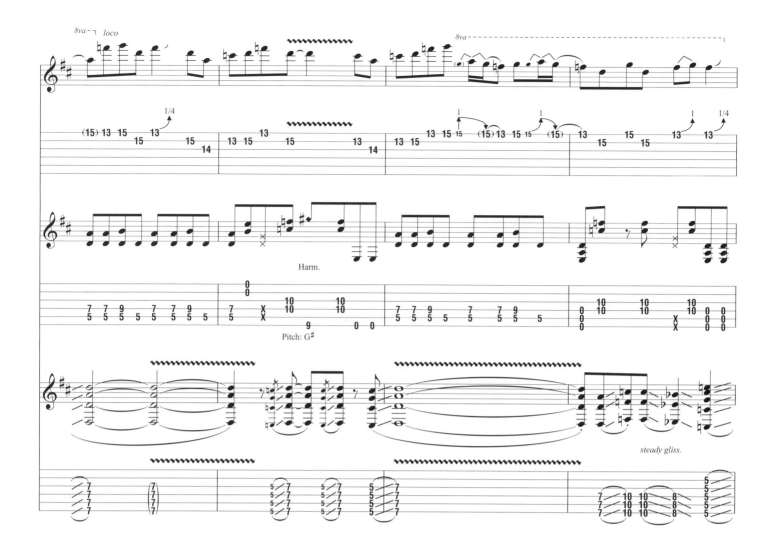

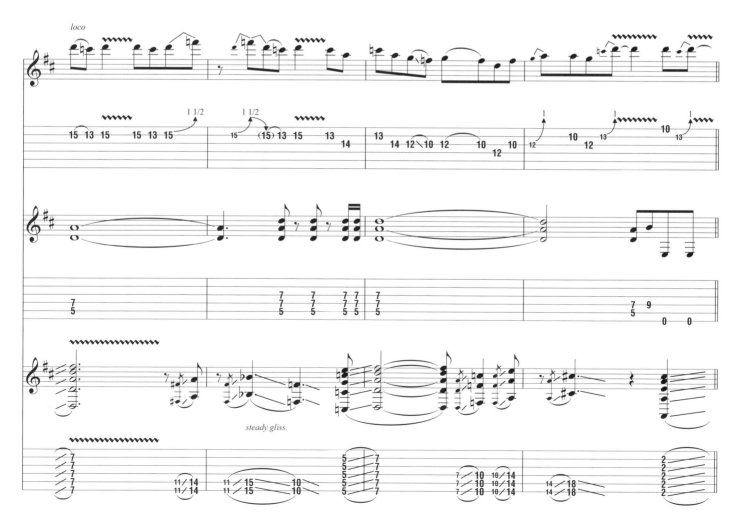

Get on your bad _____ mo-tor scoot-er.

Outro
Free time

Gtr. 3 tacet

Get on your bad _____ mo-tor scoot - er, uh,

get on your bad _____ mo - tor scoot - er,

and _____

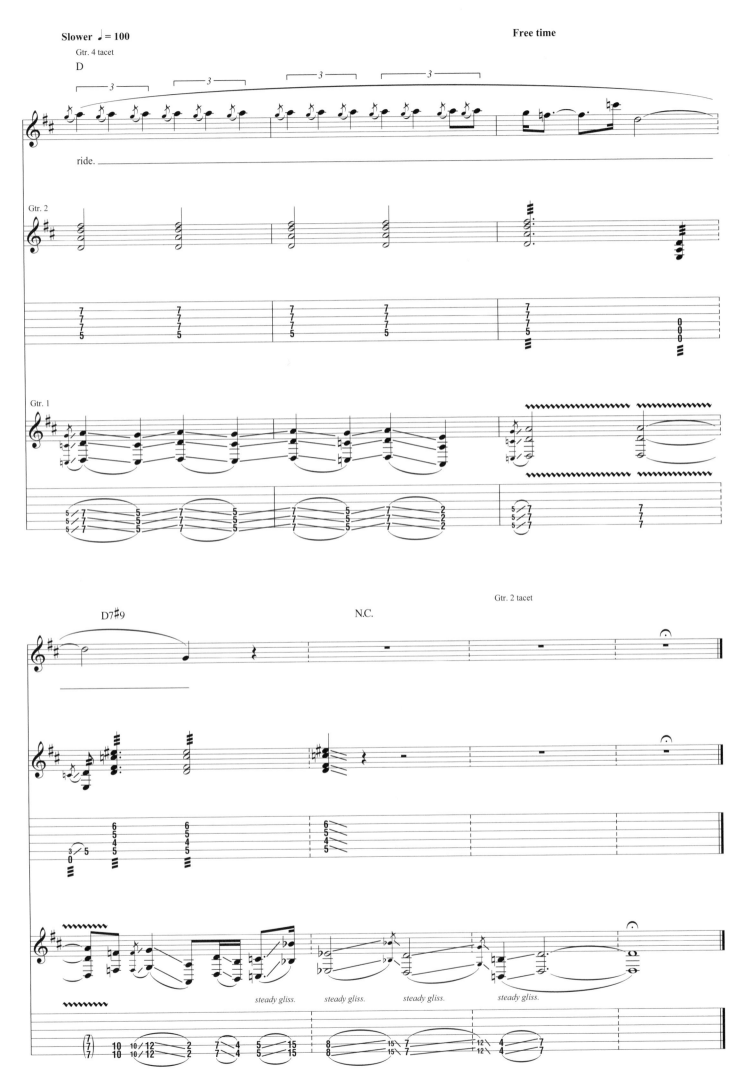

Black and Blue

Words and Music by Edward Van Halen, Alex Van Halen, Michael Anthony and Sammy Hagar

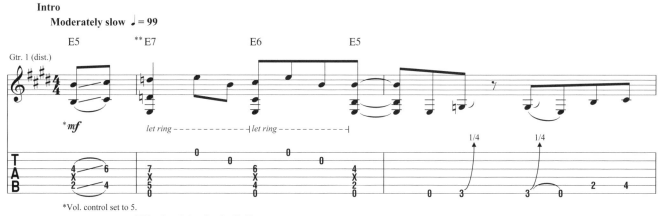

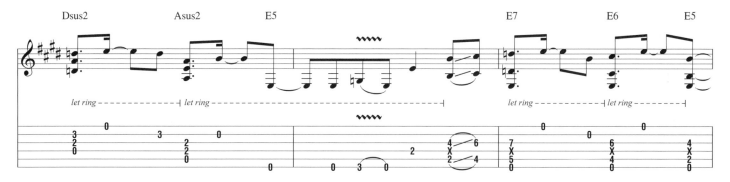

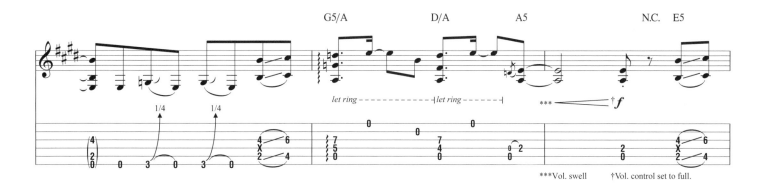

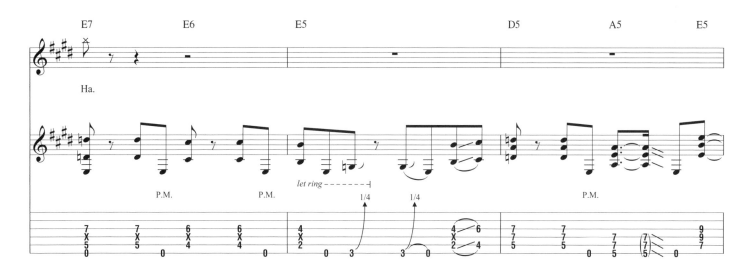

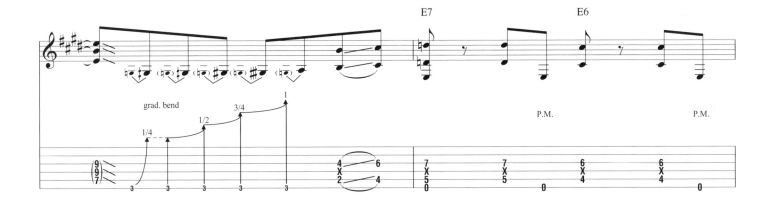

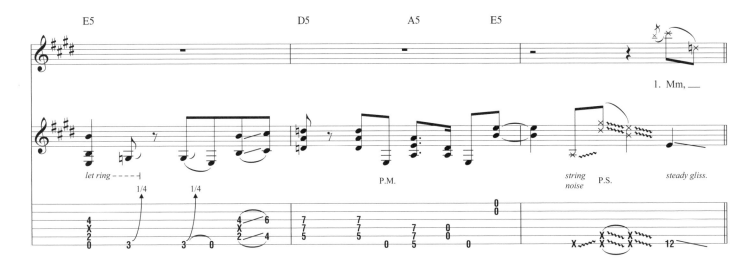

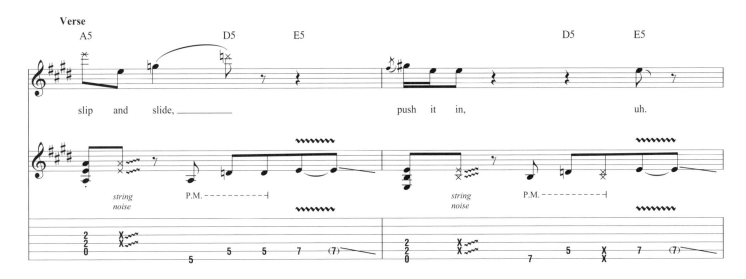

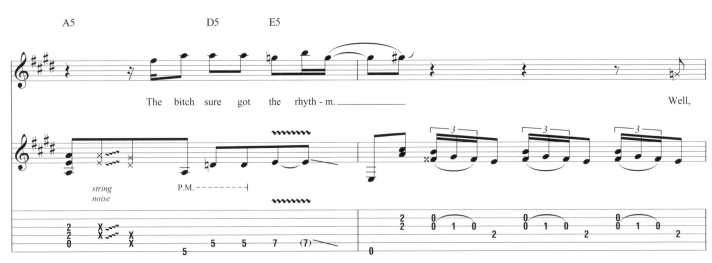

34

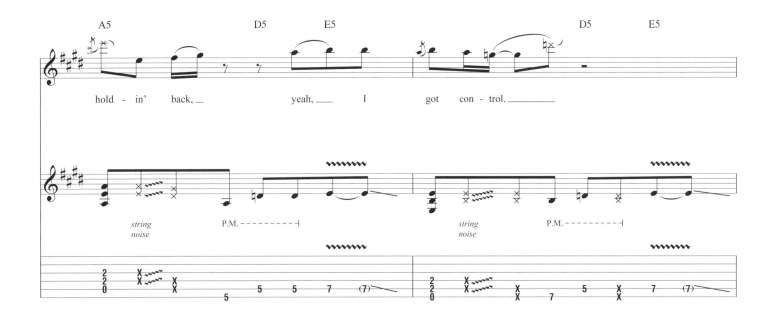

hold - in' back, ____ yeah, ____ I got con - trol. ____

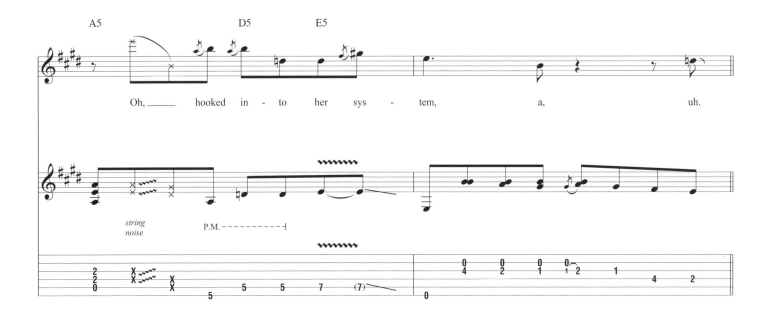

Oh, ____ hooked in - to her sys - tem, a, ____ uh.

Chorus

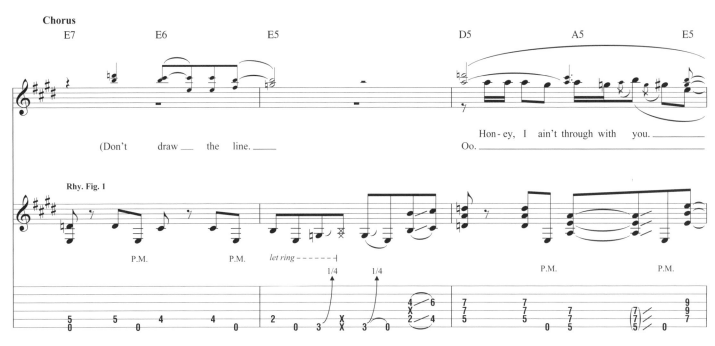

(Don't draw ____ the line. ____)

Hon - ey, I ain't through with you. ____

Oo. ____

it. _____ Lit - tle bit o' ev - 'ry - thing, _____

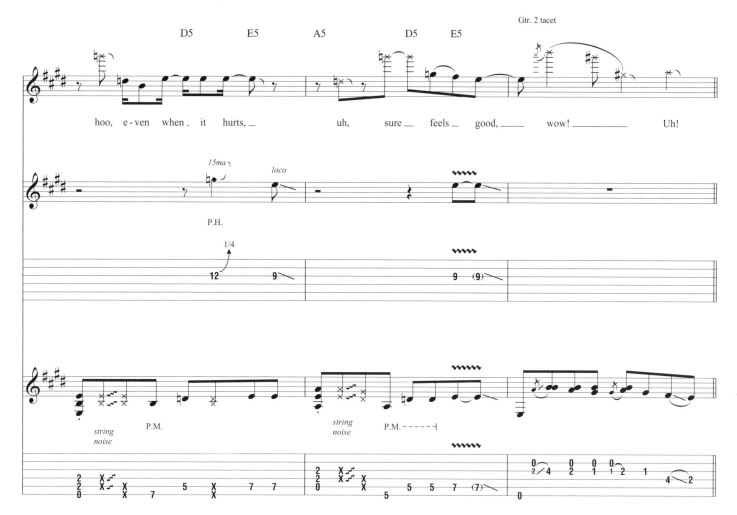

hoo, e - ven when _ it hurts, _____ uh, sure _ feels _ good, _____ wow! _____ Uh!

Chorus

(Don't draw _____ the line. _____

Hon-ey, I ain't through with you. _____ Woo!
Oo. _____

Uh, the hard-er the bet-ter... _____ Do it till we're black and _____ blue.)
...black and blue.

Bridge

Yo, ___ ma - ma, ha!

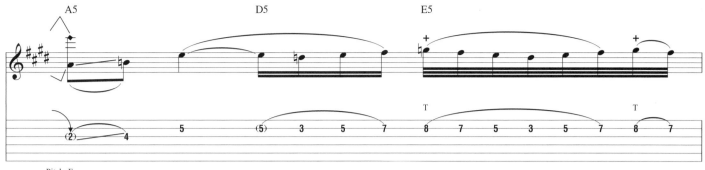

Pitch: E

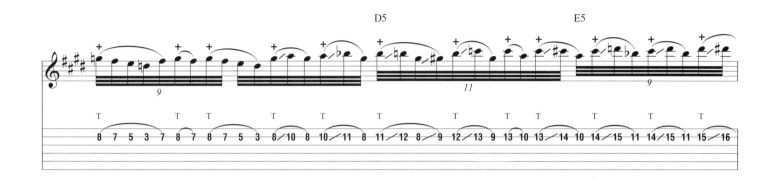

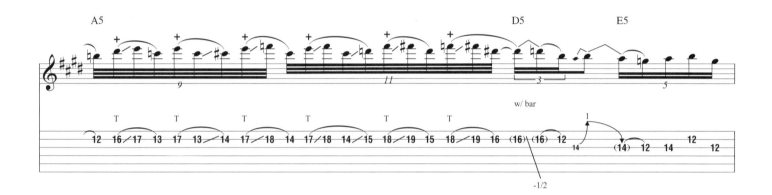

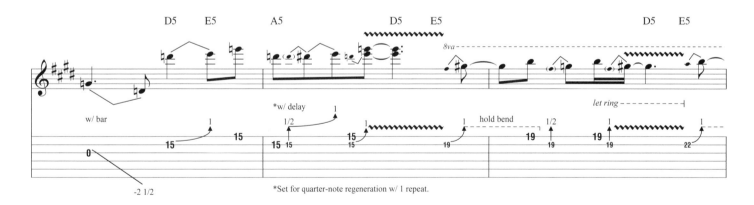

*Set for quarter-note regeneration w/ 1 repeat.

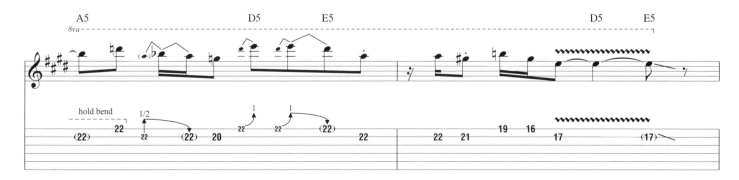

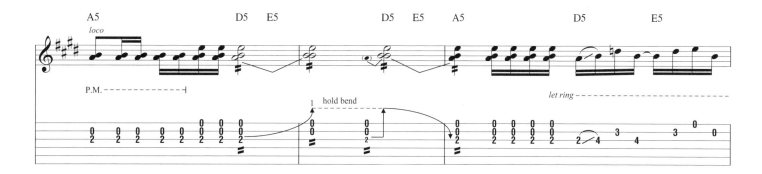

Interlude

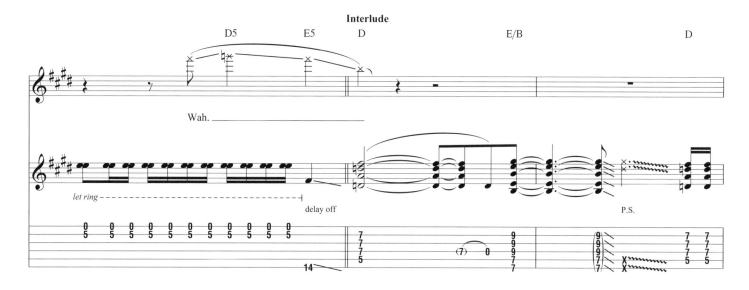

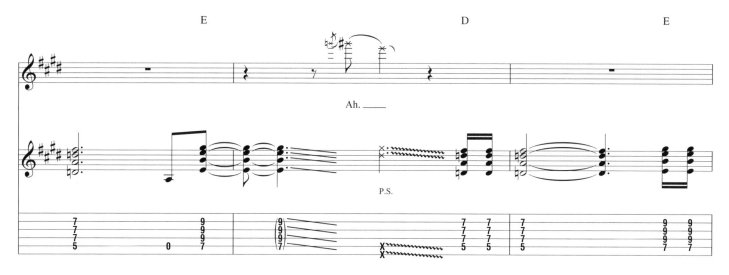

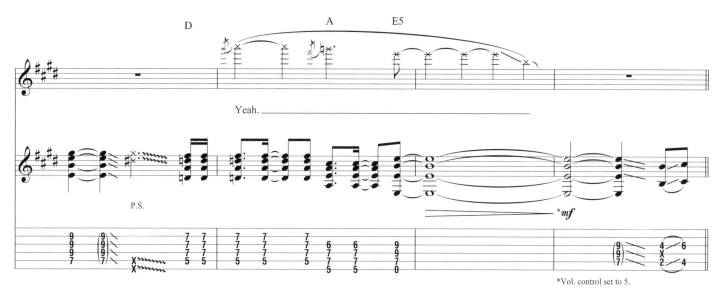

*Vol. control set to 5.

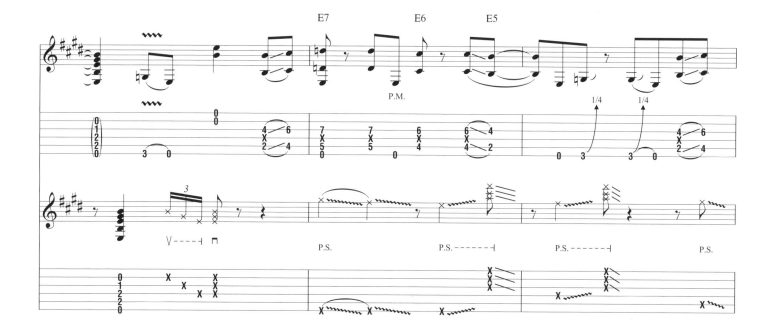

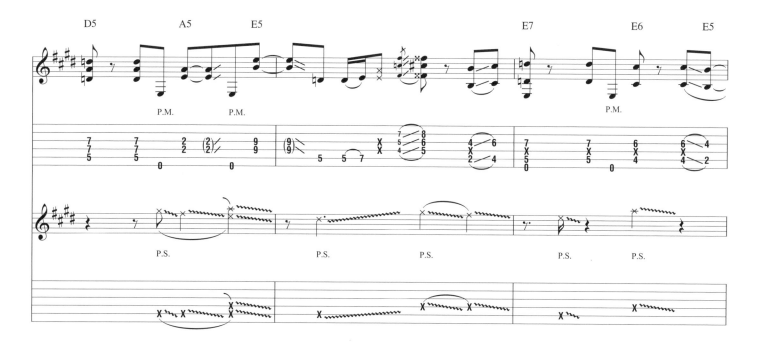

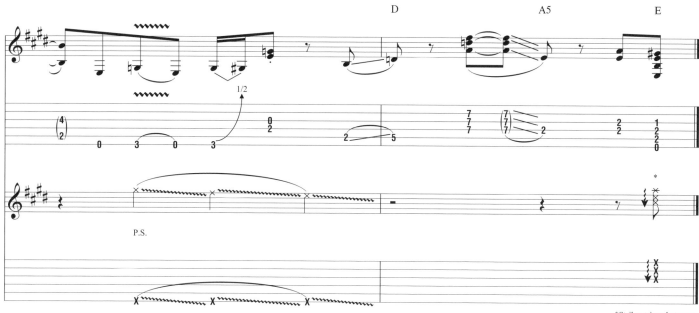

*Strike strings between
nut and tuners.

from Michael Jackson - *Number Ones*

Black or White

Words and Music by Michael Jackson

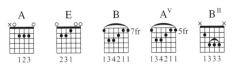

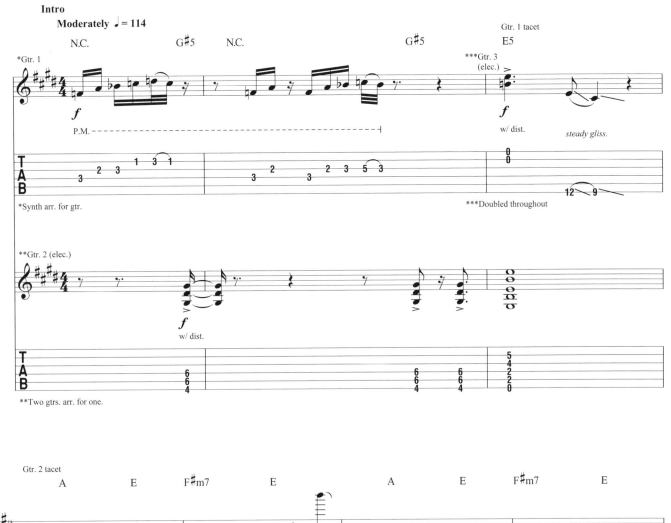

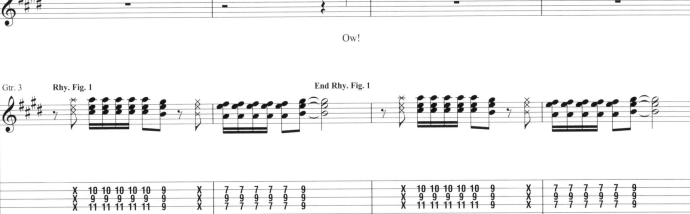

51

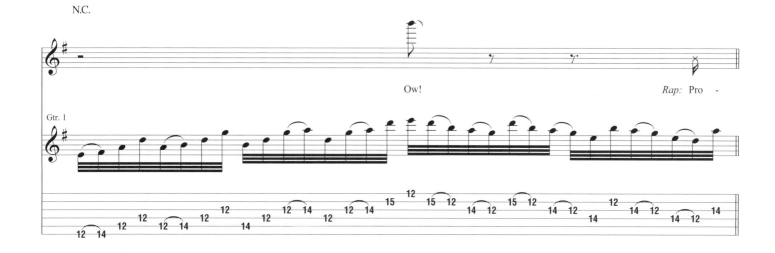

Ow!

Rap: Pro -

Breakdown

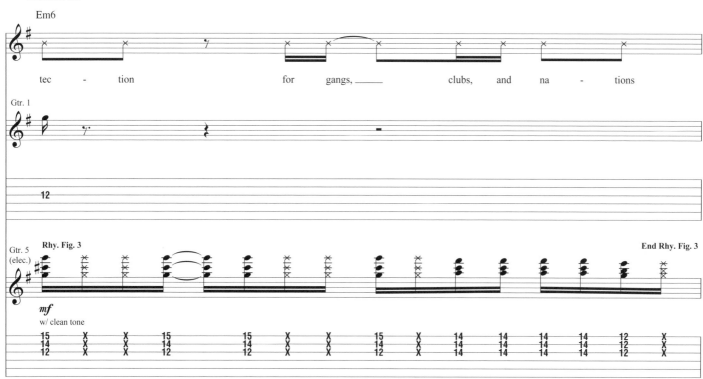

tec - tion for gangs, _____ clubs, and na - tions

Gtr. 1 tacet
Gtr. 5: w/ Rhy. Fig. 3 (6 times)

caus - ing grief in hu - man re - la - tions. It's a turf war on a glob - al scale.

I'd rath - er hear both sides of the tale. ___ See, it's not a - bout rac - es, just the plac - es,

fac - es. Where your blood comes from is where your space is. I've seen the bright get dull - er. I'm

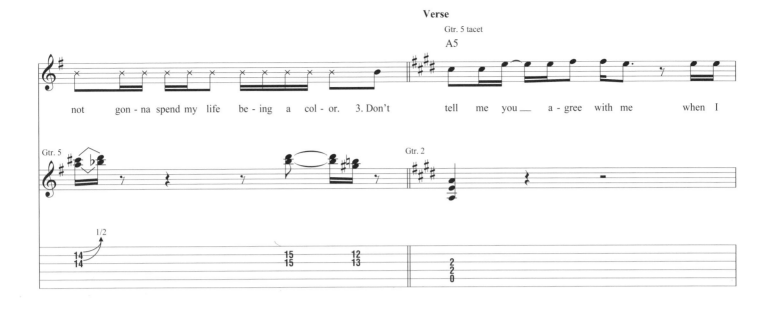

Can't You Hear Me Knocking

Words and Music by Mick Jagger and Keith Richards

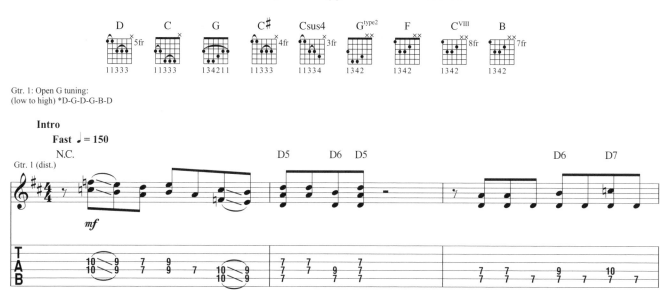

Gtr. 1: Open G tuning:
(low to high) *D-G-D-G-B-D

Intro

Fast ♩ = 150

Gtr. 1 (dist.)

*Keith Richards removes 6th string.

Half-time feel

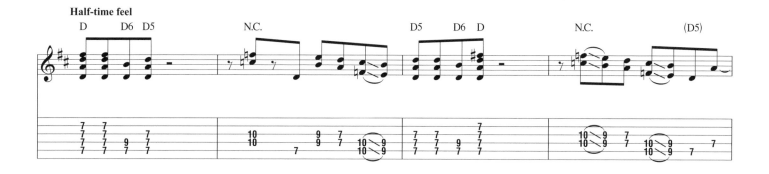

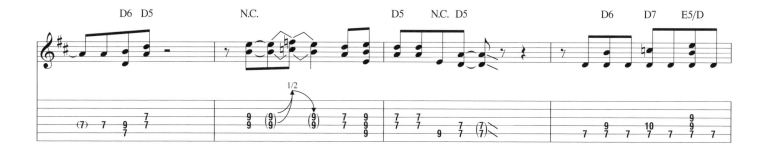

*See top of first page of song for chord diagrams pertaining to rhythm slashes.

sat - in shoes. _____   Yeah, _ you got

plas - tic boots. _____   Y'all _ got

co - caine eyes. _____   Yeah, _ you got

down your dirt - y street? ____   Yeah.

Chorus

Help me, ba - by,   ain't   no   stran - ger.

Help me, ba - by,   ain't   no   stran - ger.

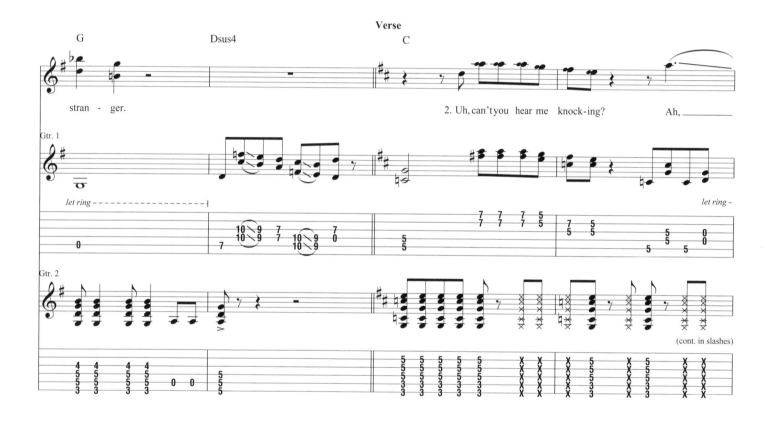

down the gas light street, now? _____ Uh, can't you hear me knock-ing? Yeah.

Well, throw me down the keys. _____ All right, now.

Chorus

Hear me ring-ing big bell tolls. _____

now. _____ And __ all, all a-round your town.
Hear me knock - ing.

Interlude

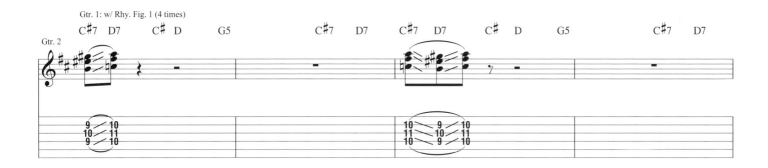

Sax Solo

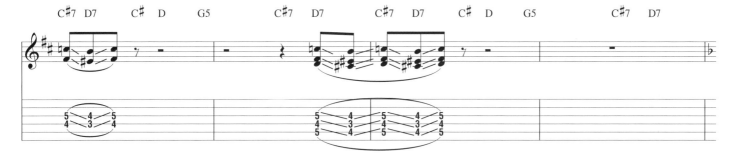

*Dm

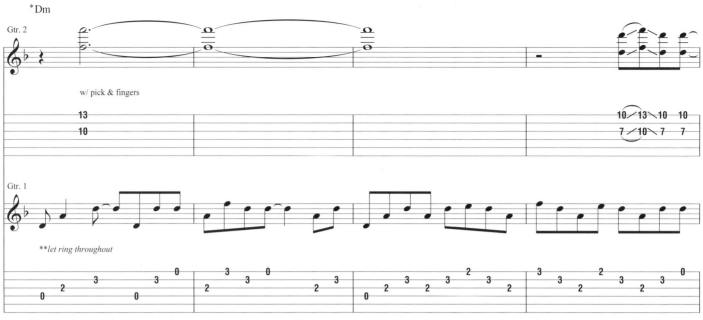

Gtr. 2

w/ pick & fingers

Gtr. 1

**let ring throughout

*Chord symbol reflects basic harmony.
  **(next 34 meas.)

let ring -

Gtr. 2: w/ Rhy. Fig. 2 (3 times)

Gtr. 1

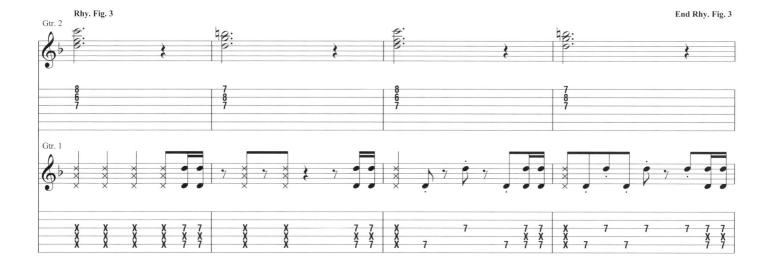

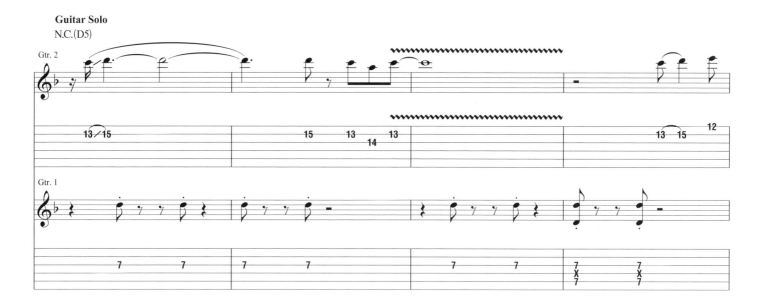

Guitar Solo

N.C.(D5)

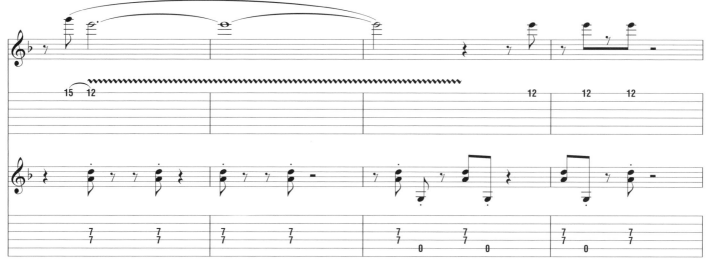

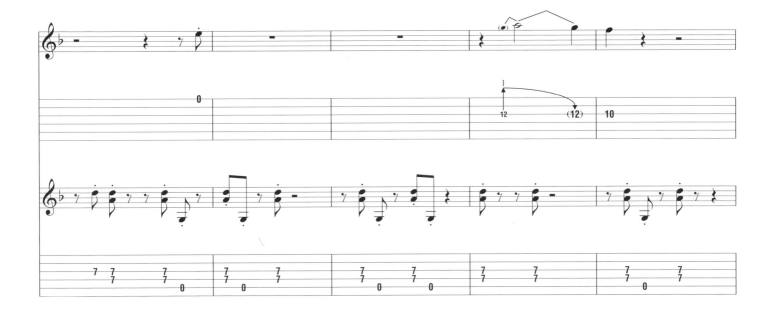

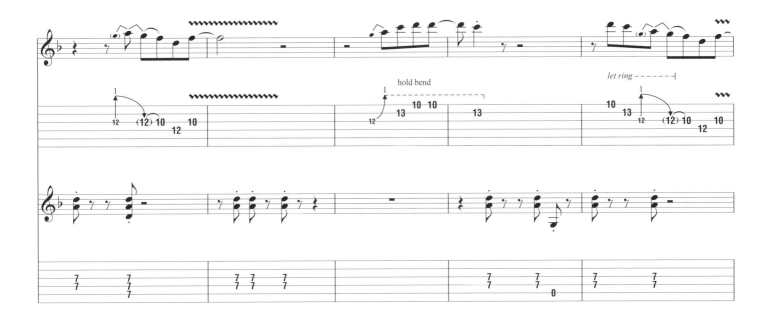

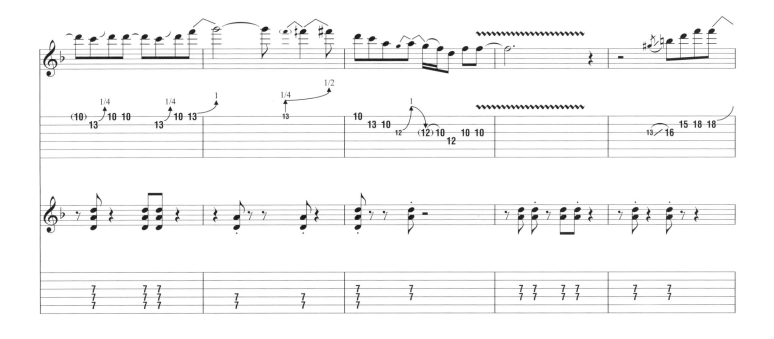

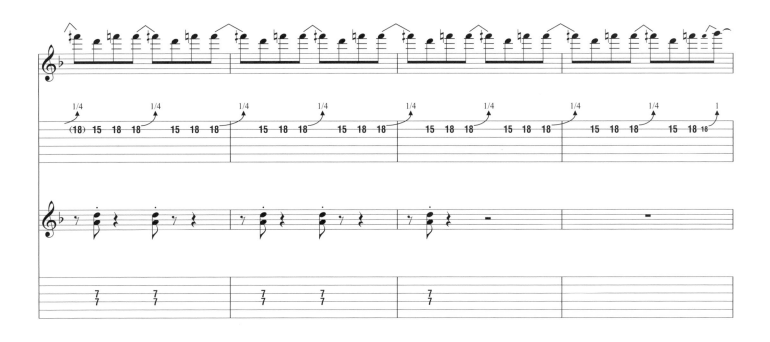

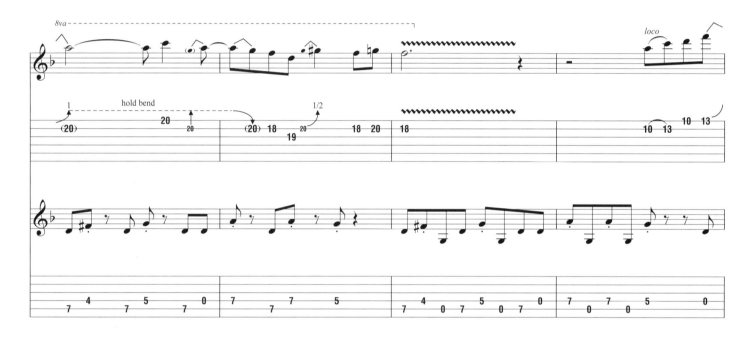

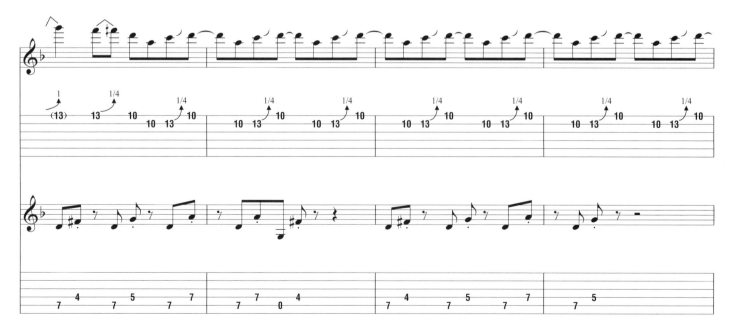

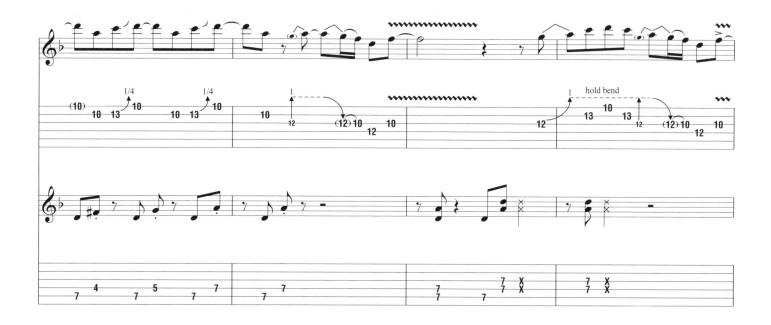

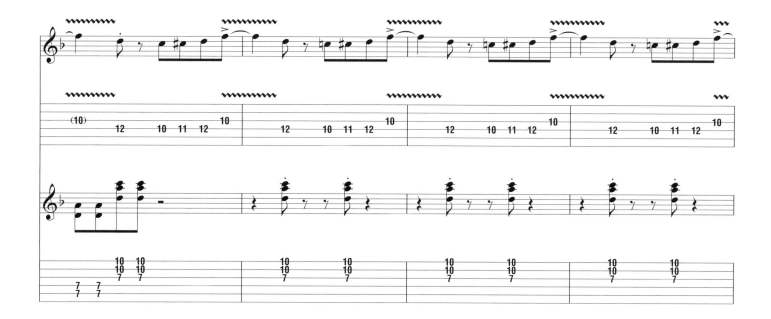

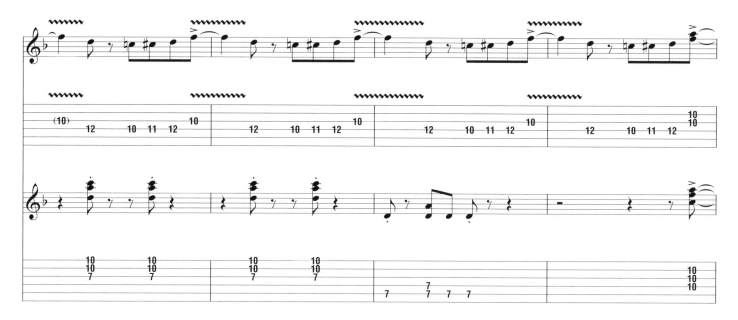

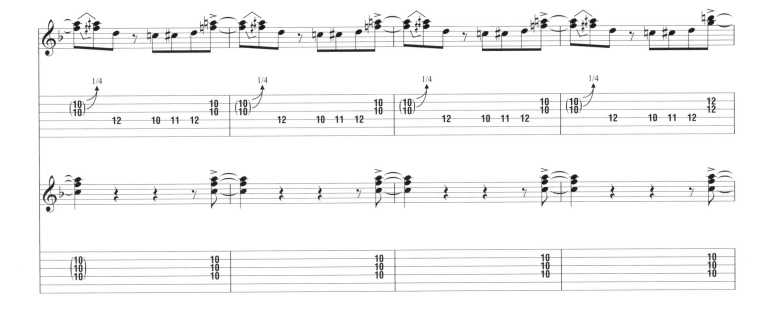

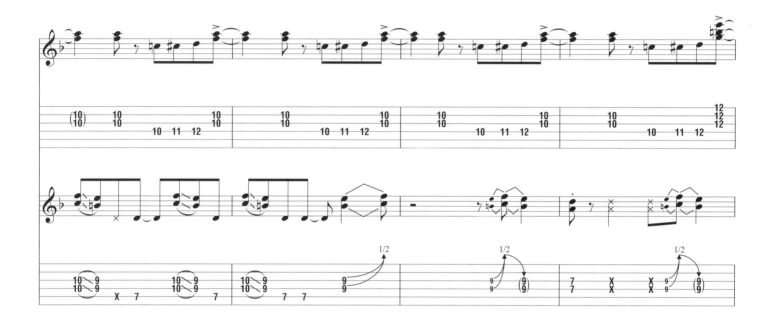

Cocaine

Words and Music by J.J. Cale

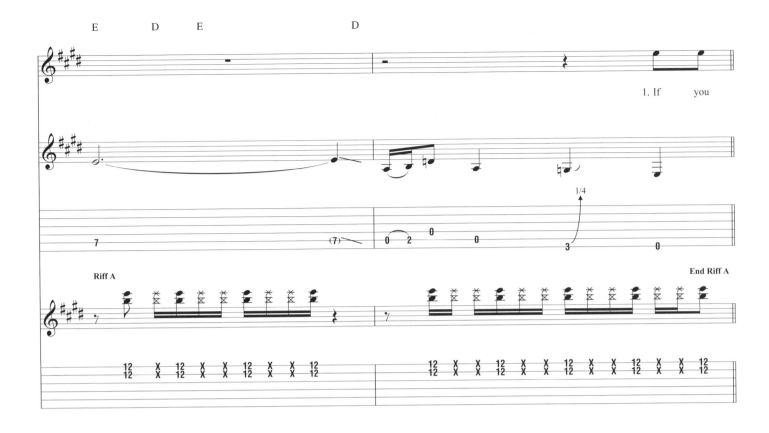

She don't lie, _____ she don't lie, _____ she don't lie, _____ co - caine. _____

2. If you

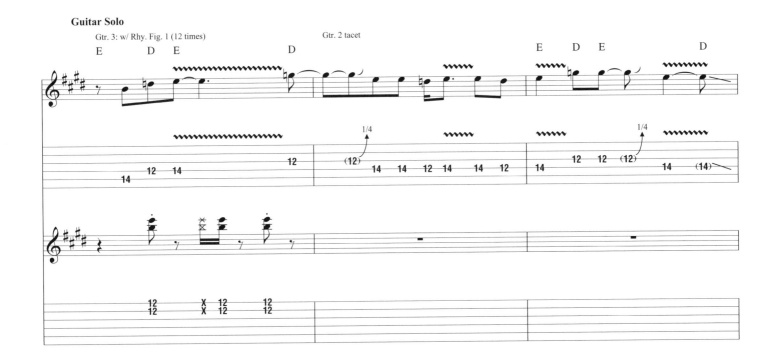

Guitar Solo

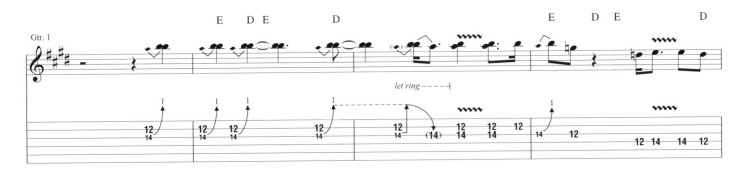

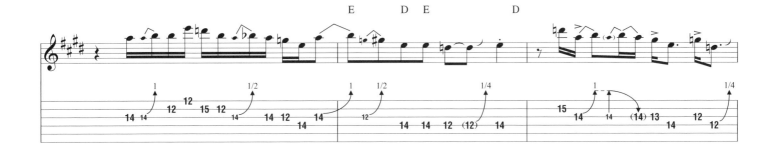

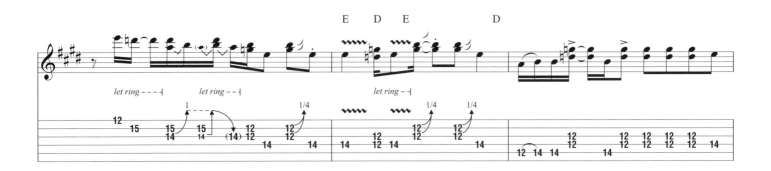

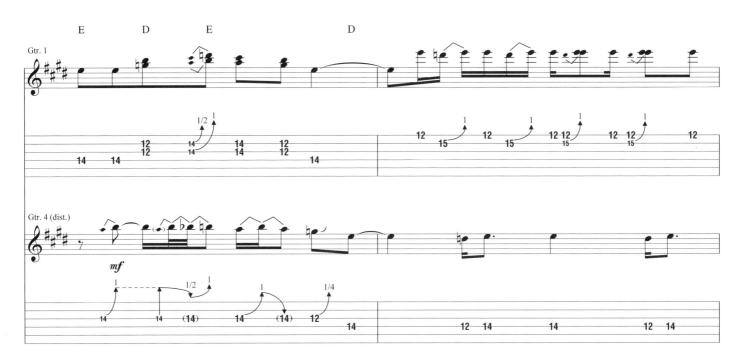

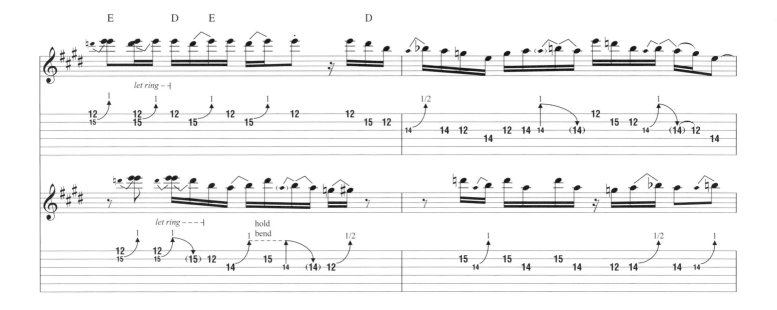

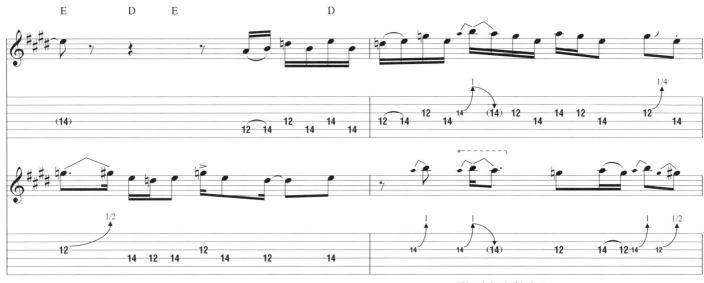

*Played ahead of the beat.

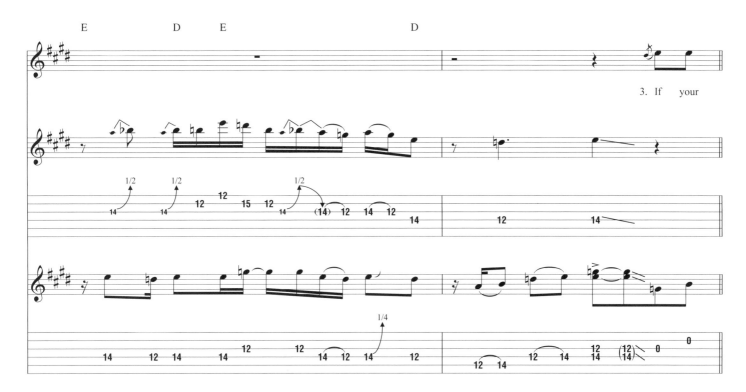

3. If your

Verse

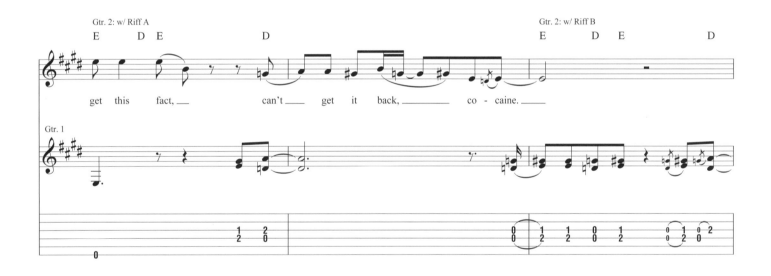

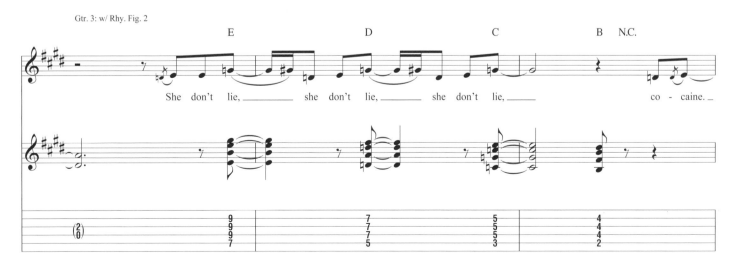

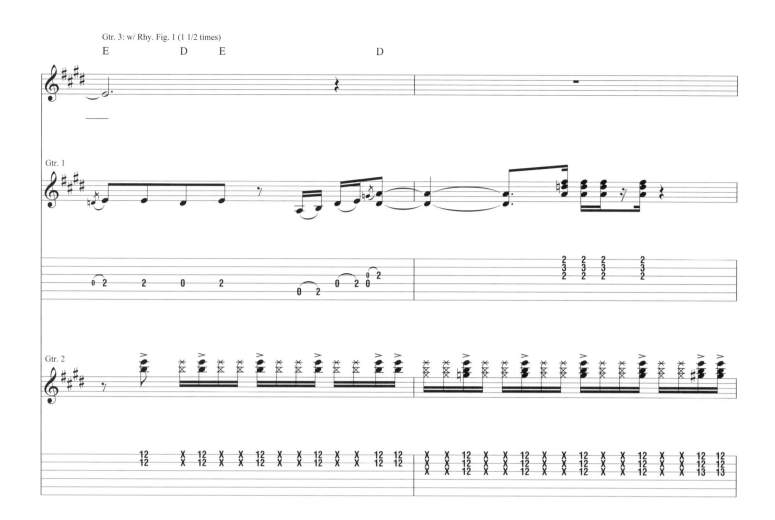

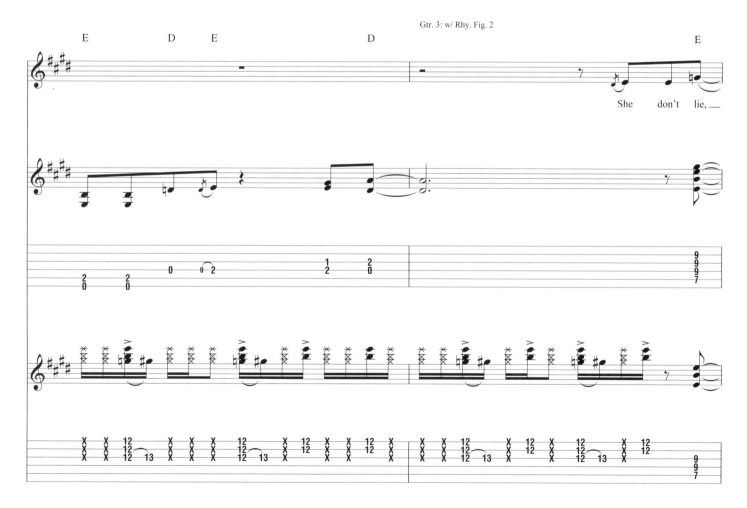

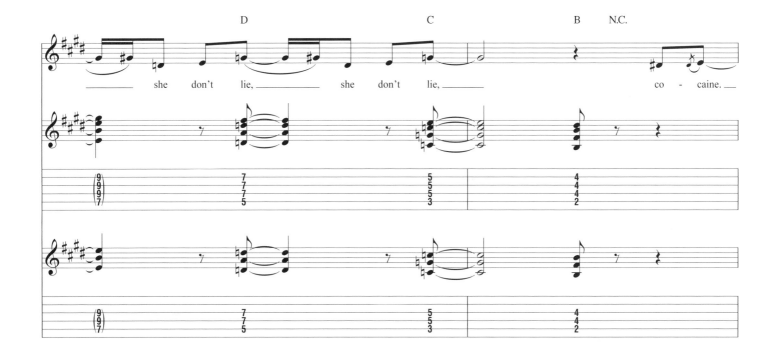

she don't lie, she don't lie, co - caine.

Gtr. 3: w/ Rhy. Fig. 1 (2 times)

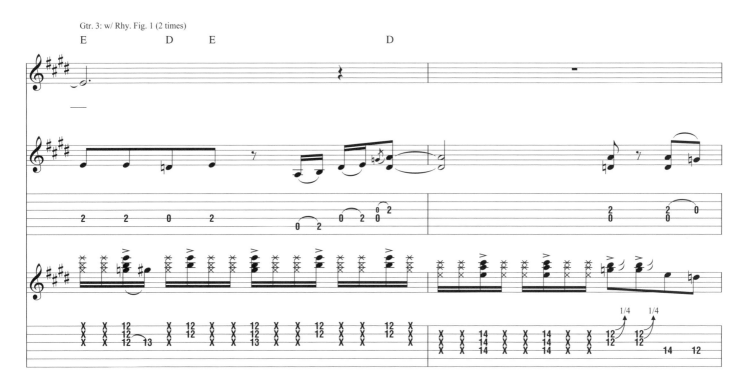

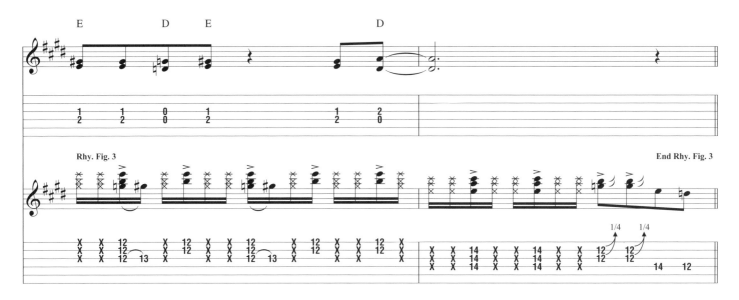

Rhy. Fig. 3

End Rhy. Fig. 3

Outro

Gtr. 2: w/ Rhy. Fig. 3 (till fade)
Gtr. 3: w/ Rhy. Fig. 1 (till fade)

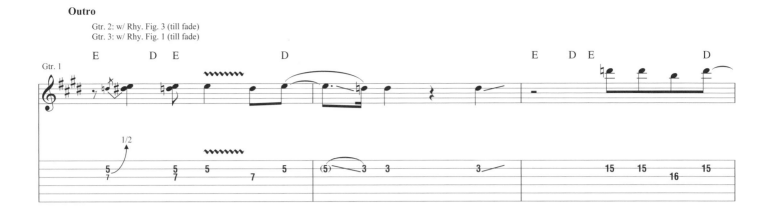

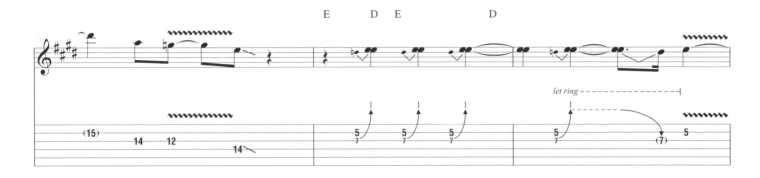

Begin fade

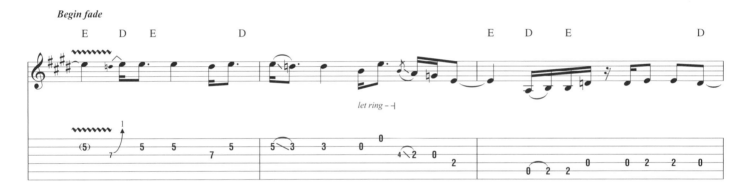

Fade out

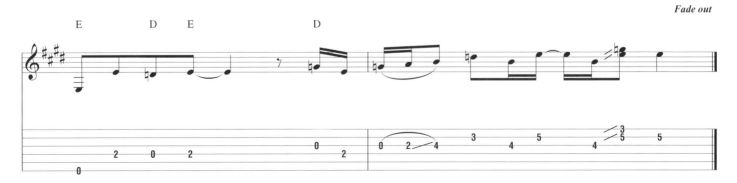

from R.E.M. - *Automatic for the People*

Everybody Hurts

Words and Music by William Berry, Peter Buck, Michael Mills and Michael Stipe

Chorus

Don't let your - self go, ___

*See top of first page of song for chord diagrams pertaining to rhythm slashes.

'cause ev - 'ry - bod-y cries. ___

And ev - 'ry - bod-y hurts ___ some -

- times. _____ Some - times ev - 'ry - thing is

wrong. Now it's time ___ to sing a -

Bridge

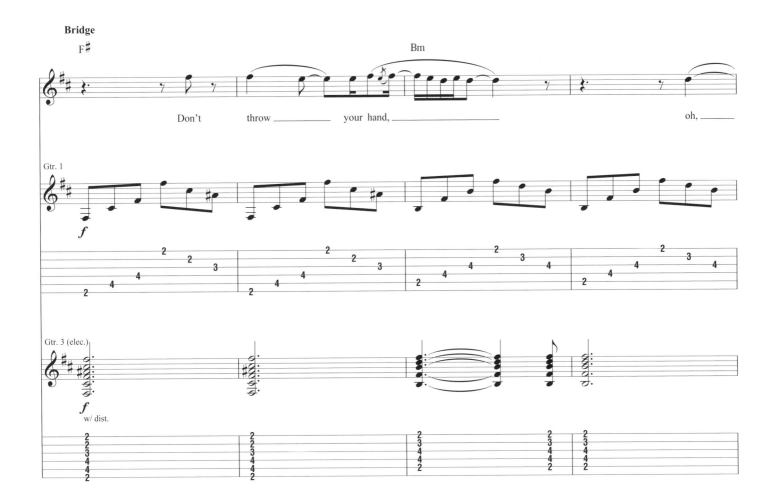

Don't throw ____ your hand, ____ oh, ____

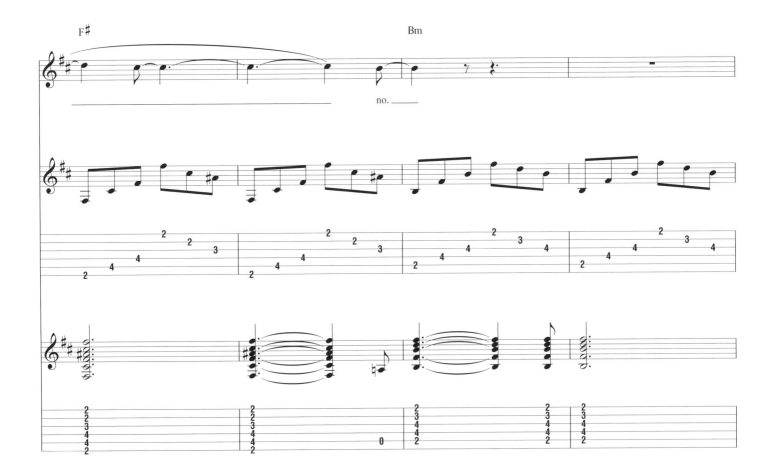

no. ____

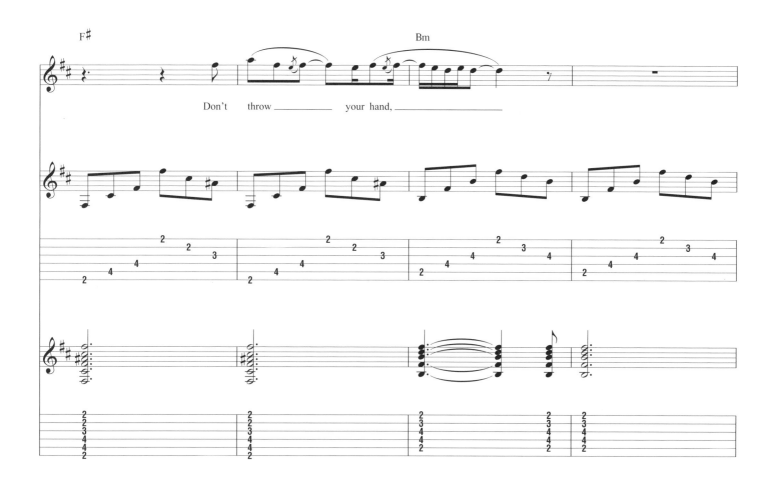

Don't throw _____ your hand, _____

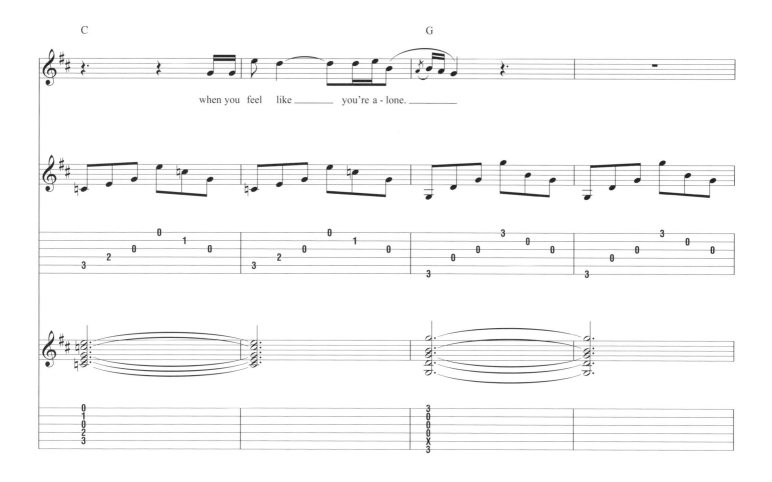

when you feel like _____ you're a - lone. _____

No, no, no, you are not a-lone.

Verse
Gtr. 1: w/ Riff A (3 3/4 times)
Gtr. 3 tacet

3. If you're on ___ your own ___ in this life, ___

___ the days and nights ___ are long. ___

When you think you've ___ had too ___ much ___ of this life ___

Gtr. 1: w/ Fill 1

___ to hang on. ___

Chorus
Gtr. 1: w/ Riff B
Gtr. 2: w/ Rhy. Fig. 1

Well, ev - 'ry - bod - y hurts. ___ Some -

Fat Bottomed Girls

Words and Music by Brian May

Drop D tuning:
(low to high) D-A-D-G-B-E

Intro
Moderately slow ♩ = 86

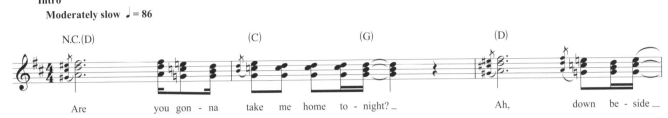

Are   you gon - na   take   me   home   to - night? ___   Ah,   down   be - side ___

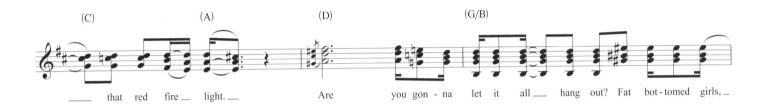

___ that   red   fire ___ light. ___   Are   you gon - na   let   it   all ___ hang   out? Fat   bot - tomed girls, ___

___   you   make   the   rock - in'   world ___   go   'round.

*Gtrs. 1 & 2 (dist.)

mf
let ring
throughout

*Composite arrangement

**D5   Csus2

**Chord symbols reflect implied harmony.

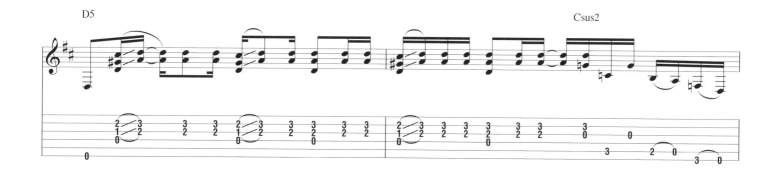

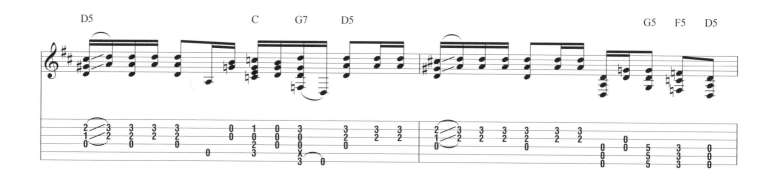

Hey. _____ 1. I was

Verse

just a skin-ny lad, ___ nev-er knew ___ no good from bad, ___ but I knew

95

life be-fore___ I left my nur-ser-y._____ Huh. Left a-lone___

___ with big fat Fan-ny, she was such a naugh-ty nan-ny, heap big

wom-an, you made a bad boy out of me._____

Interlude

Hey, hey!

96

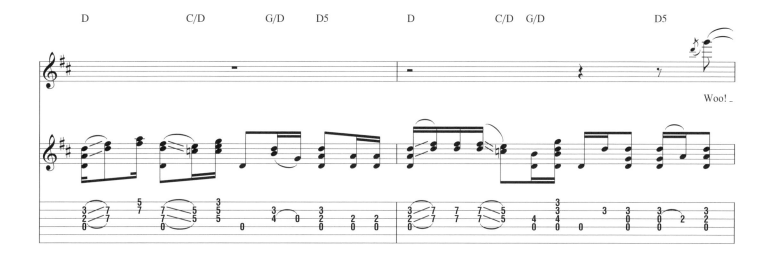

Woo! _

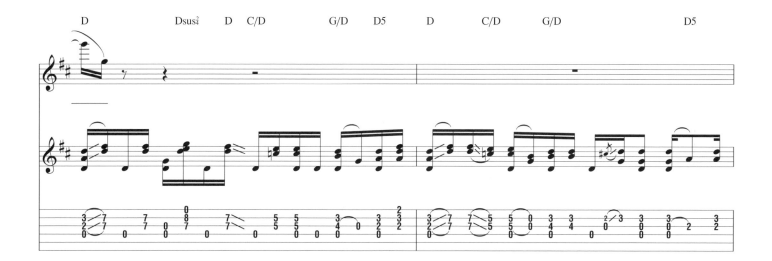

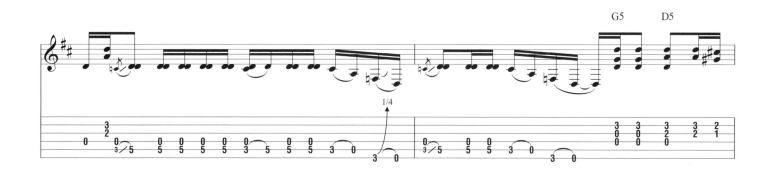

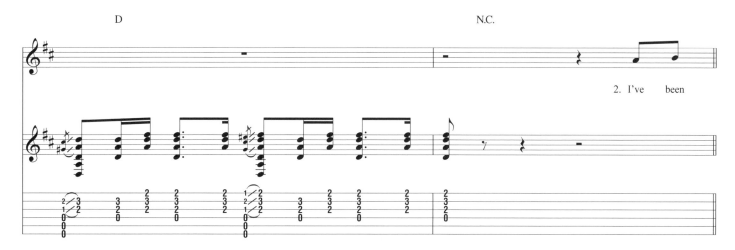

2. I've been

Verse

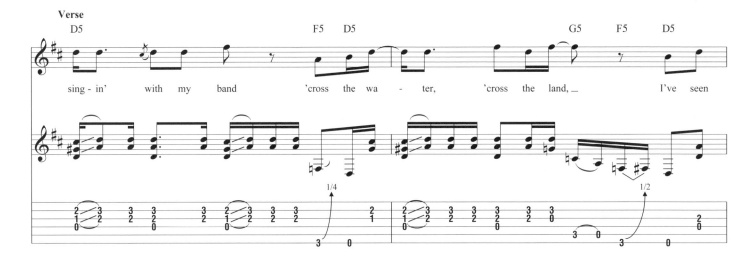

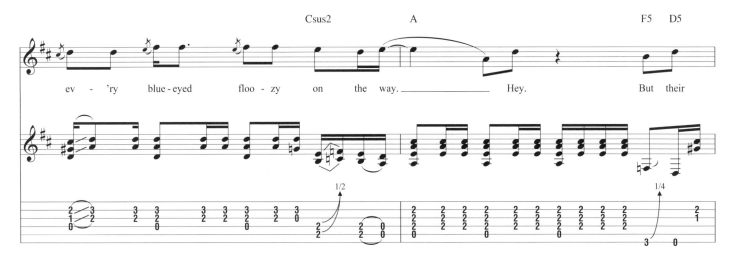

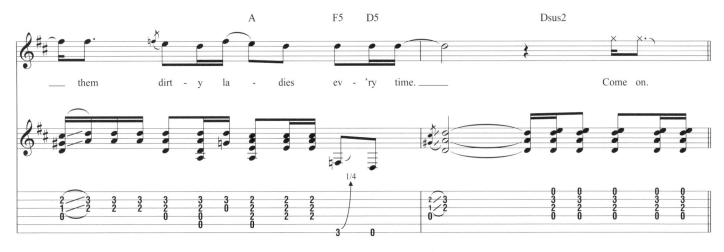

Chorus

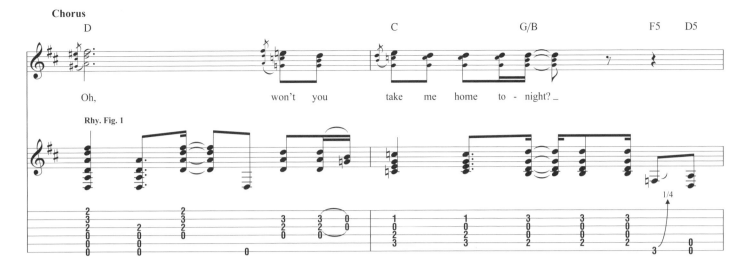

Oh, won't you take me home to-night?

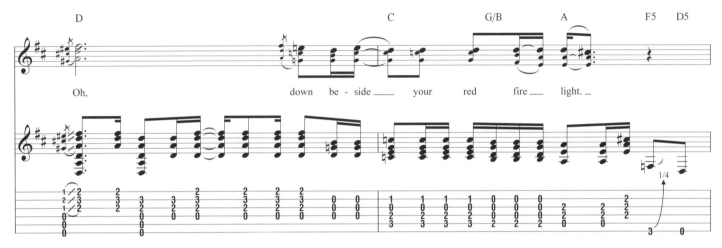

Oh, down be-side your red fire light.

Oh, and you give it all you got, fat bot-tomed girls,

you make the rock-in' world go 'round. Fat bot-tomed girls,

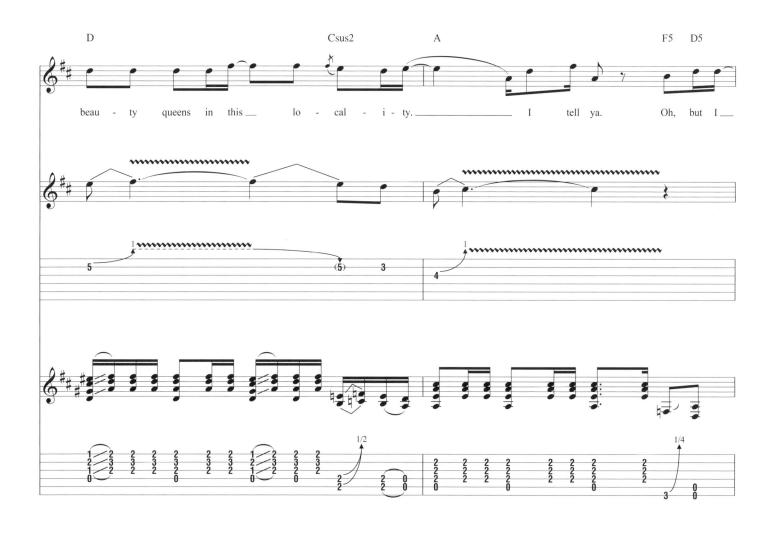

beau - ty queens in this __ lo - cal - i - ty. _____ I tell ya. Oh, but I __

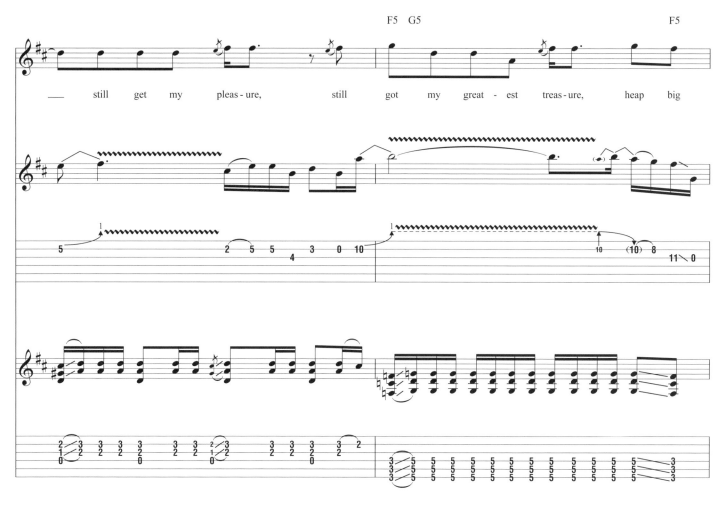

__ still get my pleas - ure, still got my great - est treas - ure, heap big

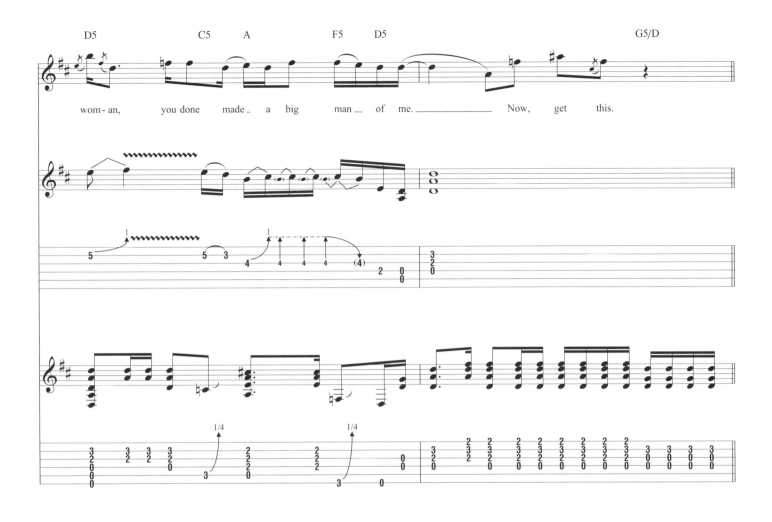

woman, you done made a big man of me. Now, get this.

Chorus

Gtrs. 1 & 2: w/ Rhy. Fig. 1
Gtr. 3 tacet

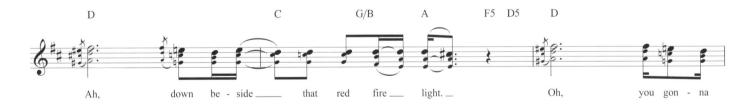

Oh, I know. Please.

Are you gon-na take me home to-night?

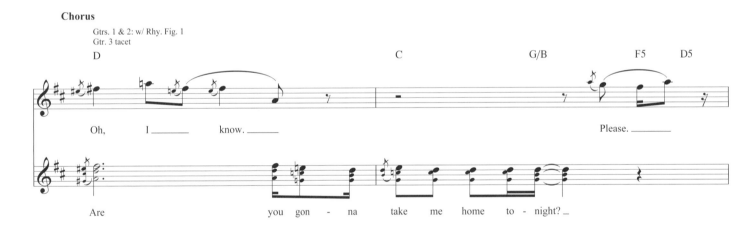

Ah, down be-side that red fire light. Oh, you gon-na

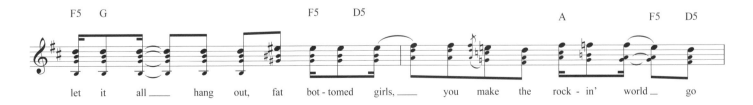

let it all hang out, fat bot-tomed girls, you make the rock-in' world go

'round. Yeah, ___ fat bot - tomed girls, ___ you make the rock - in' world ___ go

Outro

'round. ___ Get on your bikes ___ and ride.

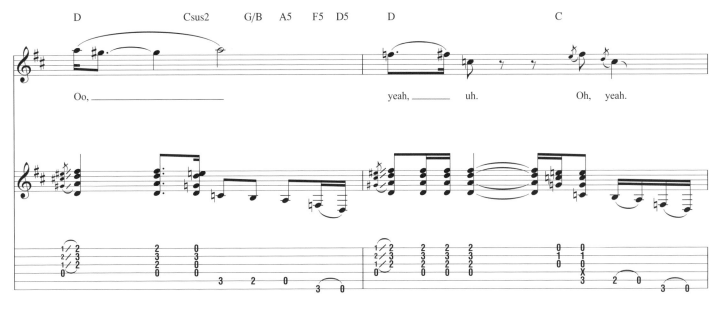

Oo, _____ yeah, ___ uh. Oh, yeah.

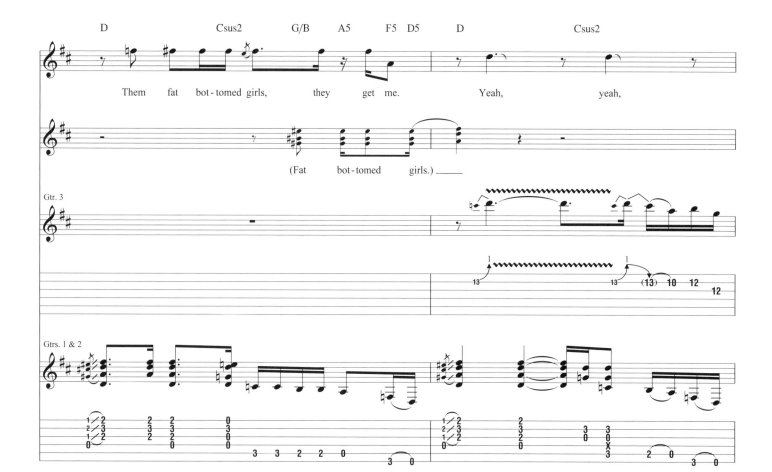

Them fat bot-tomed girls, they get me. Yeah, yeah,

(Fat bot-tomed girls.) ____

Gtr. 3

Gtrs. 1 & 2

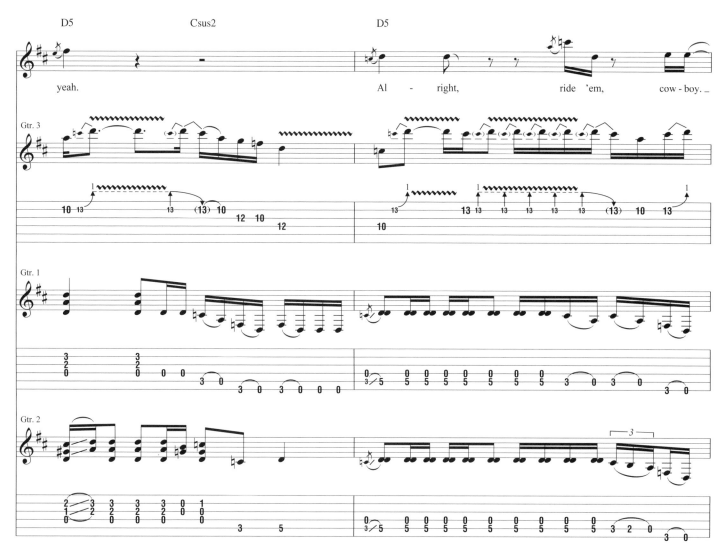

D5   Csus2   D5

yeah.   Al - right,   ride 'em,   cow-boy. __

Gtr. 3

Gtr. 1

Gtr. 2

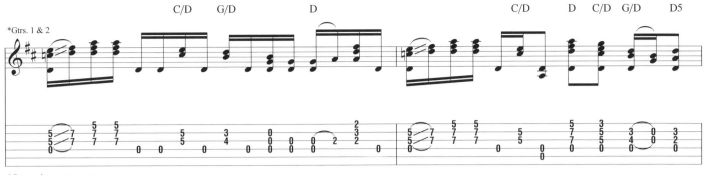

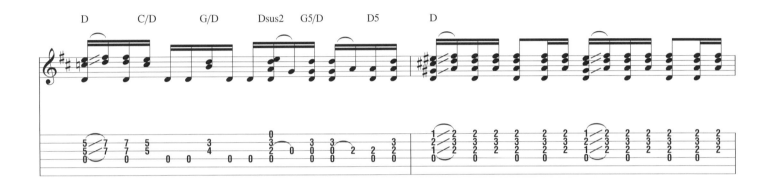

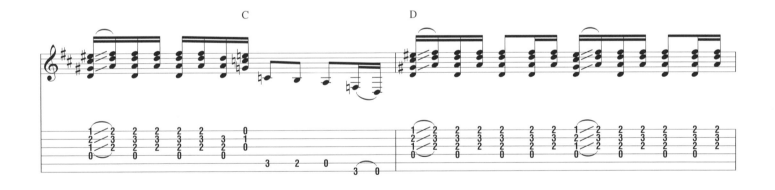

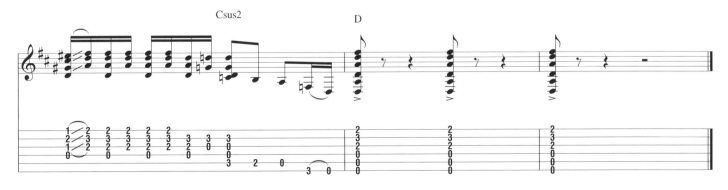

from James Gang - *Rides Again*

Funk #49

Words and Music by Joe Walsh, Dale Peters and James Fox

Intro
Moderately ♩ = 88

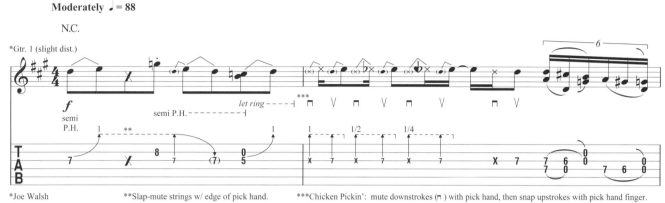

*Joe Walsh   **Slap-mute strings w/ edge of pick hand.   ***Chicken Pickin': mute downstrokes (⊓) with pick hand, then snap upstrokes with pick hand finger.

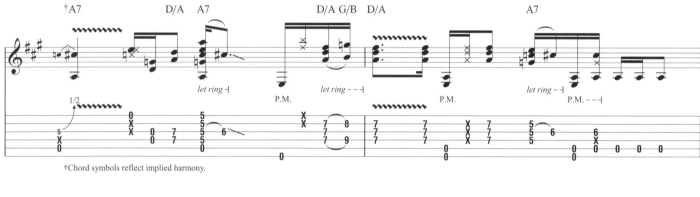

†Chord symbols reflect implied harmony.

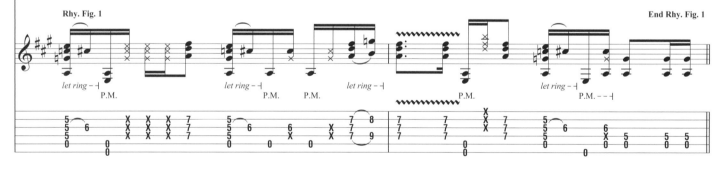

sleep all day, ___   out all night, ___   I know where you're go - in'. ___
jump - in' up, ___   fall - in' down, ___   don't mis - un - der - stand ___ me.
3. Out all night, ___   sleep all day, ___   I know what you're do - in'. ___

I don't think __ that's a, act-in' right, __ you don't think it's show-in'. __
You don't think __ that I know your plan; __ what you try'n' to hand __ me? __
If you're gon-na a, act that way, __ I think there's trou-ble brew-in'. __

Chorus

*Unintentional harm.

Interlude

Percussion Solo
Voc.: w/ ad. lib jungle screams
Gtr. 1 tacet

Breakdown

w/ heavy reverb   reverb off

108

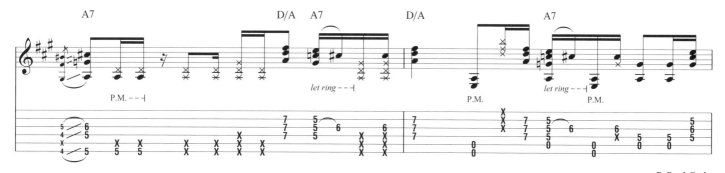

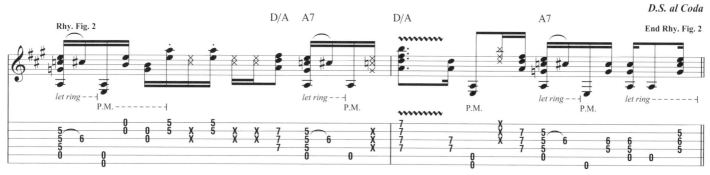

D.S. al Coda

Coda

Outro

Gtr. 1: w/ Rhy. Fig. 1 (4 times) Gtr. 1: w/ Rhy. Fig. 2 (2 times)

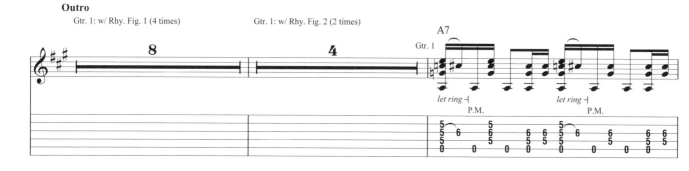

Begin fade

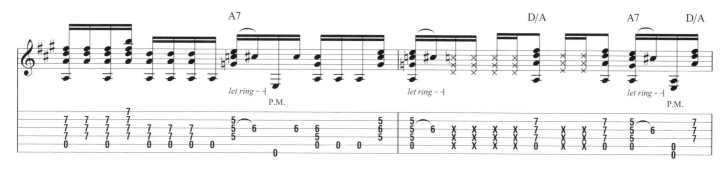

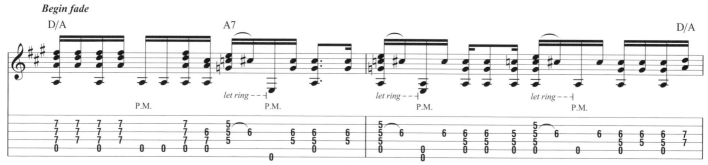

Fade out

Hey You

Words and Music by Roger Waters

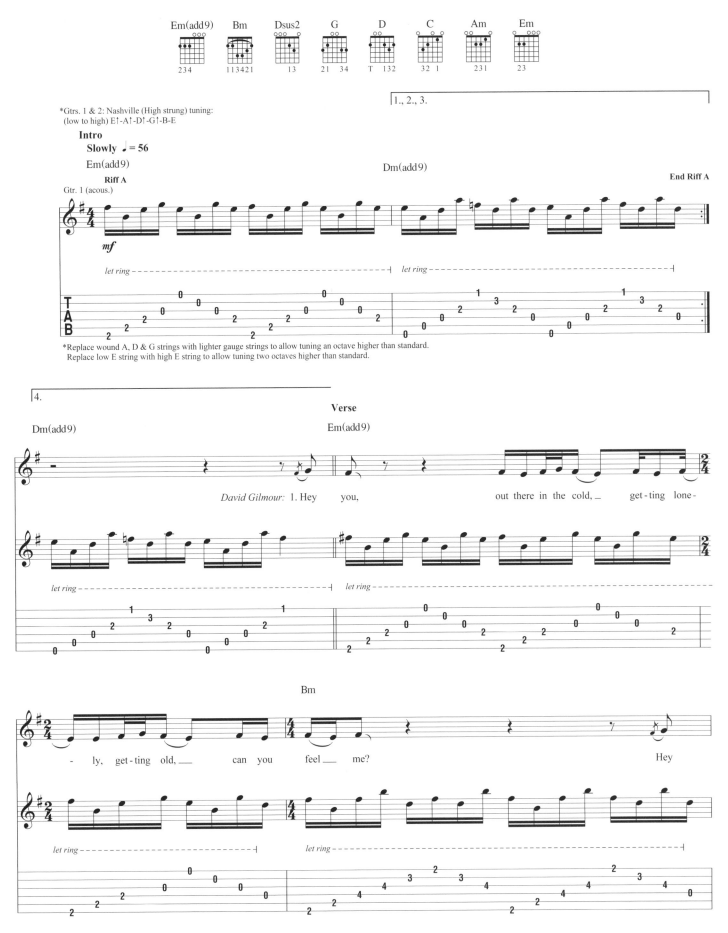

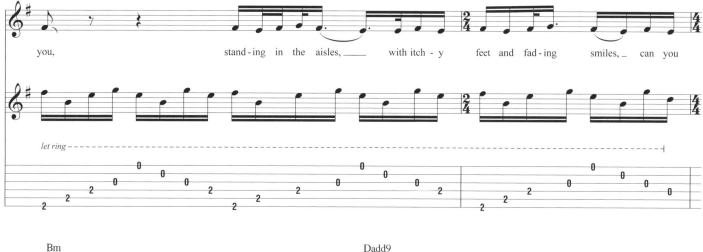

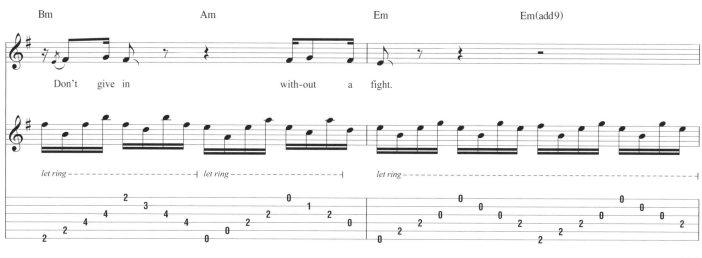

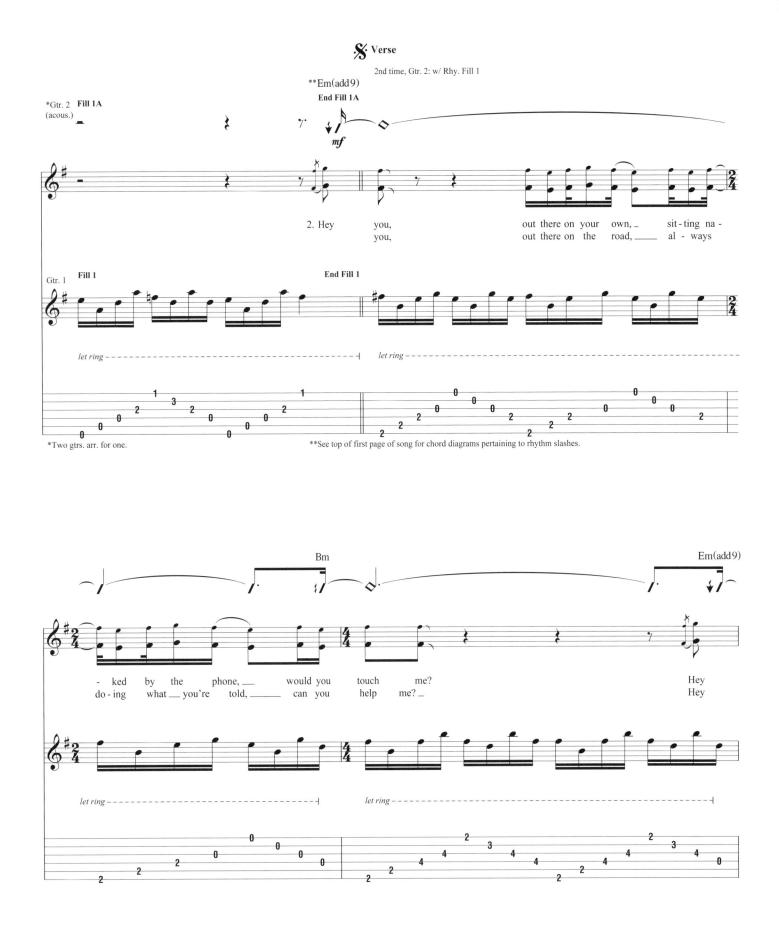

*Two gtrs. arr. for one.   **See top of first page of song for chord diagrams pertaining to rhythm slashes.

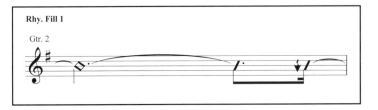

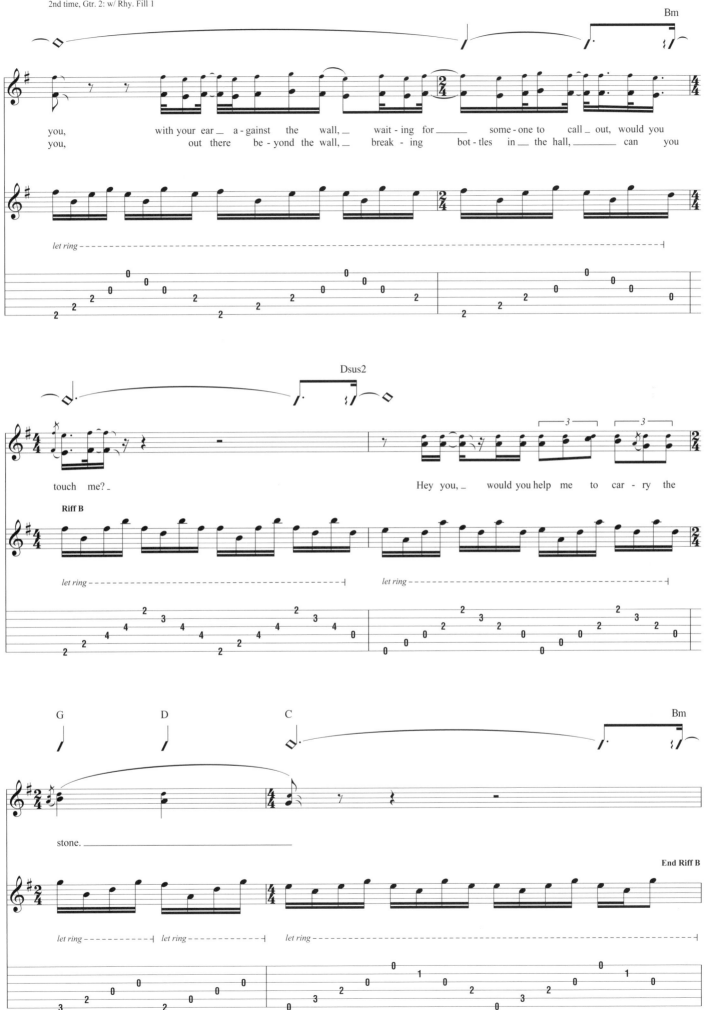

Open your heart, I'm coming home.

Guitar Solo

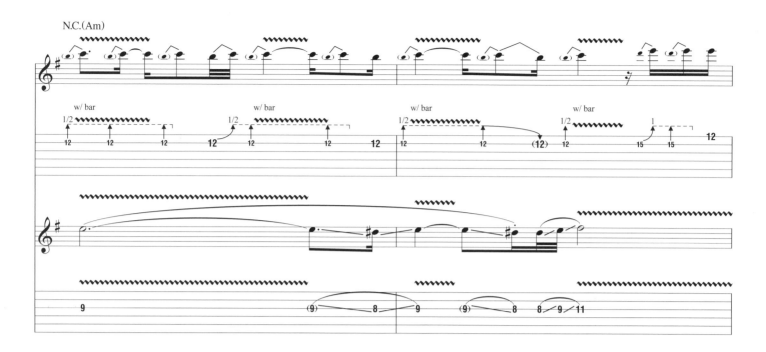

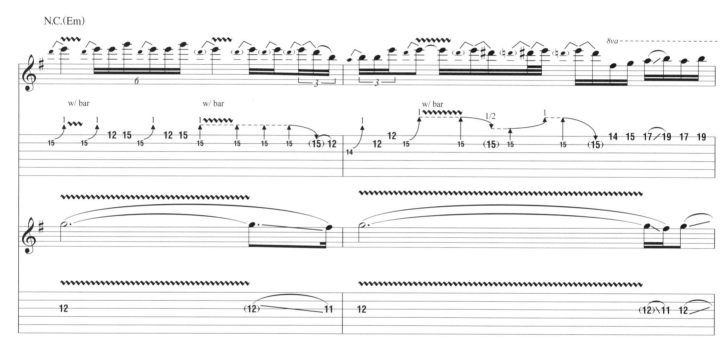

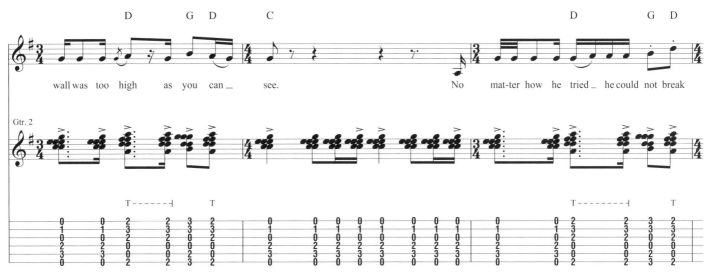

I Wanna Be Sedated

Words and Music by Jeffrey Hyman, John Cummings and Douglas Colvin

*Chord symbols reflect basic harmony.

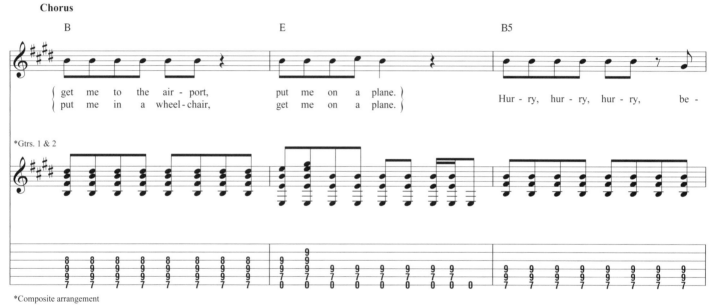

*Composite arrangement

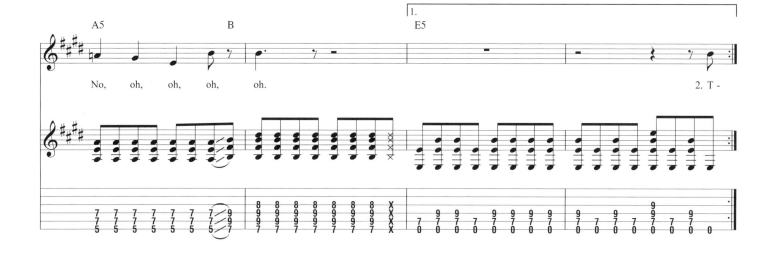

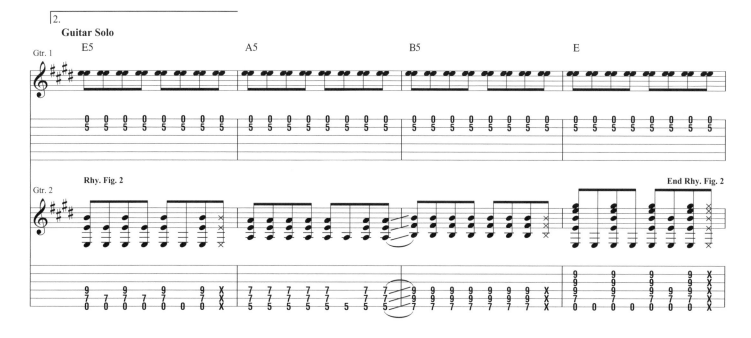

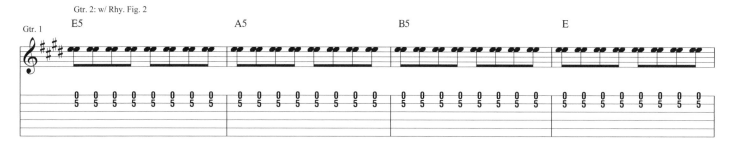

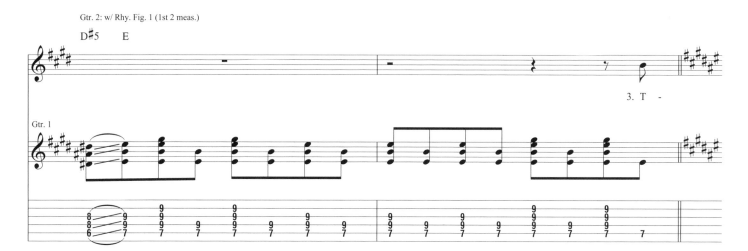

Verse

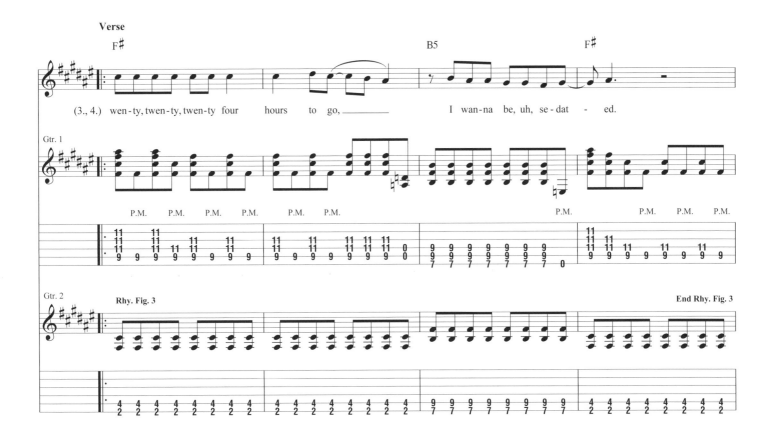

(3., 4.) wen-ty, twen-ty, twen-ty four hours to go, _____ I wan-na be, uh, se - dat - ed.

Noth in' to do, __ no - where __ to go, __ oh. __ I wan-na be se - dat - ed. Just

Chorus

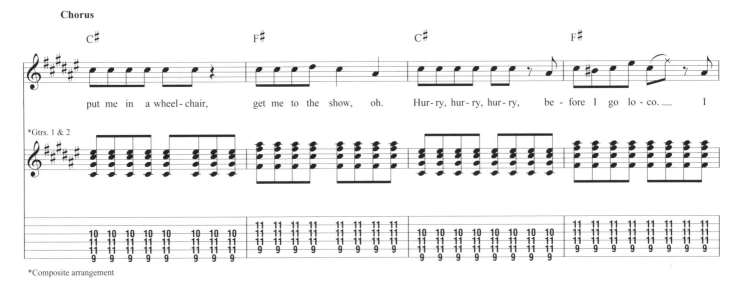

put me in a wheel-chair, get me to the show, oh. Hur-ry, hur-ry, hur-ry, be-fore I go lo - co. __ I

*Composite arrangement

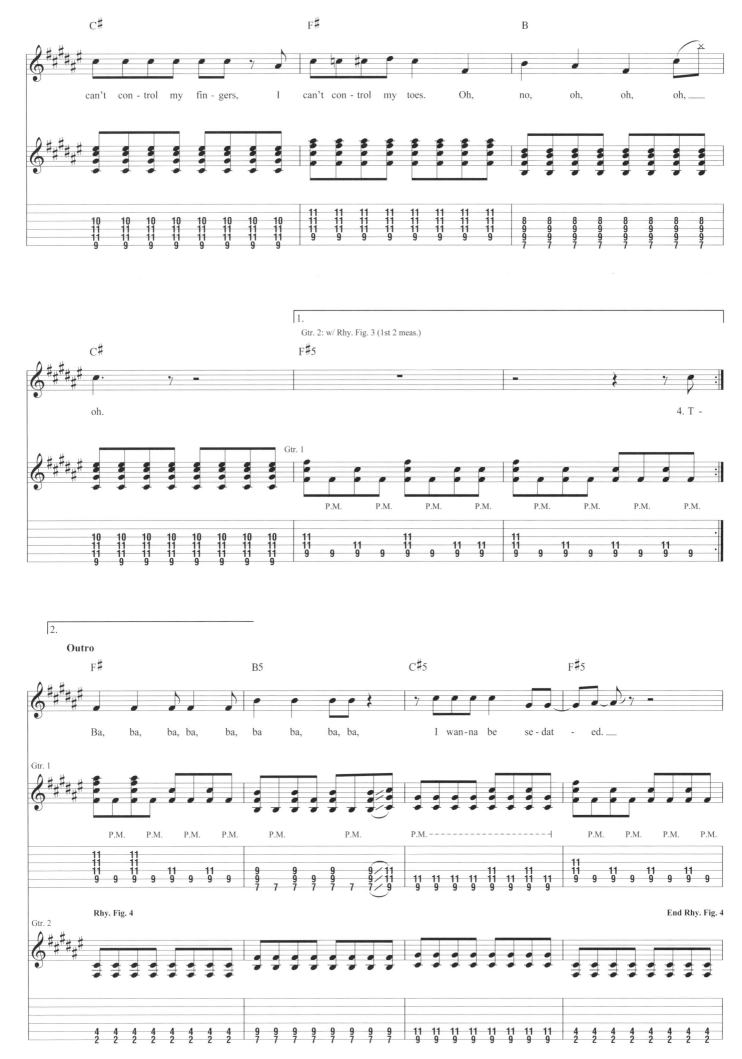

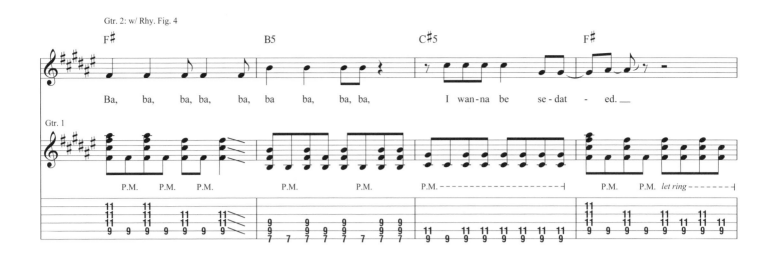

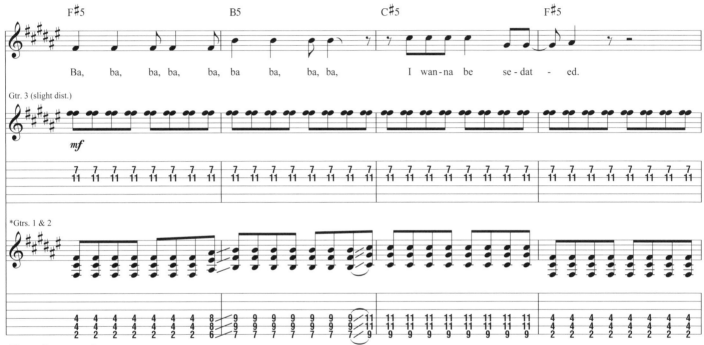

*Composite arrangement

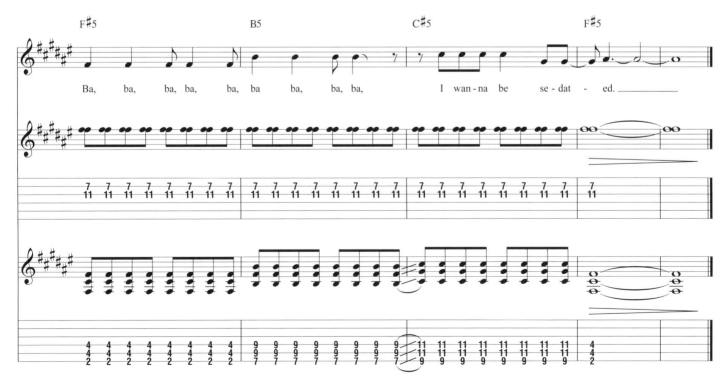

from Ten Years After - *Stonedhenge*

I'm Going Home

Words and Music by Alvin Lee

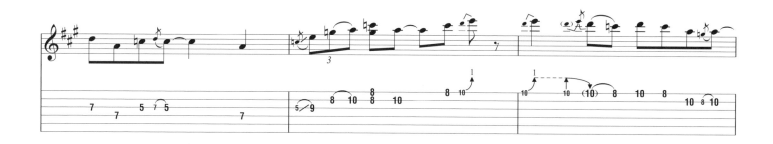

*Chord symbols reflect overall harmony.

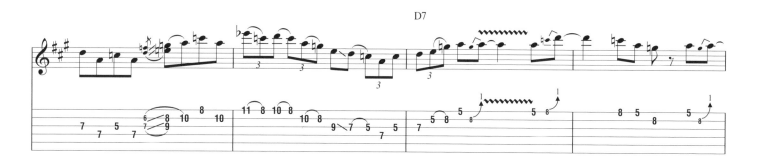

1. Go - in' home, __

Verse

__ my ba - by. Go - in' home, __

__ my ba - by. Go - in' home, __

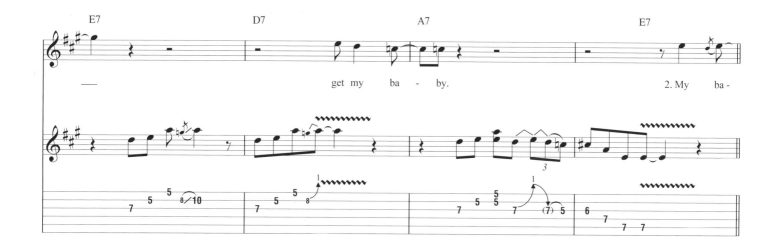

get my ba - by.　　　　　　　2. My ba -

Verse

- by,　　　　　my girl. ___　　　　　　　My ba -

- by,　　　　　be good. ___　　　　　　　I'm go'n'

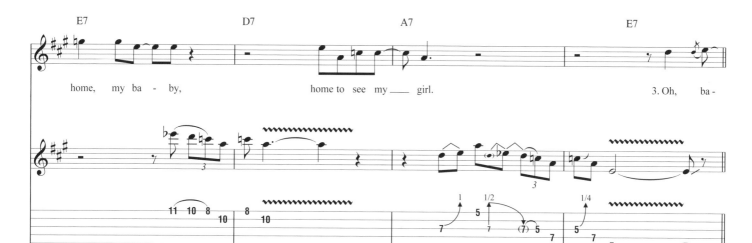

home, my ba - by,　　　　home to see my ___ girl.　　　　3. Oh, ba -

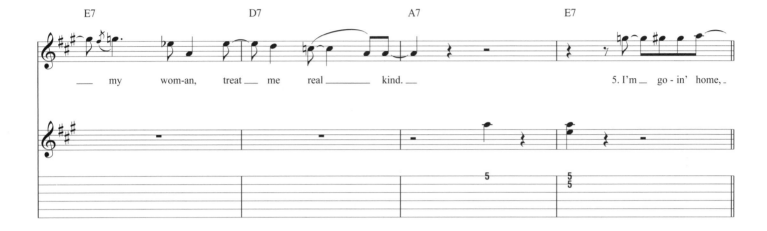

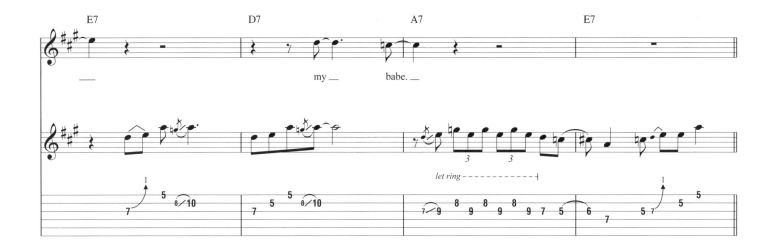

Guitar Solo

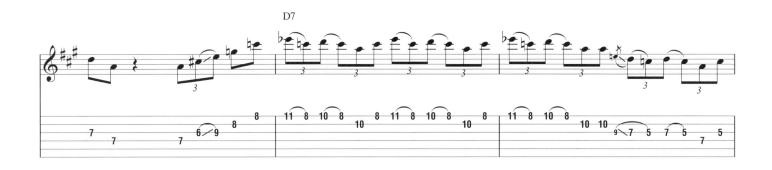

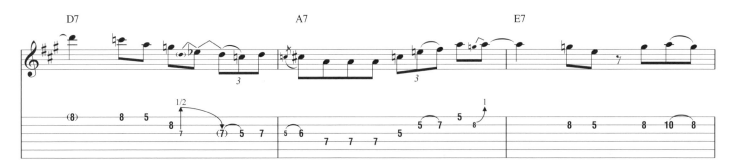

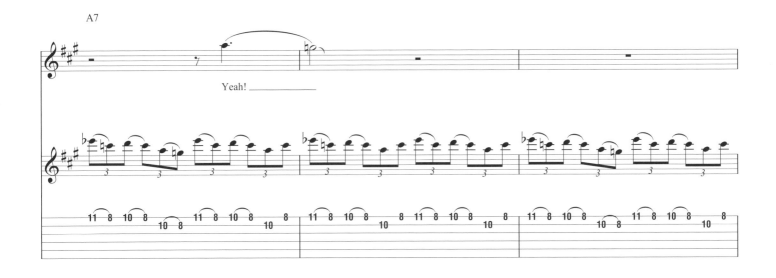

Yeah! _____

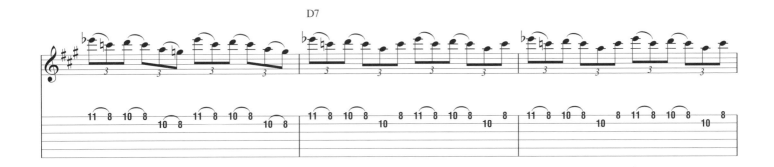

6. Go - in' home, ___

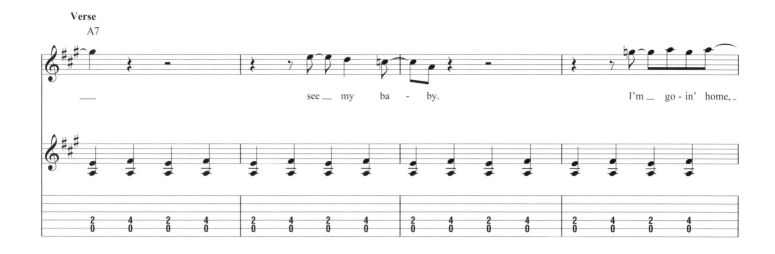

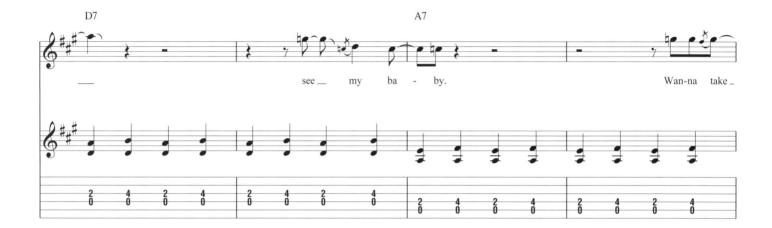

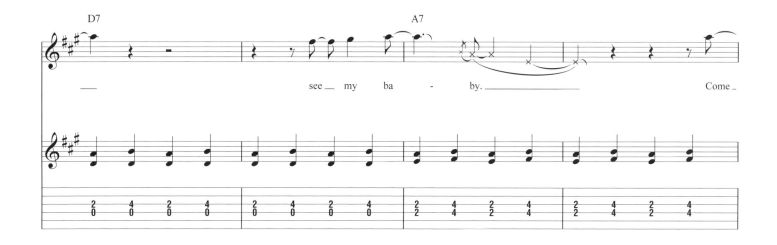

see my ba - by. _____ Come _

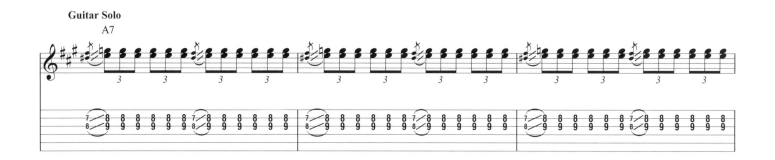

_ on, take _ me. Ow! _____ Yeah. _____

Guitar Solo

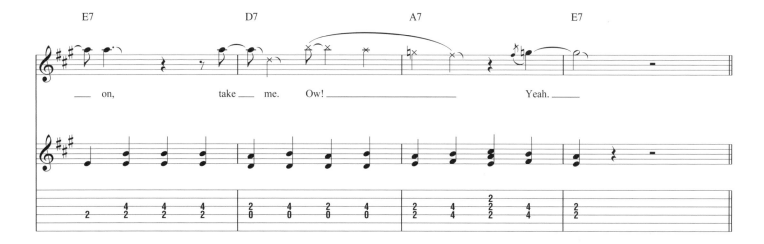

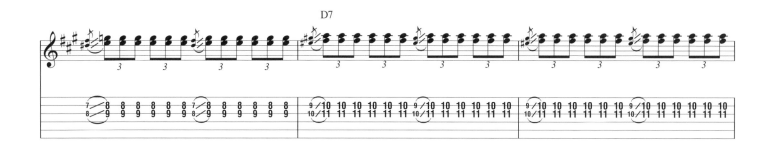

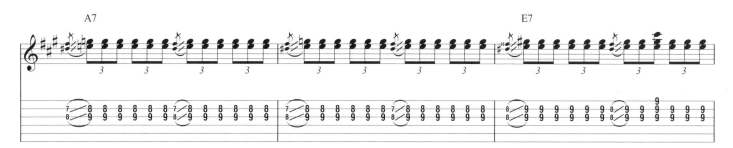

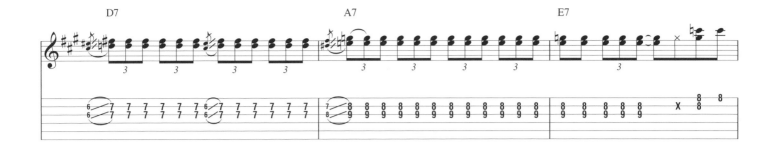

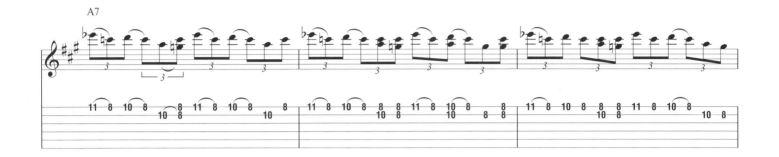

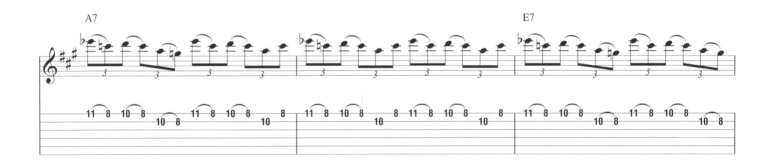

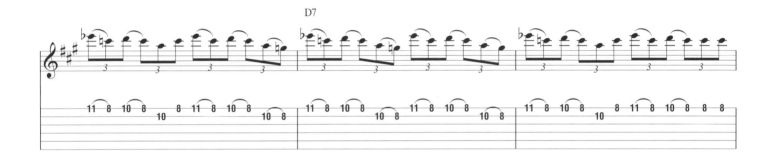

8. I'm ___ go - in' home. ___

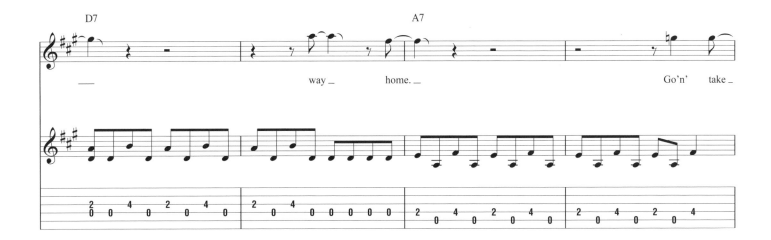

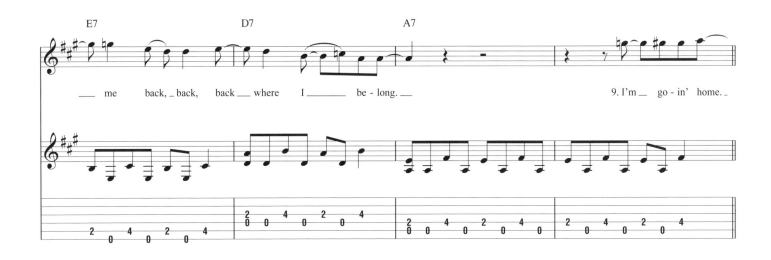

I'm __ go'n' home. __   Well,   home, __

__   home, __   back __ where   I __   be - long. __

Outro

Free time

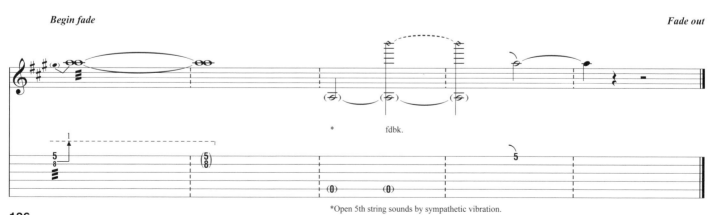

Begin fade   *Fade out*

* fdbk.

Open 5th string sounds by sympathetic vibration.

from The Black Crowes - *Shake Your Money Maker*

Jealous Again

Words and Music by Chris Robinson and Rich Robinson

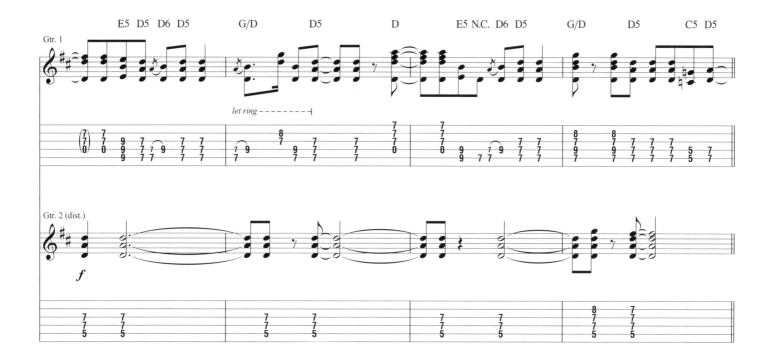
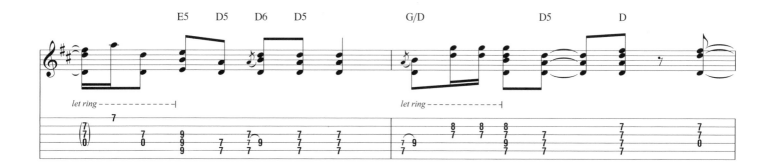
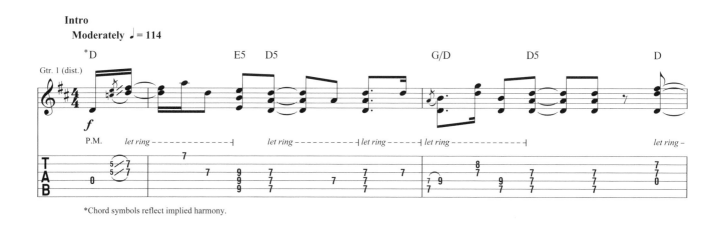

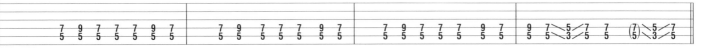

138

Verse

Interlude

Hey.

Verse

3. Nev-er felt like smil-in', sug-ar wan-na kill me yet. Mm, yeah. Found me

loose - lipped and laugh - in', sing-in' songs, ain't got no re - grets. _____ Oh, _____ yeah, _ yeah. _ I'm jeal-

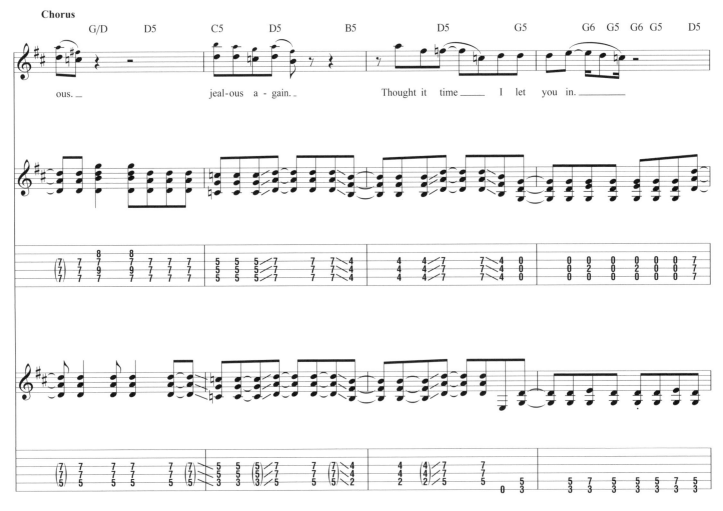

Chorus

ous. _ jeal-ous a - gain. _ Thought it time _____ I let you in. _____

Breakdown

Gtr. 1 tacet

Gtr. 3

*Gtrs. 1 & 4: w/ Fill 1

Don't__ you think I want to,__ don't__ you think I would?__ Don't__

Gtrs. 1, 3 & 4

*Gtr. 1: w/ slight dist.; Gtr. 4 (slight dist.) played *mf*.

__ you think I'd tell you, ba - by, if__ I on - ly could? __ Am I act - ing cra - zy, __

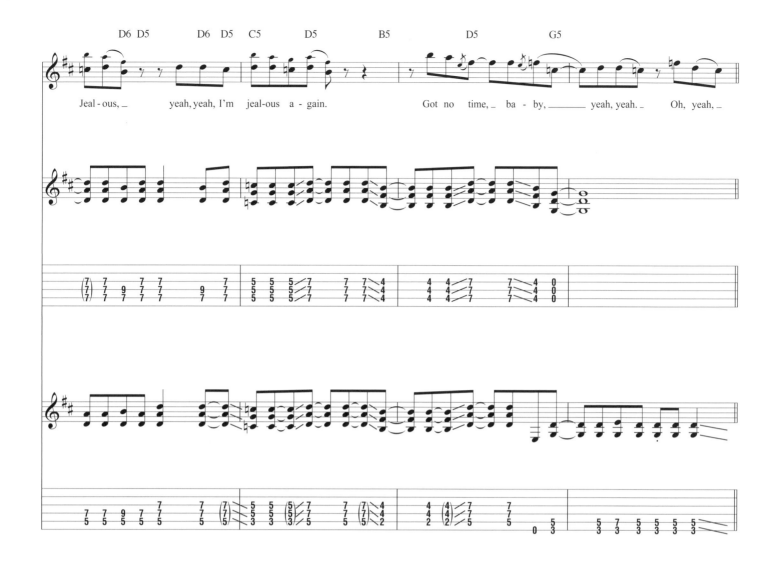

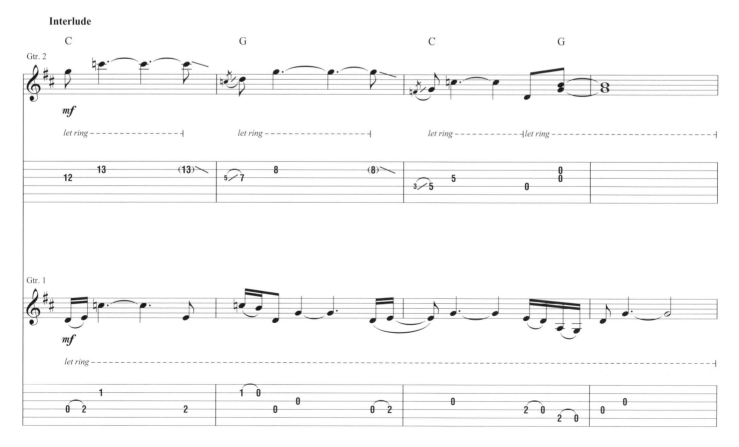

Outro-Guitar Solo

jeal - ous ____ with a jeal - ous heart. ____

Rhy. Fig. 1

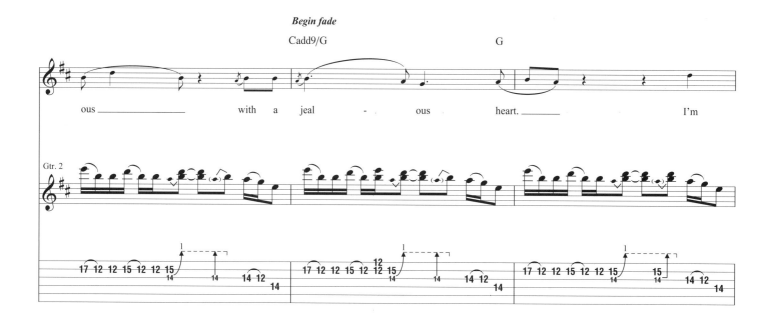

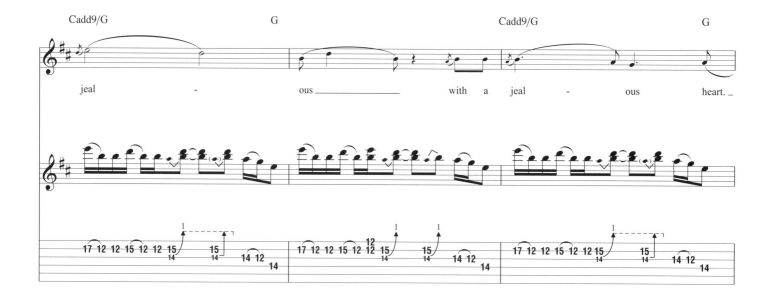

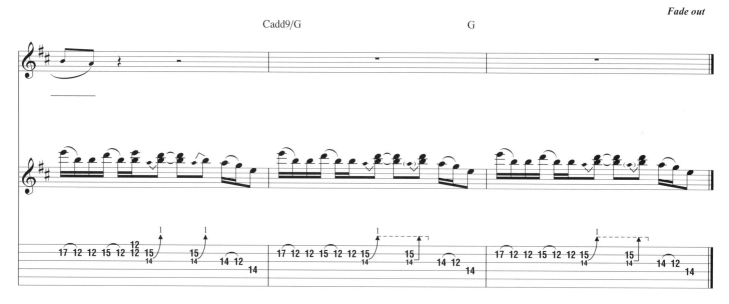

La Grange

Words and Music by Billy F Gibbons, Dusty Hill and Frank Lee Beard

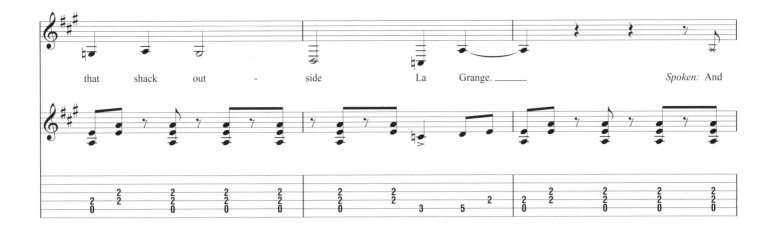

that shack out - side La Grange. _____ *Spoken:* And

you know what I'm talk - in' a - bout. Just let me know if you ___ wan - na go ___

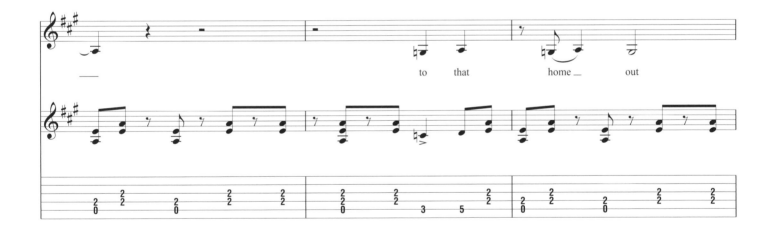

to that home ___ out

on ___ the range. *Spoken:* They got - ta lot - ta nice girls.

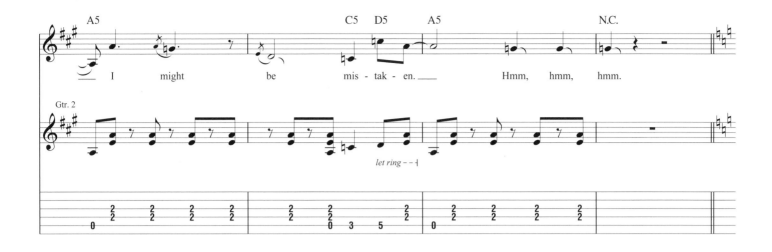

I might be mis-tak-en. ___ Hmm, hmm, hmm.

Guitar Solo

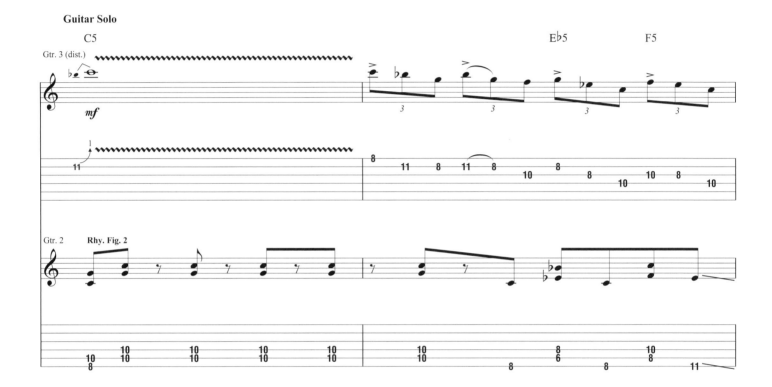

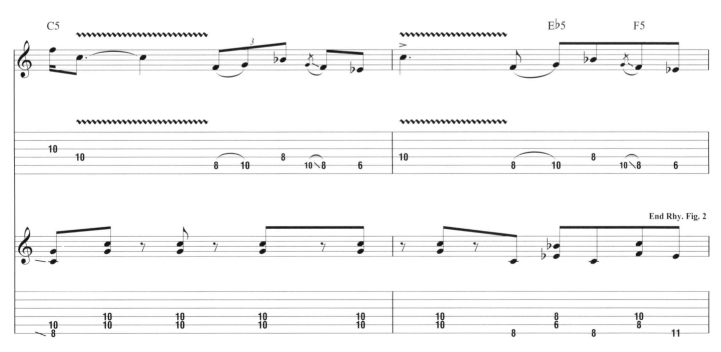

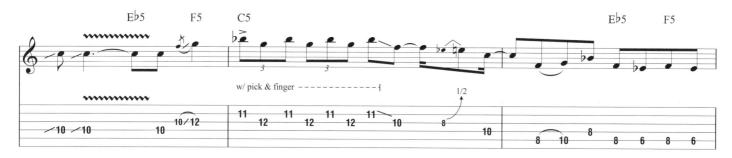

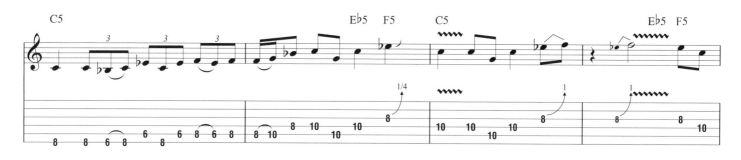

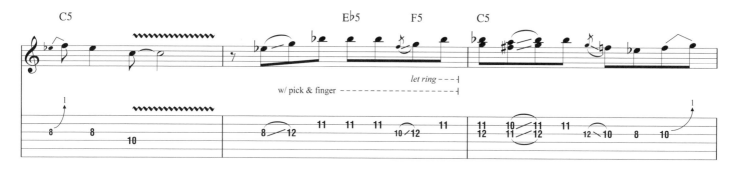

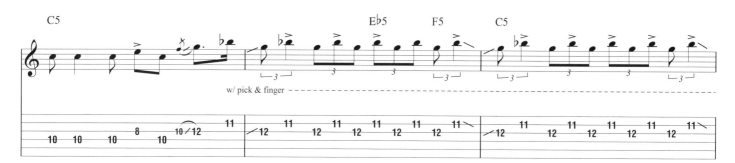

Interlude

*Composite arrangement

Outro-Guitar Solo

Gtr. 1 tacet

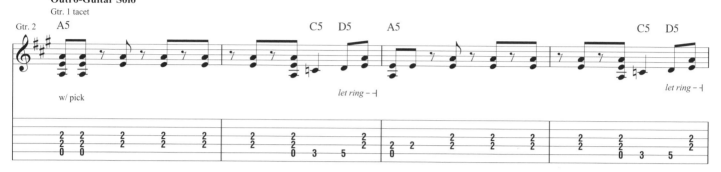

Gtr. 2: w/ Rhy. Fig. 1 (till fade)

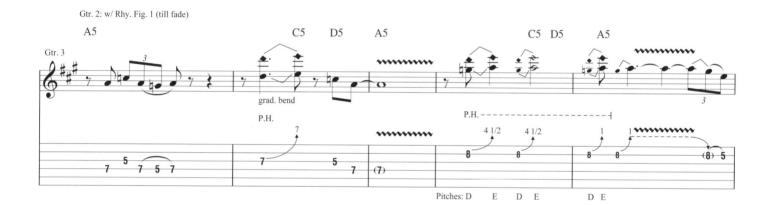

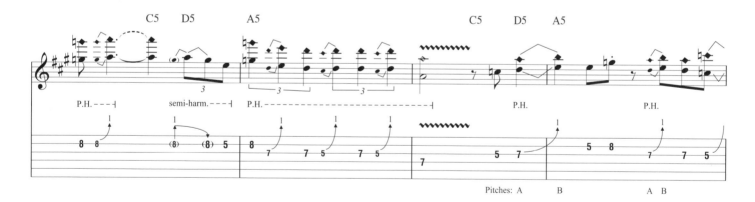

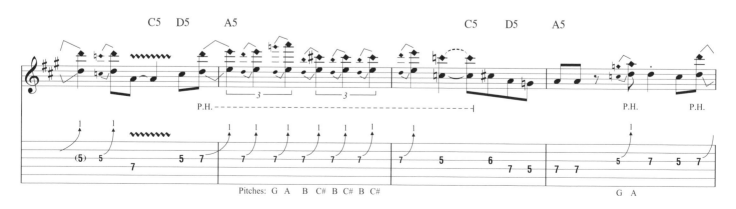

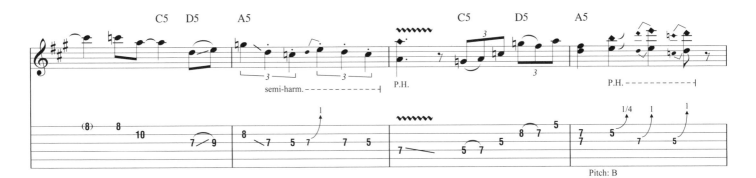

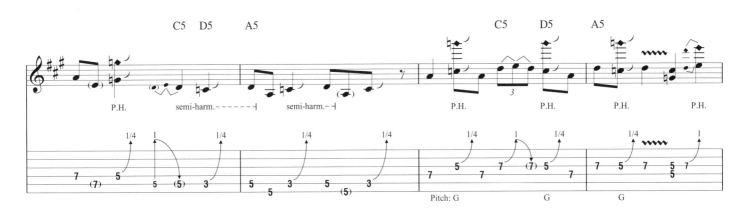

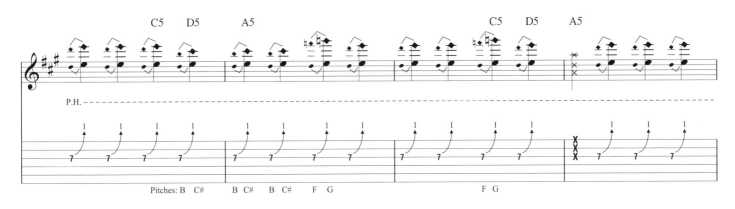

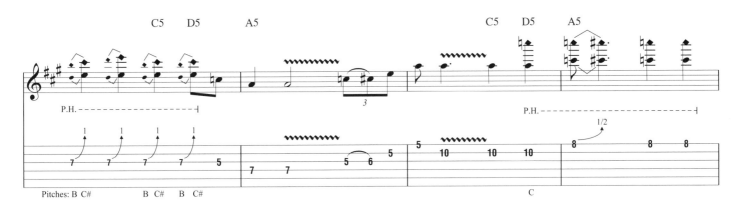

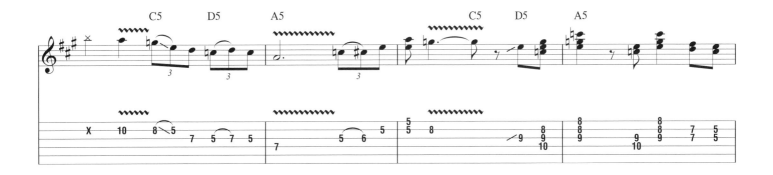

from Yes - *Fragile*

Long Distance Runaround

Words and Music by Jon Anderson

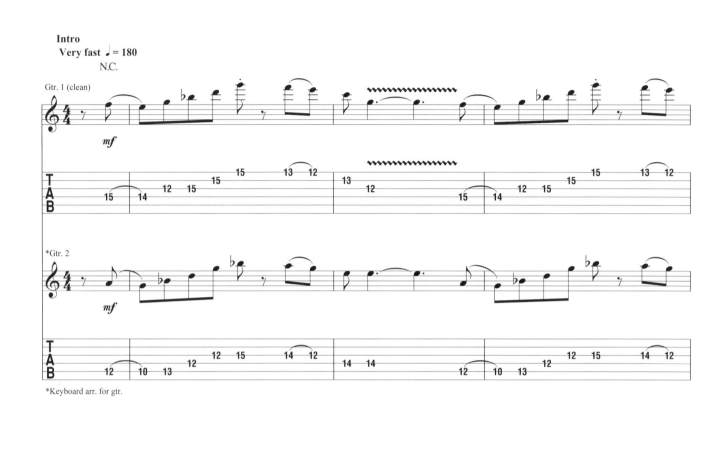

*Keyboard arr. for gtr.

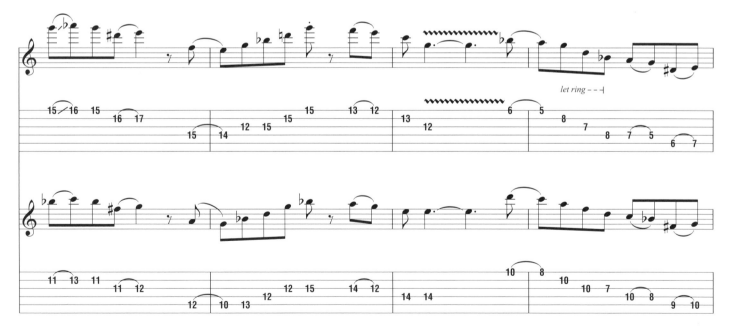

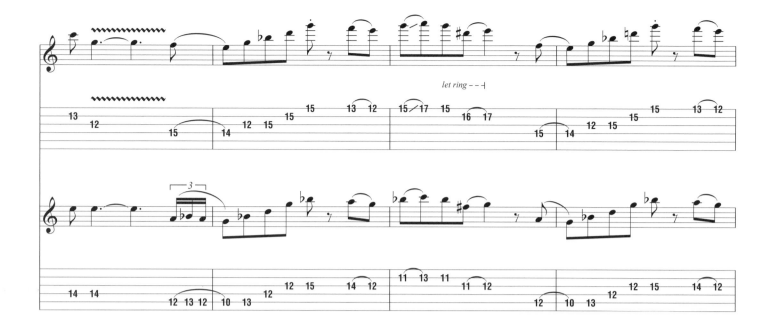

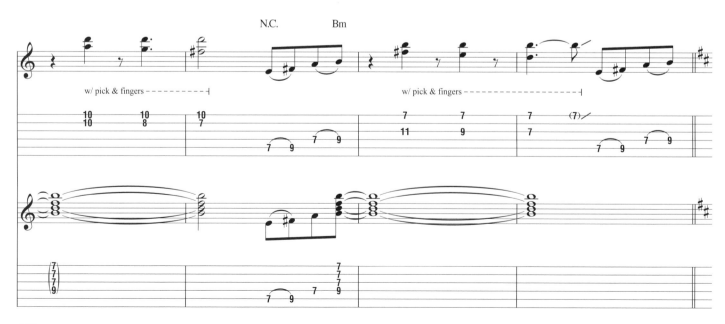

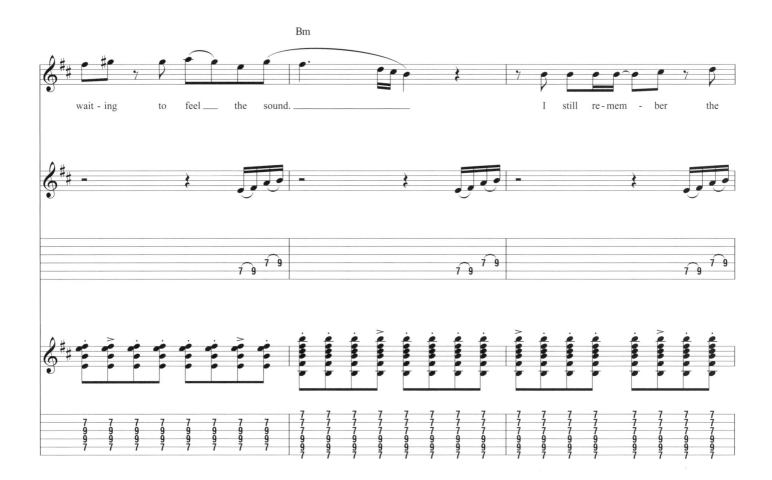

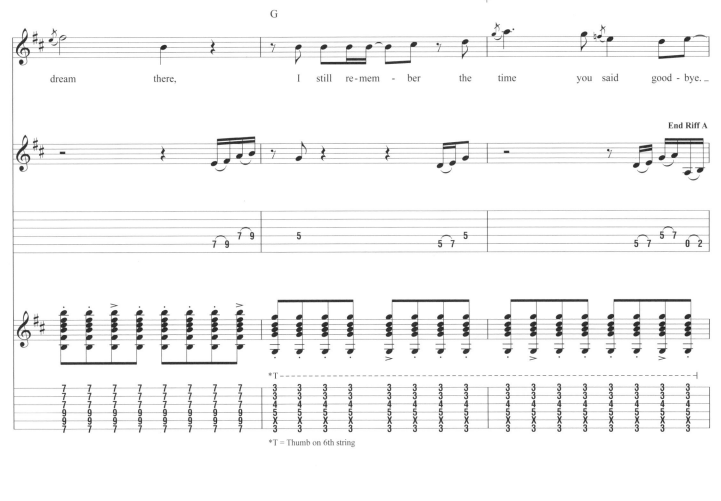

*T = Thumb on 6th string

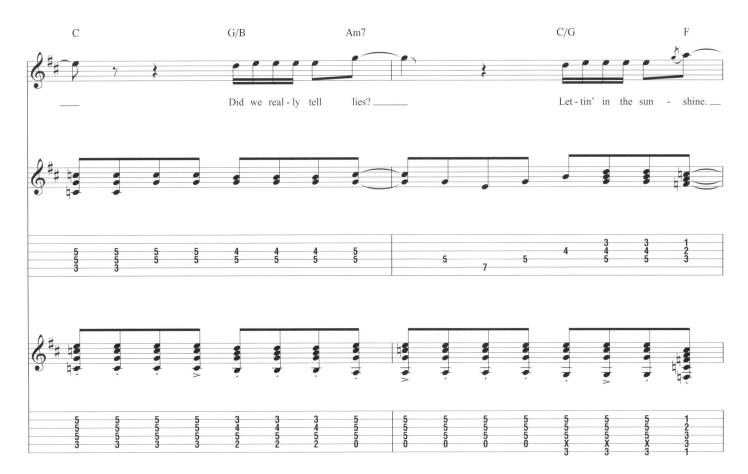

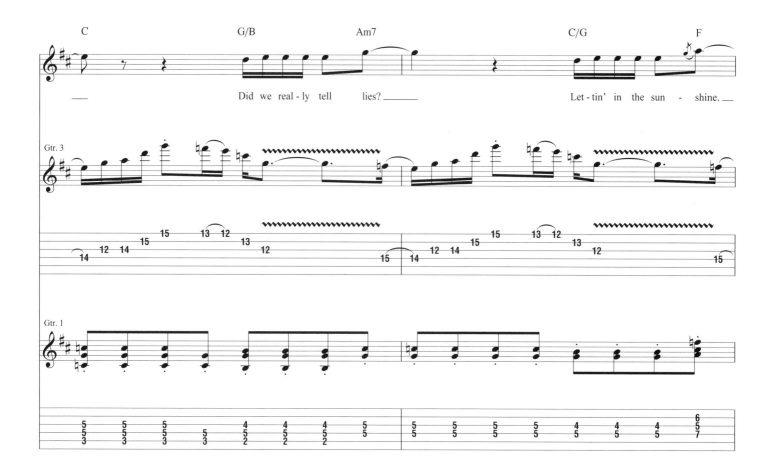

Did we real - ly tell lies? _____   Let - tin' in the sun - shine. _____

D.S. al Coda

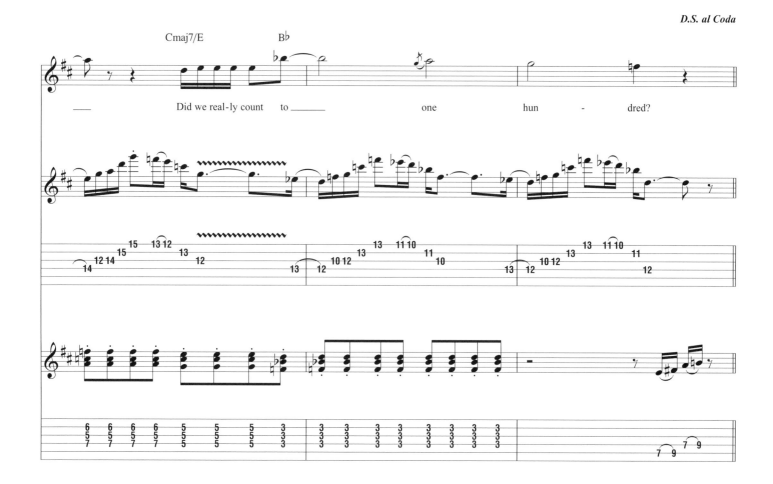

Did we real - ly count to _____ one hun - dred?

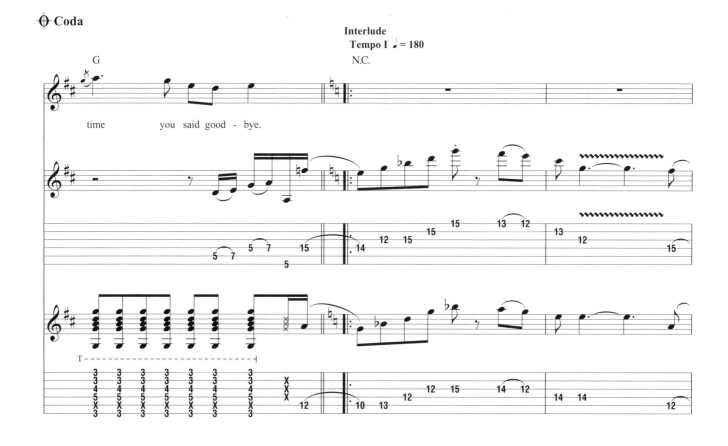

time   you said good - bye.

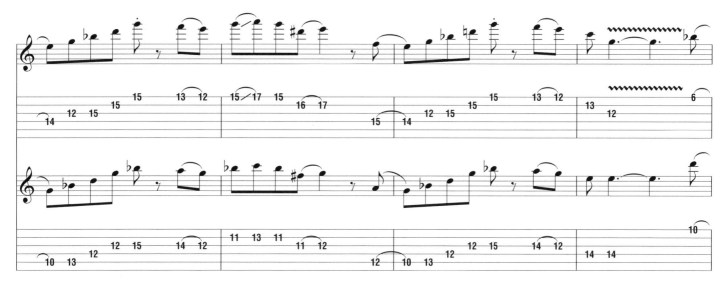

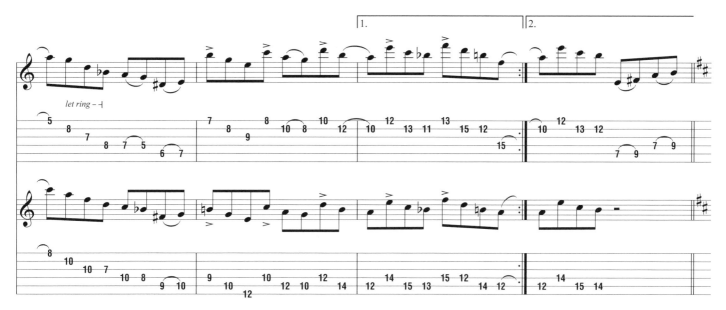

Verse
Half-time ♩ = 90

Gtr. 1: w/ Riff A
Gtr. 2: w/ Rhy. Fig. 1 (1st 13 meas.)

Esus2   Bm   Esus2

4. Cold sum - mer glis - ten - ing, ___ hot col - or

melt - ing the an - ger to stone. ___ I still re - mem - ber the

G

dream there, ___ I still re - mem - ber the time you said good - bye. ___

Gtr. 3

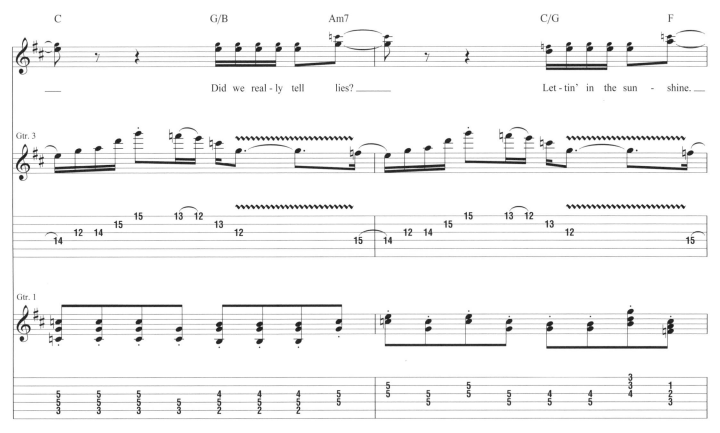

C   G/B   Am7   C/G   F

___ Did we real - ly tell lies? ___ Let - tin' in the sun - shine. ___

Gtr. 3

Gtr. 1

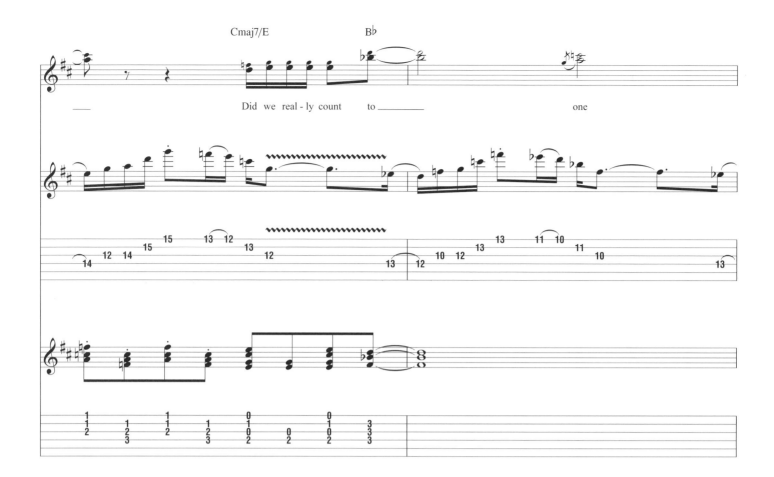

Did we real-ly count to _____ one

hun - dred? Look-in' for the sun - shine.

Gtr. 1 tacet

Gtr. 3

Gtr. 2

Outro

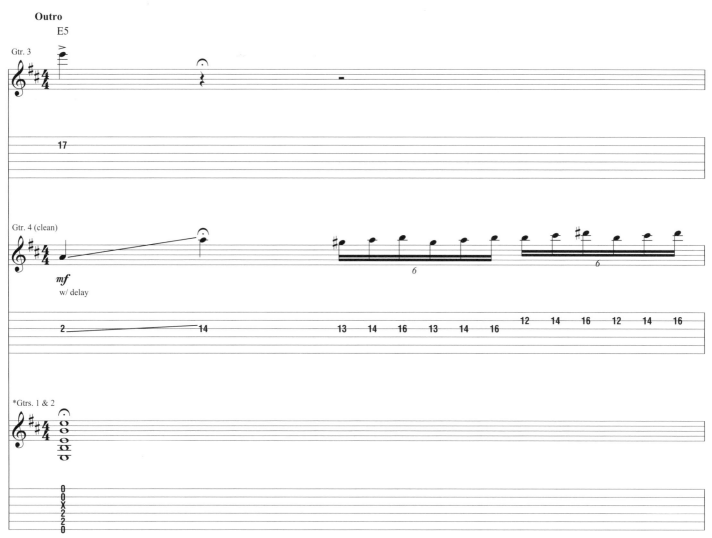

*Composite arrangement

Gtrs. 1, 2 & 3 tacet

N.C.

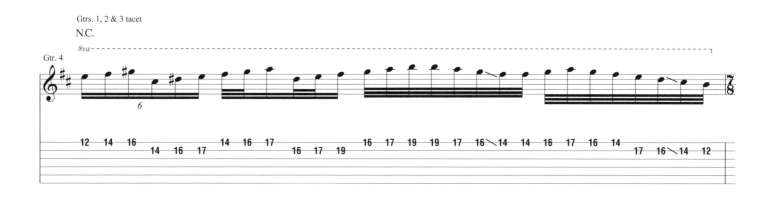

Segue to "The Fish (Schindleria Praematurus)"

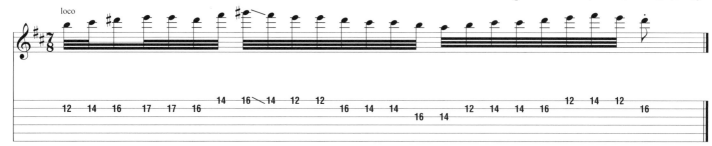

One Way to Rock

Words and Music by Sammy Hagar

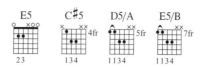

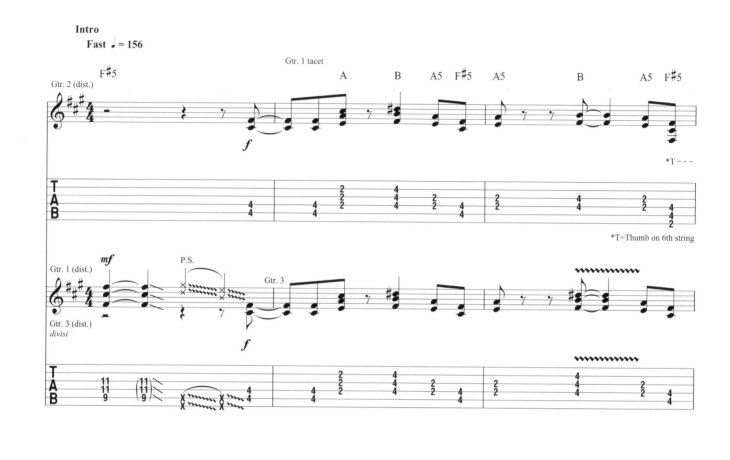

Verse

1. I've heard it called by dif - f'rent names ___ all o - ver the world ___ but it's all ___ the ___ same. ___

*Composite arrangement
**See top of first page of song for chord diagrams pertaining to rhythm slashes.

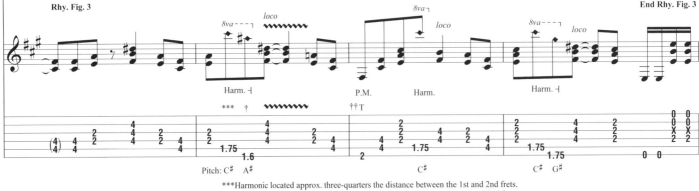

Now, there's so

***Harmonic located approx. three-quarters the distance between the 1st and 2nd frets.
†Harmonic located approx. six-tenths the distance between the 1st and 2nd frets.
††T = Thumb on 6th string

174

Verse

Gtrs. 2 & 3: w/ Rhy. Fig. 2
Gtrs. 4 & 5: w/ Rhy. Fig. 1

how man-y things can get ___ you high? ___ I'm gon-na try 'em all just once ___

Gtrs. 4 & 5 tacet — Gtrs. 2 & 3: w/ Rhy. Fig. 3

___ be - fore I ___ die. ___

Gtr. 1

Pitch: D♯ E♯ D♯

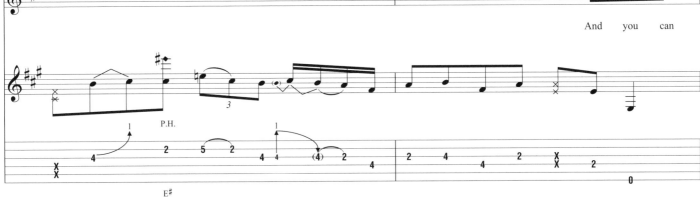

And you can

E♯

Gtr. 1 tacet
Gtrs. 2 & 3: w/ Rhy. Fig. 1
Gtrs. 4 & 5: w/ Rhy. Fig. 2

an - a - lyze ___ the sit - u - a - tion, to me it's all just men - tal mas - tur - ba-

Gtrs. 4 & 5: w/ Rhy. Fig. 4

- tion, ___ a. Huh. ___

Chorus

Gtrs. 2 & 3: w/ Rhy. Fig. 6 (1st 3 meas.)
Gtrs. 4 & 5: w/ Rhy. Fig. 5

There's on - ly one way, ____ there's on - ly

one way _ to rock. _____

There's on - ly one way, _ there's on - ly one way _ to rock.

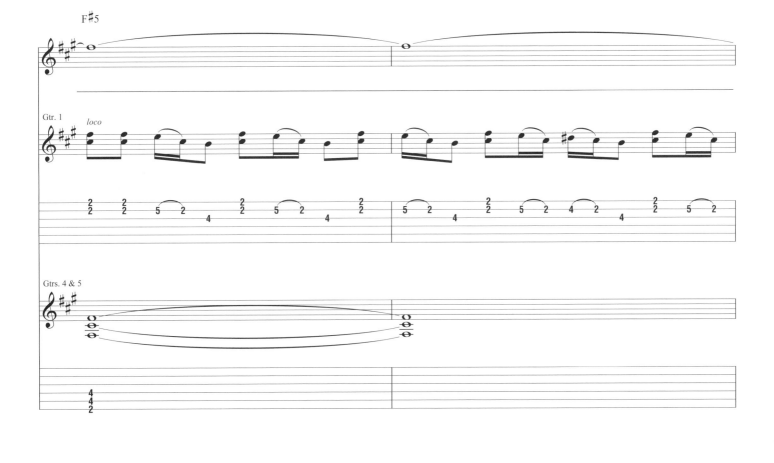

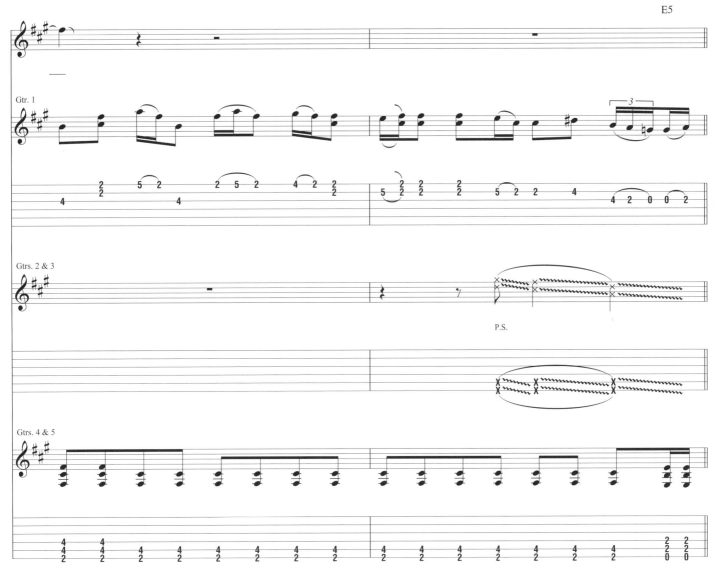

Chorus

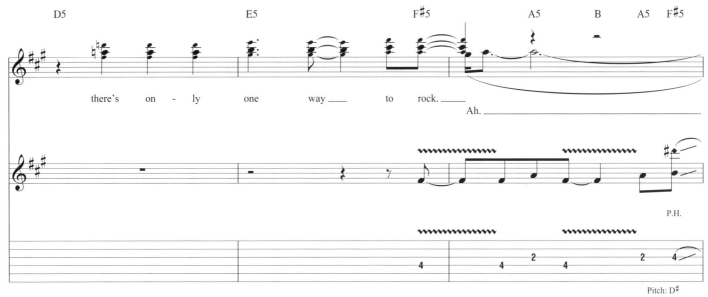

Pitch: D#

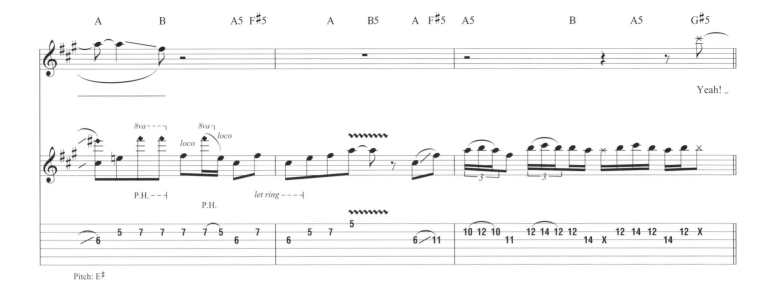

Pitch: E#

Bridge
Gtr. 1 tacet
Gtrs. 4 & 5: w/ Rhy. Fig. 10

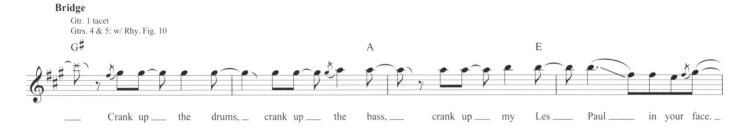

Crank up __ the drums, __ crank up __ the bass, __ crank up __ my Les __ Paul __ in your face. __

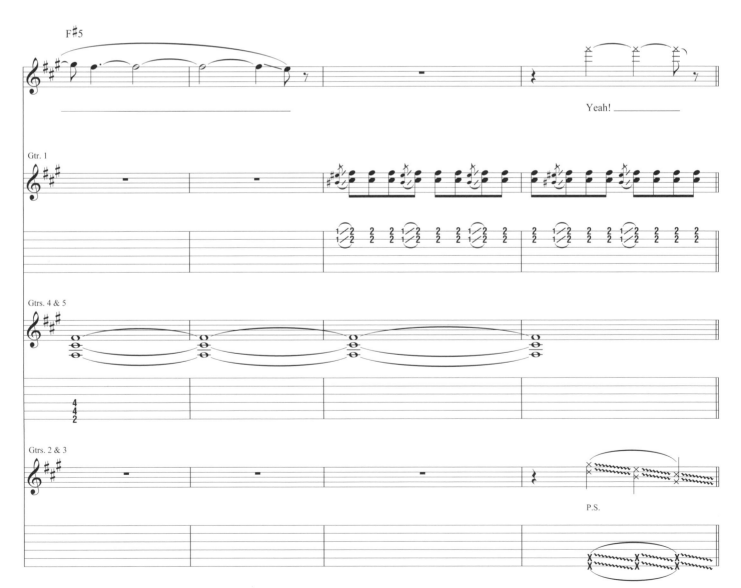

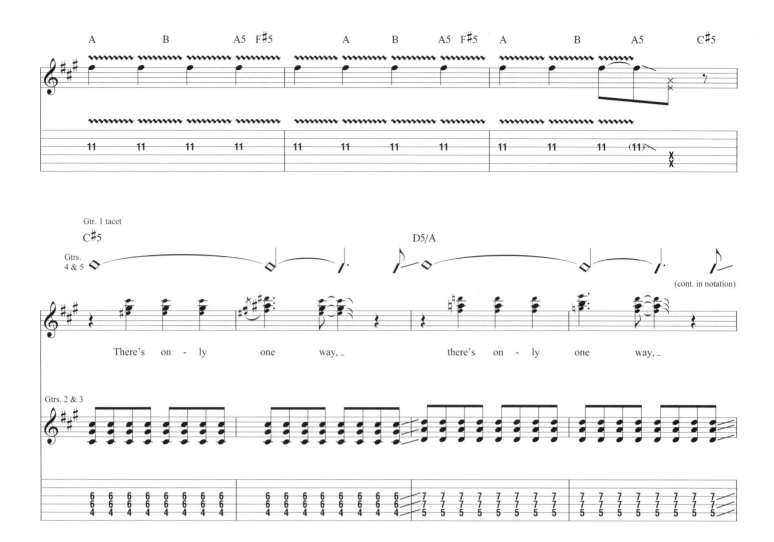

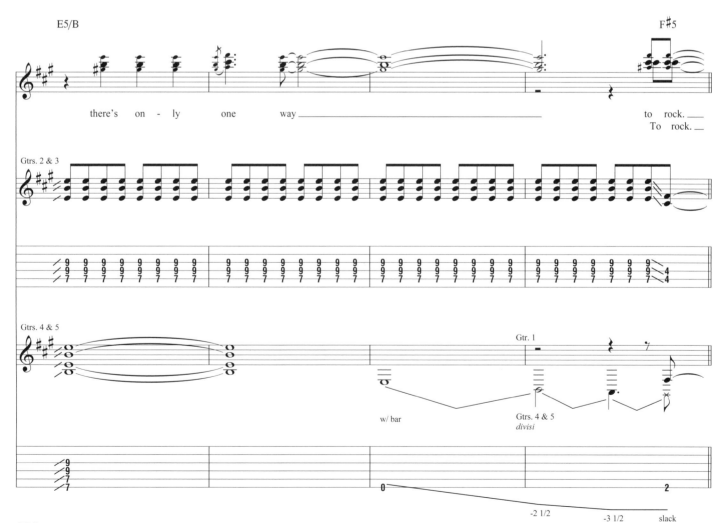

Outro-Guitar Solo

Gtrs. 4 & 5 tacet

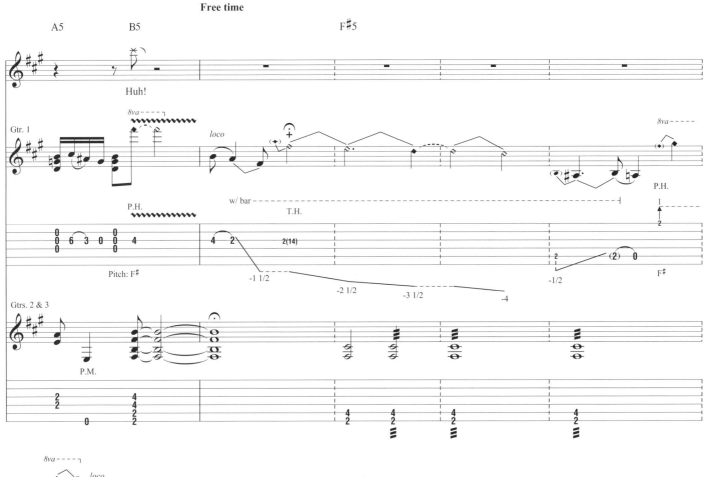

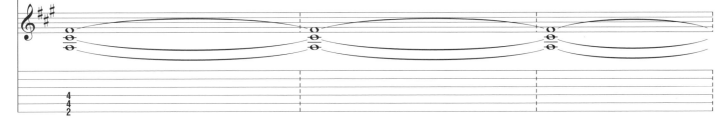

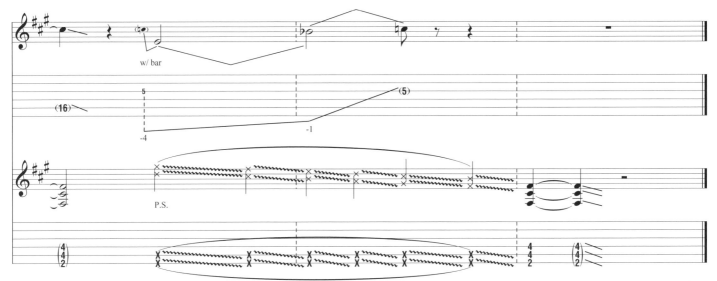

from Asia - *Asia*

Only Time Will Tell

Words and Music by Geoffrey Downes and John Wetton

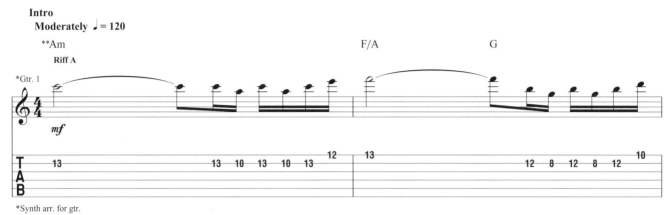

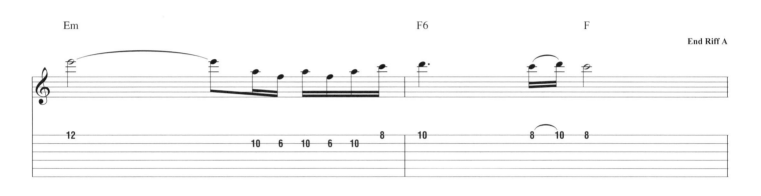

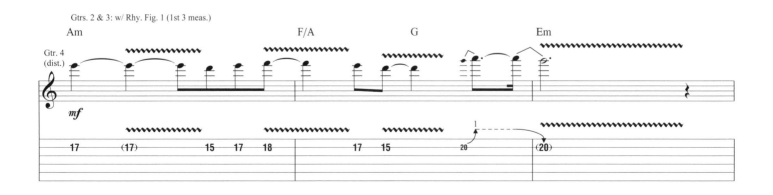

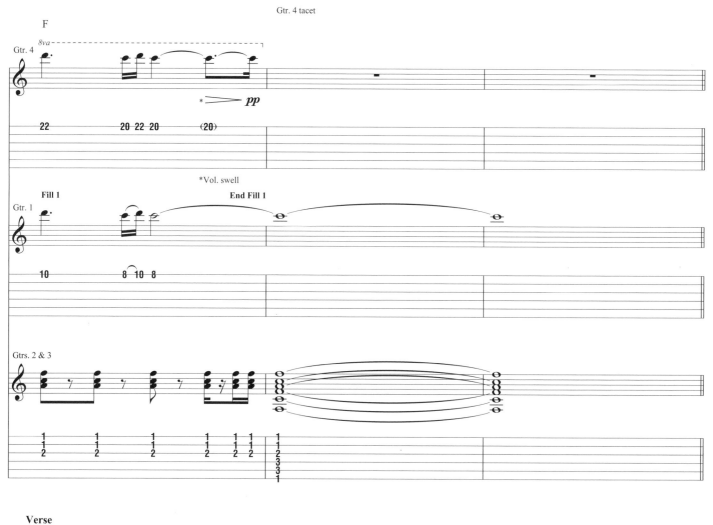

Verse

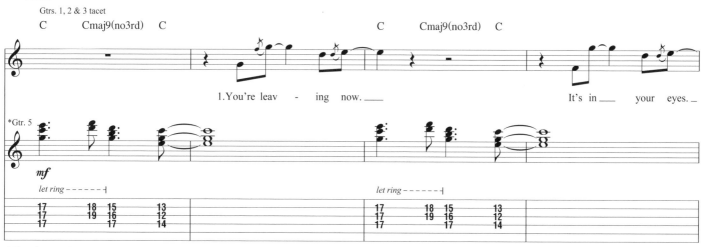

*Elec. piano arr. for gtr.

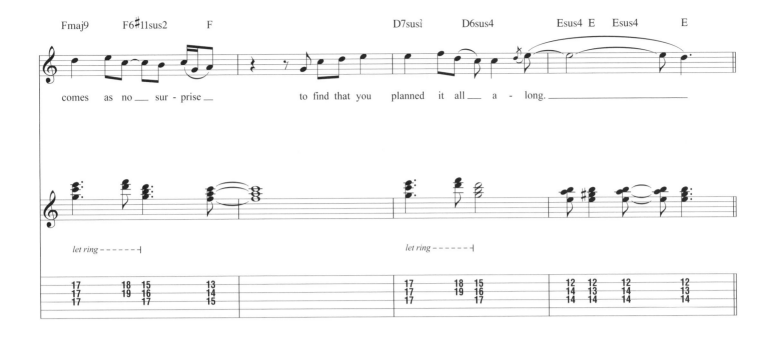

comes as no sur-prise ___ to find that you planned it all ___ a - long. ___

Verse

Gtr. 5 tacet

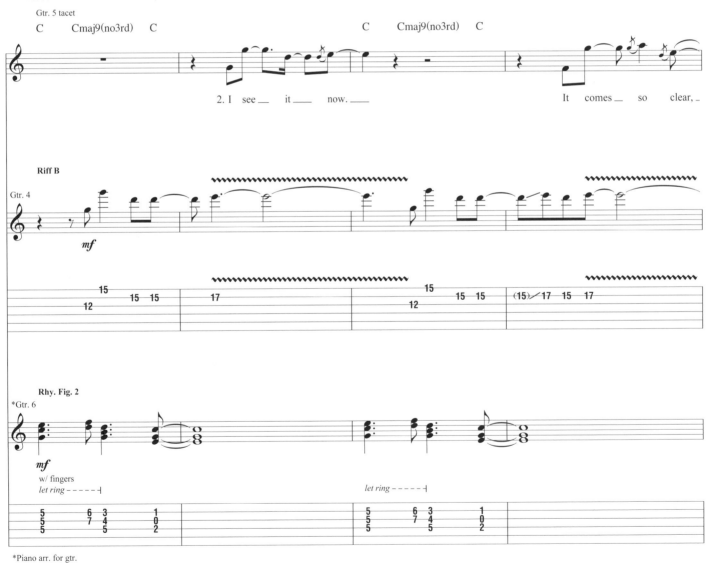

2. I see ___ it ___ now. ___ It comes ___ so clear, ___

Riff B

Gtr. 4

mf

Rhy. Fig. 2

*Gtr. 6

mf

w/ fingers

let ring - - - - - -|

*Piano arr. for gtr.

Chorus

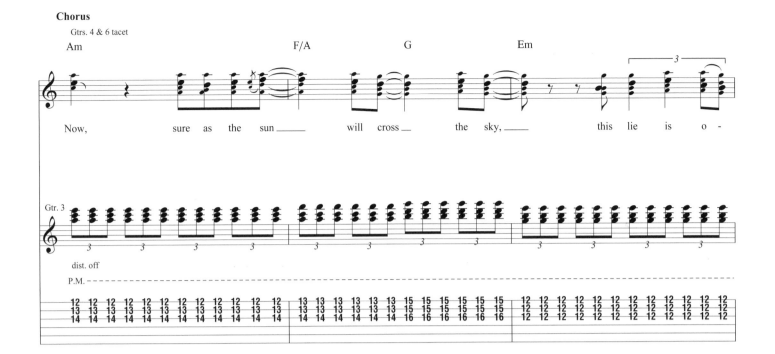

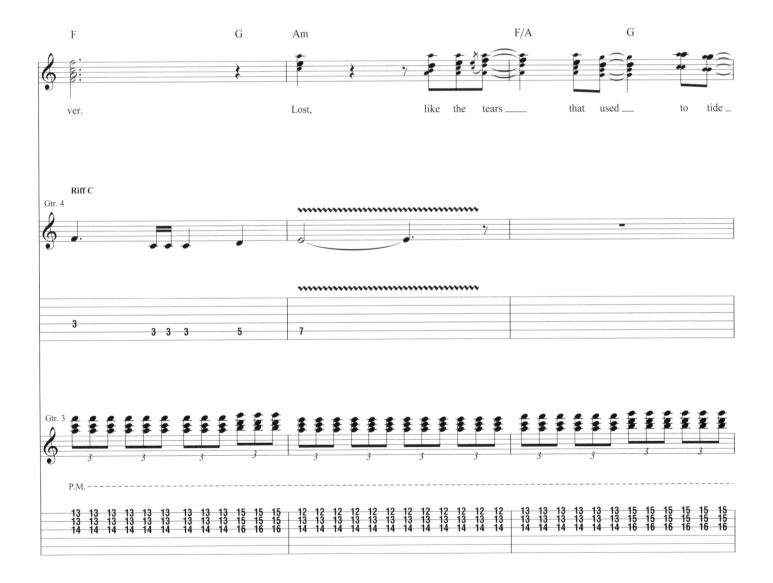

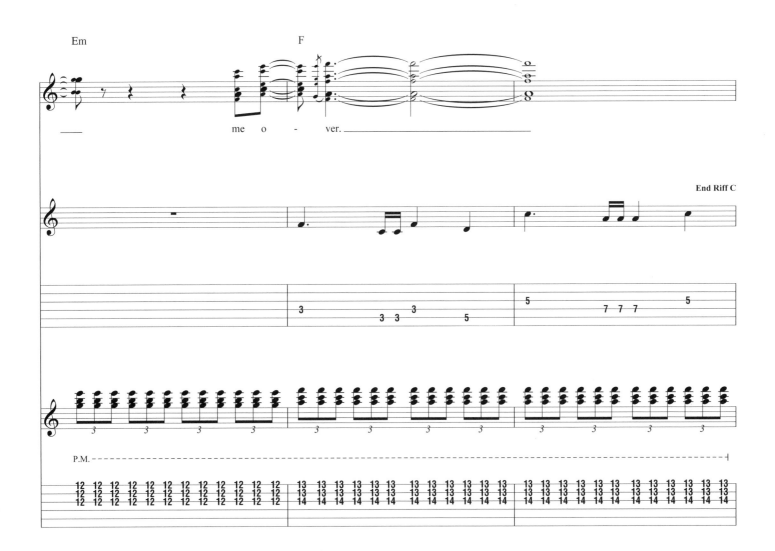

A7sus⁴ Am   A7sus⁴ Am   G7sus4

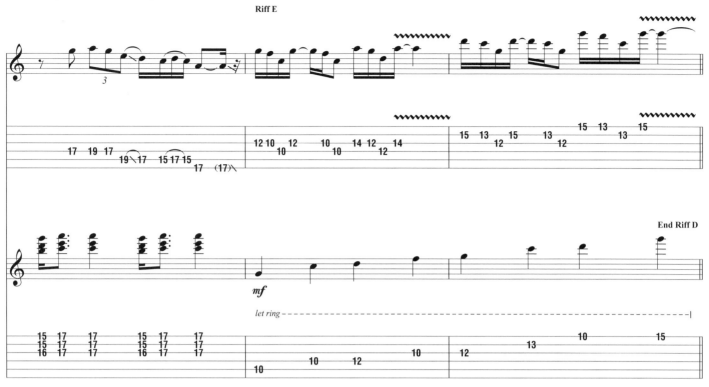

Verse

Gtr. 6: w/ Rhy. Fig. 2
Gtr. 7 tacet

C   Cmaj9(no3rd)   C   C   Cmaj9(no3rd)   C

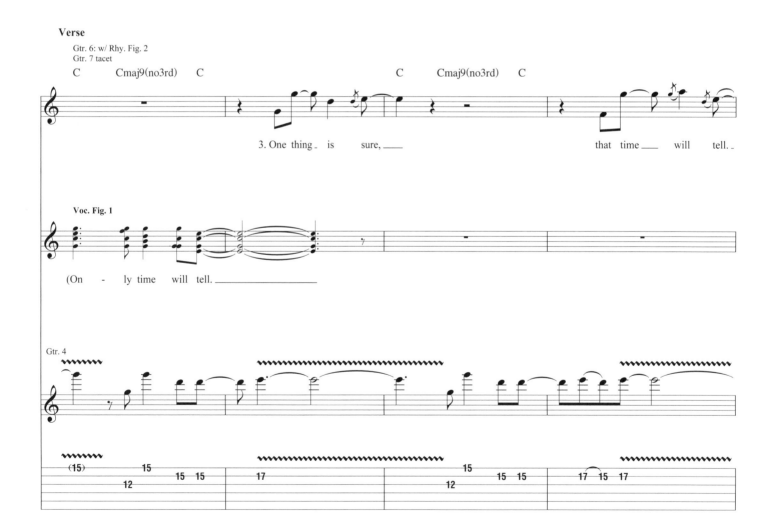

3. One thing _ is   sure, ___   that time ___ will   tell. _

Voc. Fig. 1

(On - ly time will tell. ___

Gtr. 4

If you _ were wrong _ the bright - est

On - ly time will tell.) _____

ring a - round _ the moon _ will dark - en when _ I die. _____

Interlude

Gtr. 1: w/ Riff A (1 3/4 times)
Gtr. 2: w/ Rhy. Fig. 1 (2 times)

***Chord symbols reflect overall harmony.

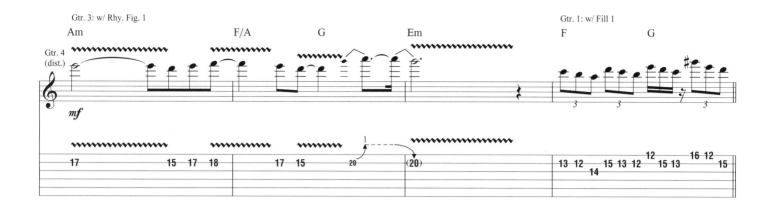

Chorus

Now,   sure as the sun _____ will cross _____ the sky, _____ the lie is o -

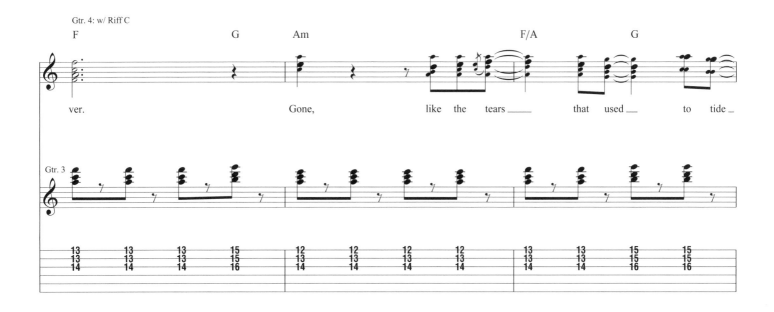

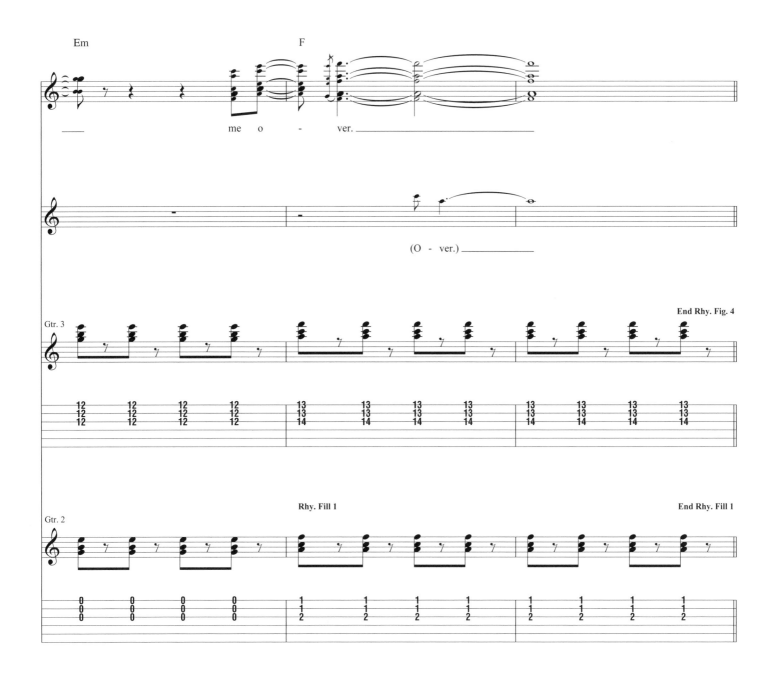

Interlude

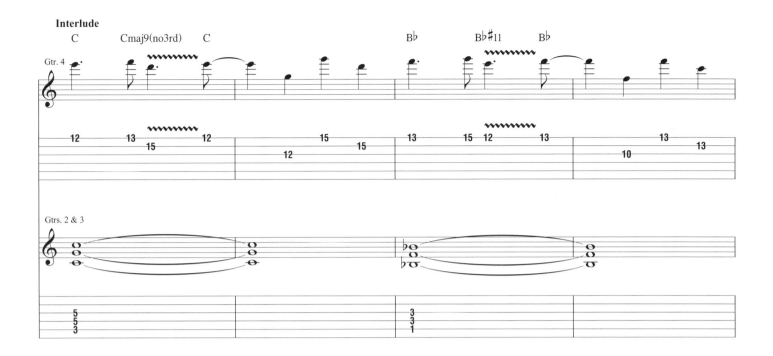

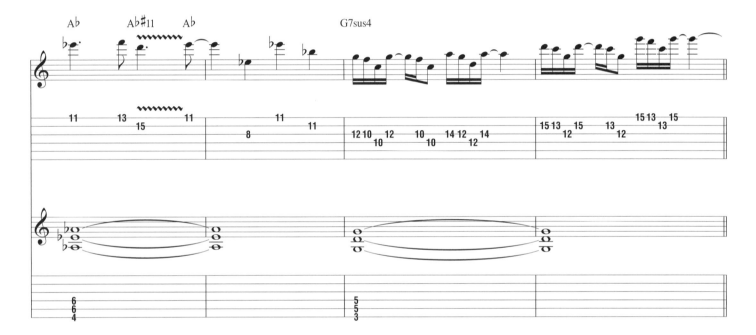

Verse

Gtrs. 2 & 3 tacet
Gtr. 7: w/ Rhy. Fig. 2 (1st 8 meas.)

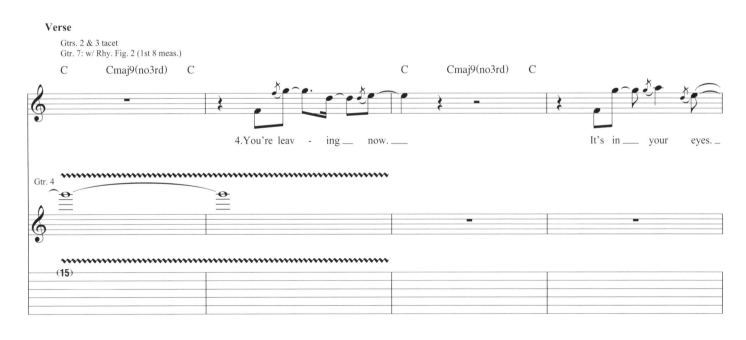

4. You're leav - ing ___ now. ___   It's in ___ your eyes. ___

from Guns N' Roses - *Appetite for Destruction*

Paradise City

Words and Music by W. Axl Rose, Slash, Izzy Stradlin', Duff McKagan and Steven Adler

Tune down 1/2 step:
(low to high) E♭-A♭-D♭-G♭-B♭-E♭

Intro
Moderately slow ♩ = 94

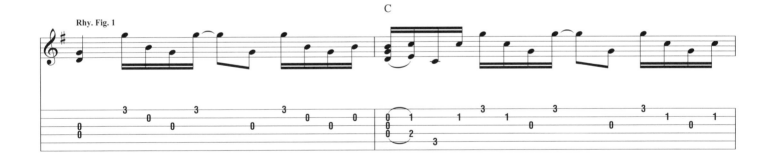

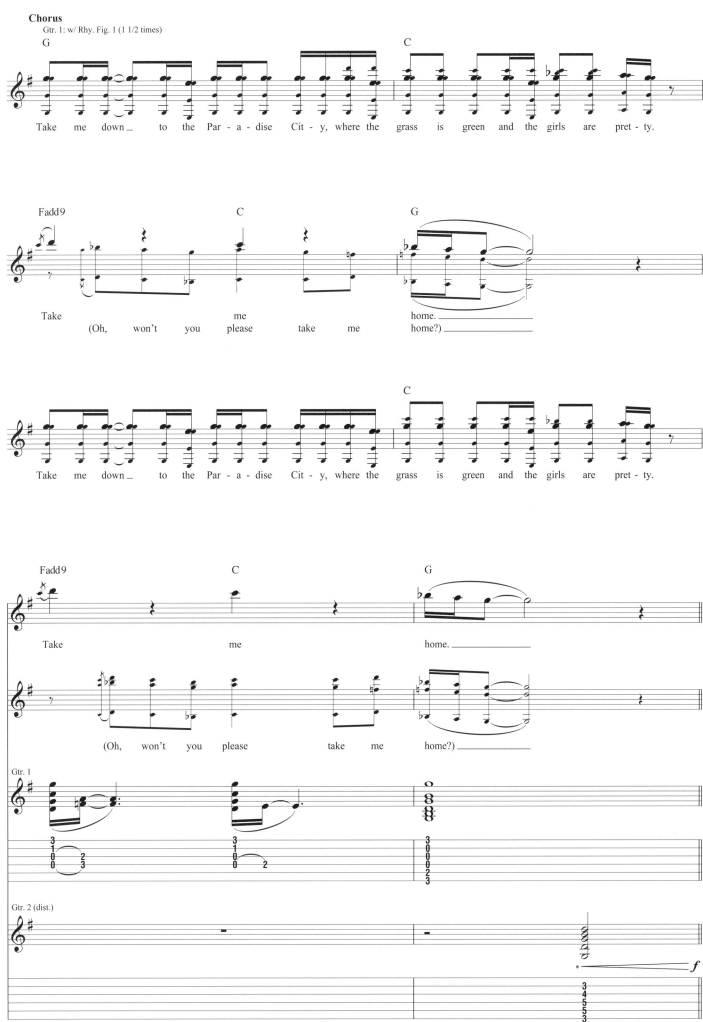

Chorus

Interlude

Gtr. 1 tacet

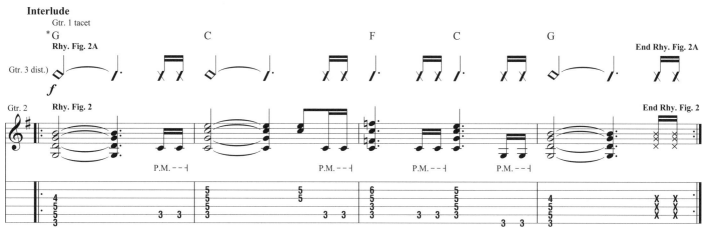

*See top of first page of song for chord diagrams pertaining to rhythm slashes.

Gtrs. 2 & 3: w/ Rhy. Figs. 2 & 2A (1 1/4 times)

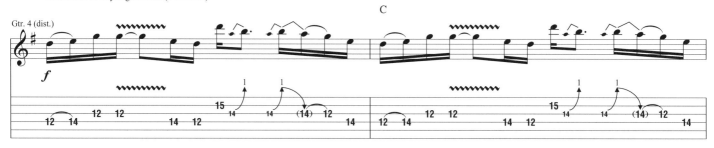

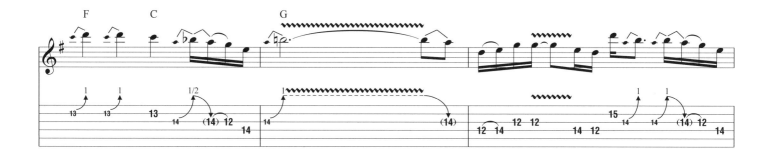

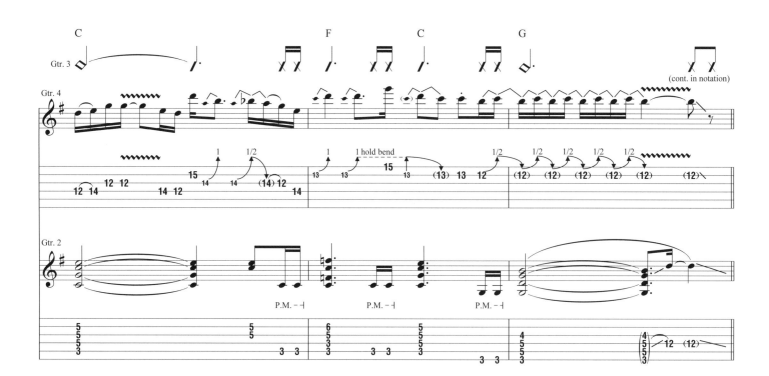

Interlude

Gtr. 4 tacet

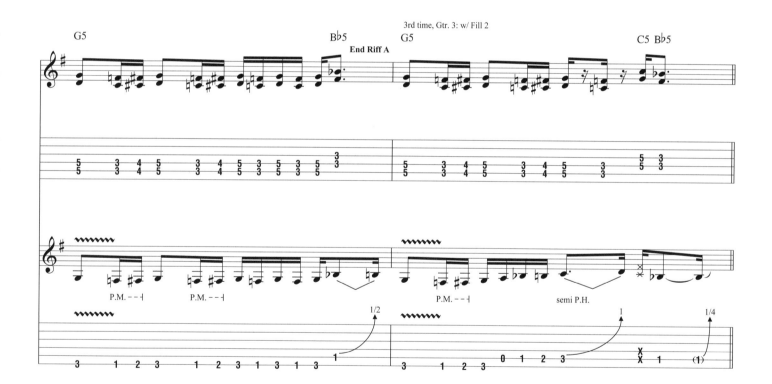

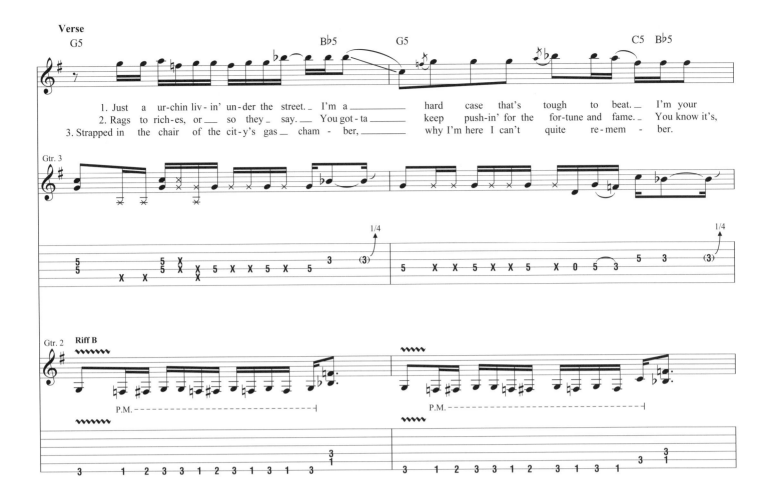

1. Just a ur-chin liv-in' un-der the street. I'm a hard case that's tough to beat. I'm your
2. Rags to rich-es, or so they say. You got-ta keep push-in' for the for-tune and fame. You know it's,
3. Strapped in the chair of the cit-y's gas cham-ber, why I'm here I can't quite re-mem-ber.

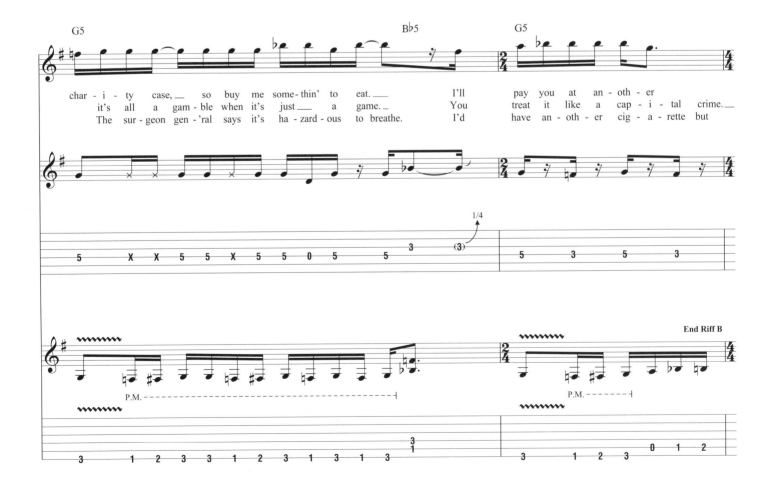

char - i - ty case, so buy me some-thin' to eat. I'll pay you at an - oth - er
it's all a gam - ble when it's just a game. You treat it like a cap - i - tal crime.
The sur - geon gen - 'ral says it's ha - zard - ous to breathe. I'd have an - oth - er cig - a - rette but

time. _____

I can't see. _____

Take it to the end of the line. _____

Tell me who you're gon - na be - lieve. _____

Ev - 'ry - bod - y's do - in' their time. _____

Chorus
Gtrs. 2 & 3: w/ Rhy. Figs. 2 & 2A (1 1/2 times)

Take me down _ to the Par - a - dise Cit - y, where the grass is green and the girls are pret - ty.

Oh, won't you please take me home? _____ Yeah, _ yeah. _____

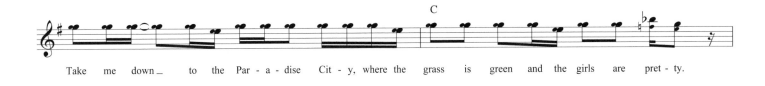

Take me down __ to the Par - a - dise Cit - y, where the grass is green and the girls are pret - ty.

D.S. al Coda
(take 1st ending)

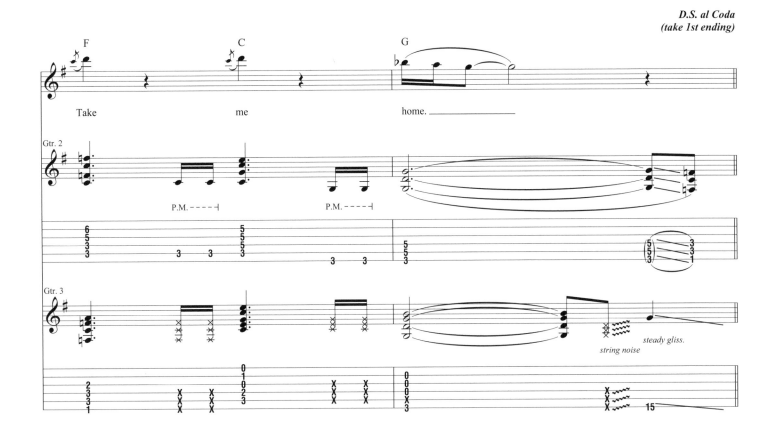

Take me home. _____

Gtr. 2

P.M. ---- ┤   P.M. ---- ┤

Gtr. 3

steady gliss.
string noise

⊕ Coda

Chorus

Gtrs. 2 & 3: w/ Rhy. Figs. 2 & 2A (1 1/2 times)

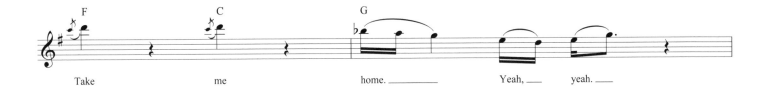

Take me down __ to the Par - a - dise Cit - y, where the grass is green and the girls are pret - ty.

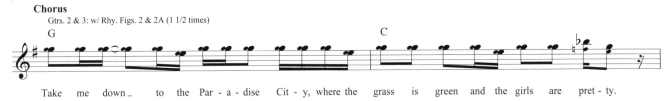

Take me home. _____ Yeah, ___ yeah. ___

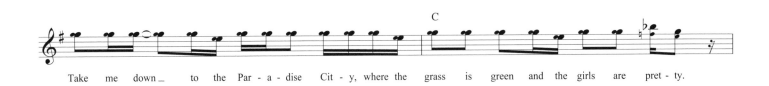

Take me down __ to the Par - a - dise Cit - y, where the grass is green and the girls are pret - ty.

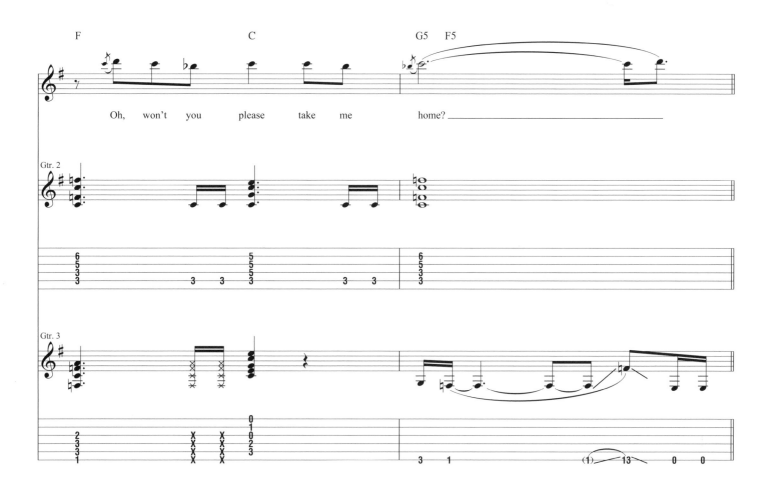

Oh, won't you please take me home? _____

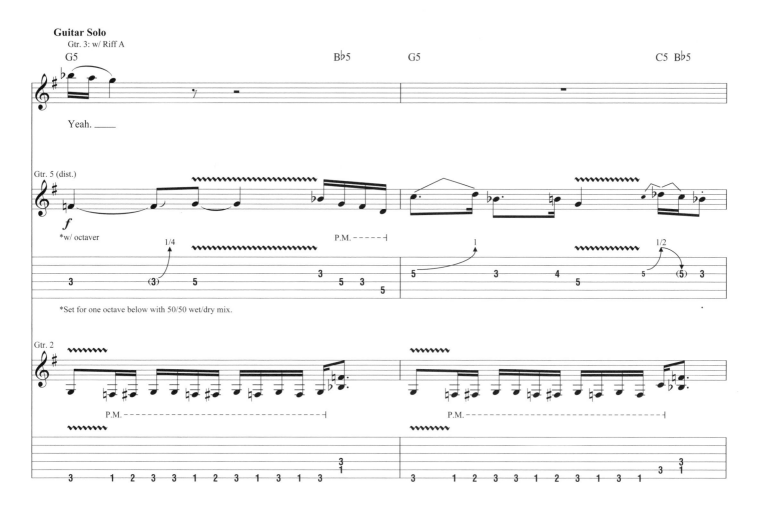

Guitar Solo

Yeah. _____

*w/ octaver

*Set for one octave below with 50/50 wet/dry mix.

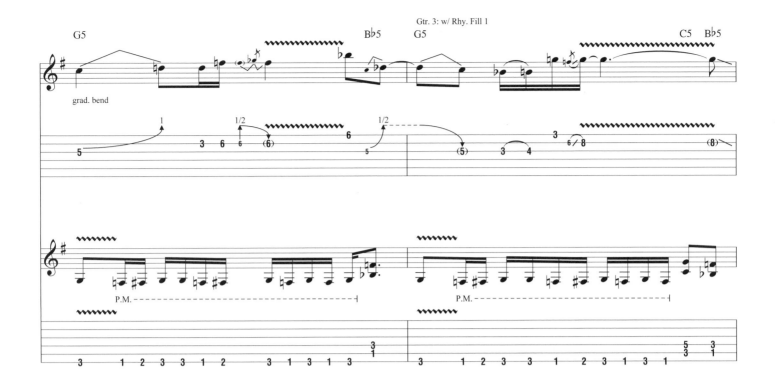

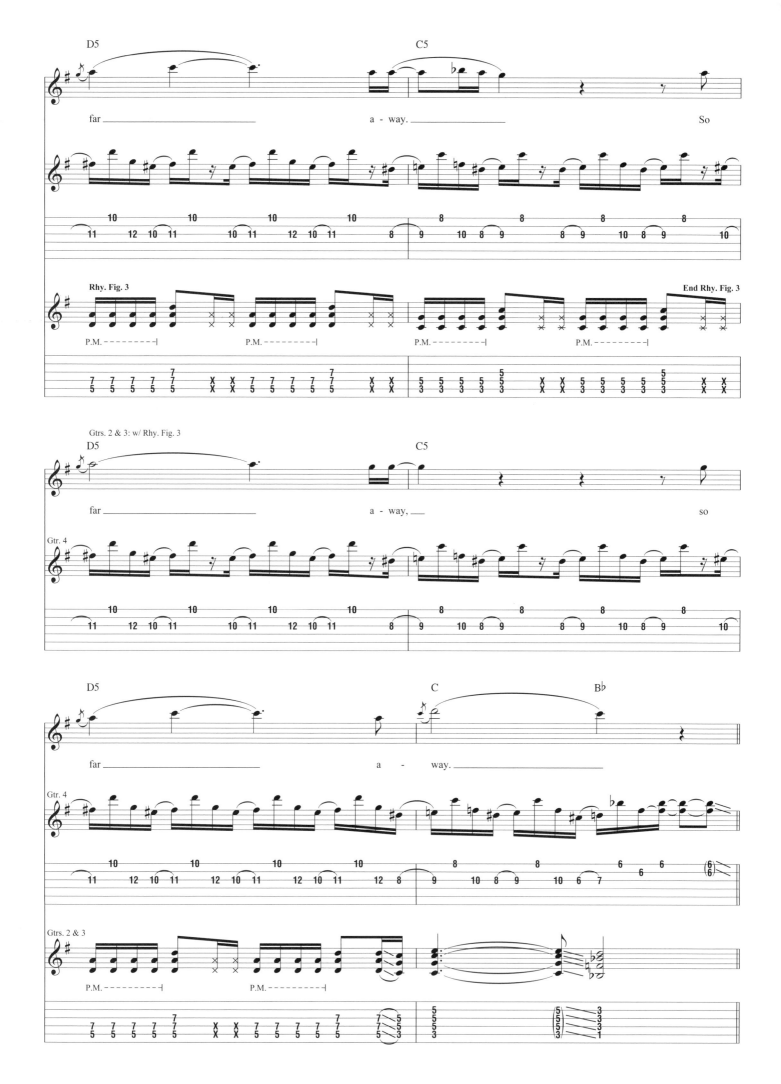

Verse

Gtr. 2: w/ Riff B

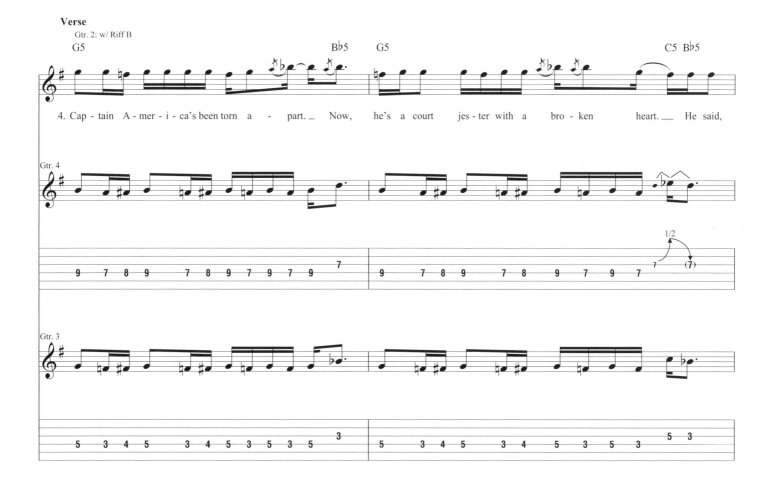

4. Cap - tain A - mer - i - ca's been torn a - part.___ Now, he's a court jes - ter with a bro - ken heart.___ He said,

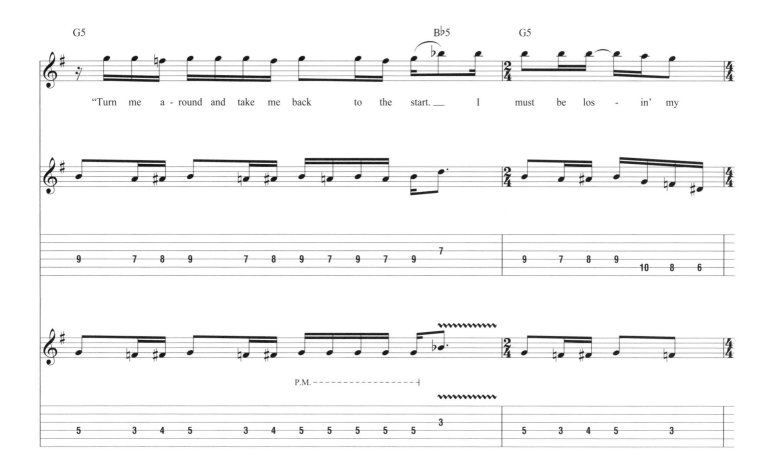

"Turn me a - round and take me back to the start.___ I must be los - in' my

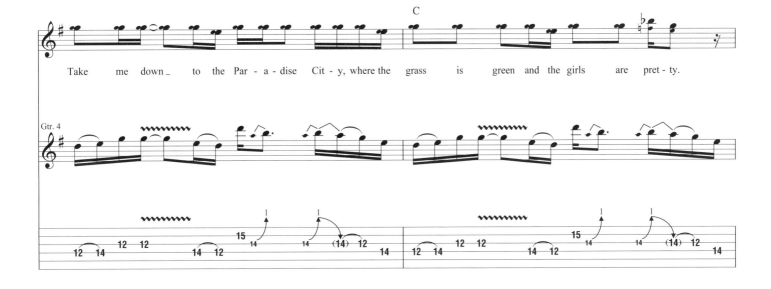

Take me down to the Par - a - dise Cit - y, where the grass is green and the girls are pret - ty.

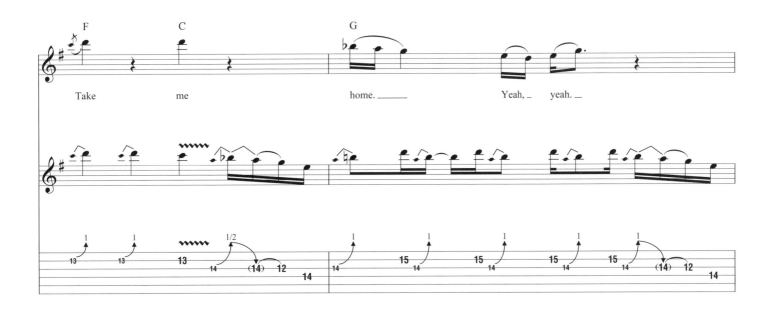

Take me home. Yeah, yeah.

Take me down to the Par - a - dise Cit - y, where the grass is green and the girls are pret - ty.

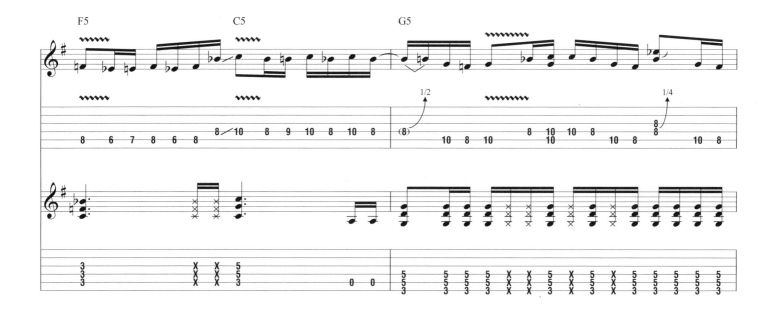

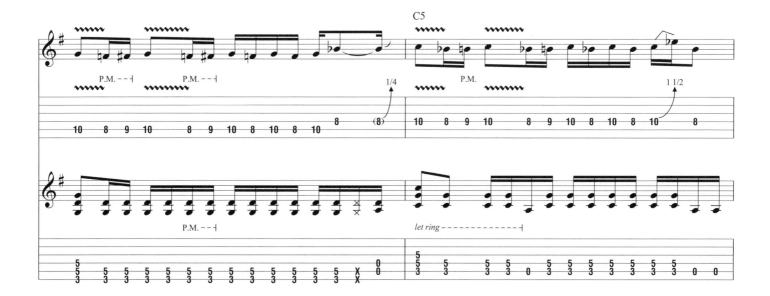

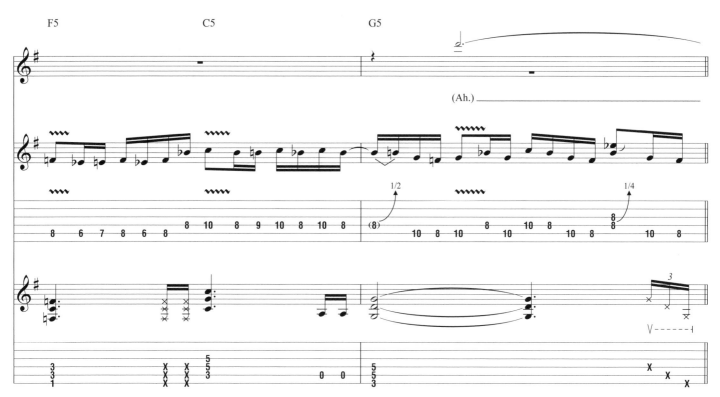

Outro-Guitar Solo

Bkgd. Voc.: w/ voc. ad lib (next 24 meas.)

I wan-na go, ___ I wan-na know. ___

Oh, won't you please ___ take ___ me home? _____

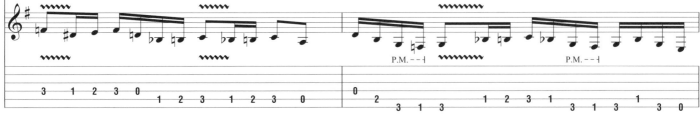

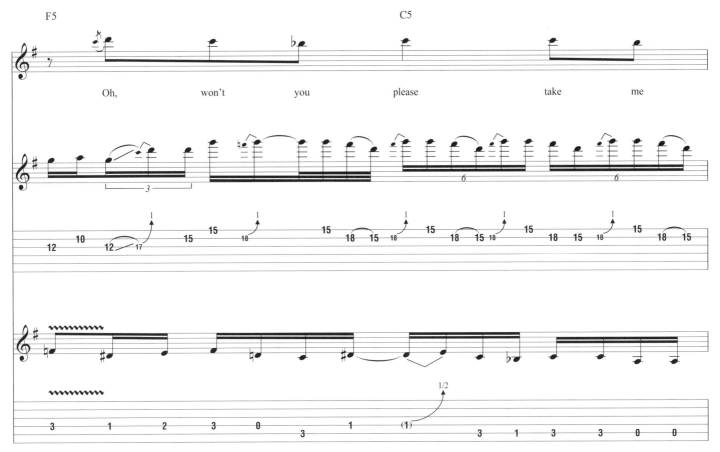

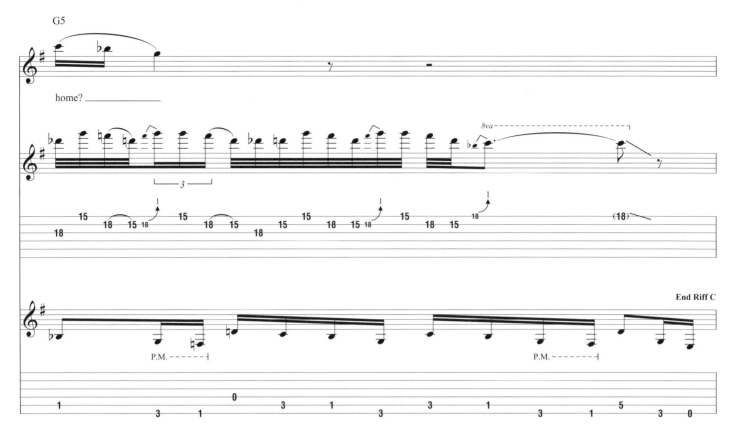

home? _____

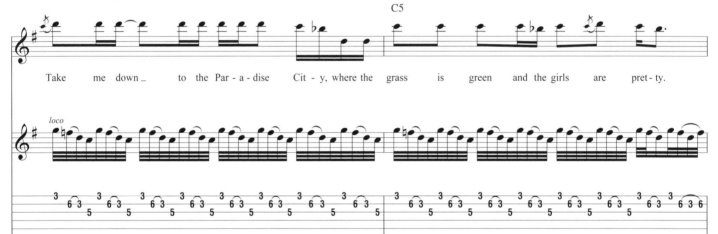

End Riff C

Gtr. 2: w/ Riff C (7 1/2 times)

C5

Take me down _ to the Par - a - dise Cit - y, where the grass is green and the girls are pret - ty.

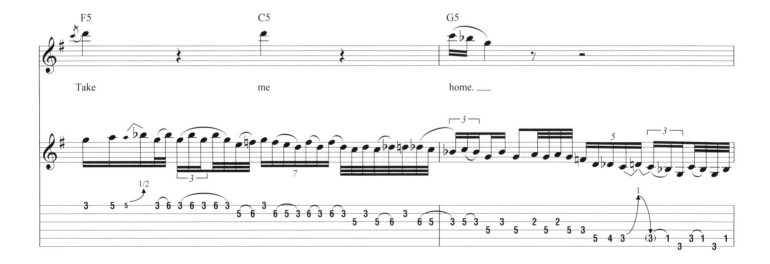

F5   C5   G5

Take   me   home. __

Take me down ___ to the Par - a - dise Cit - y, where the grass is green and the girls are pret - ty.

Oh, won't you please _____ take me home? _____

Take me down, ___ beat me 'round. _____

Oh, won't you please _____ take me home? _____

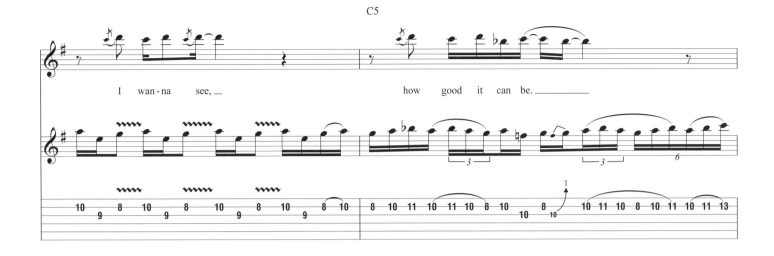

I wan-na see, __ how good it can be. __

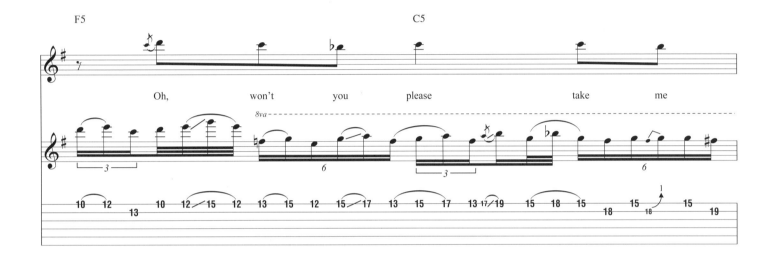

Oh, won't you please take me

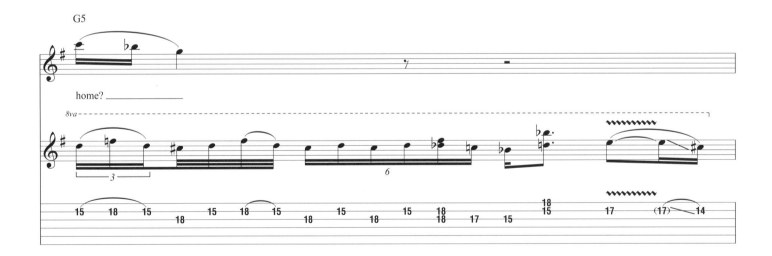

home? __

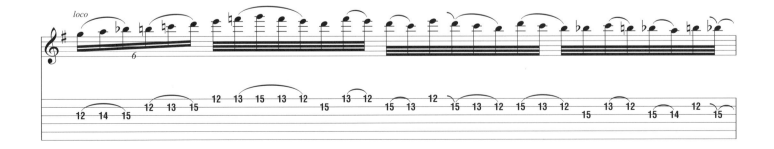

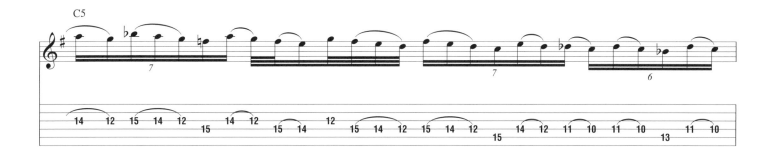

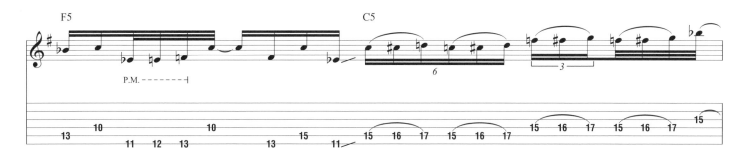

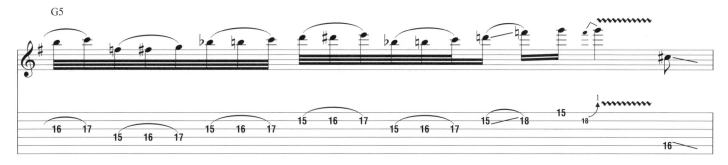

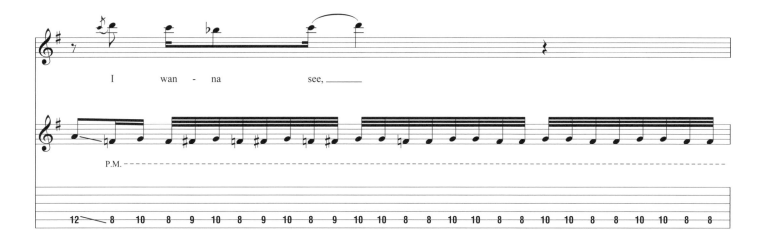

I wan - na see, _____

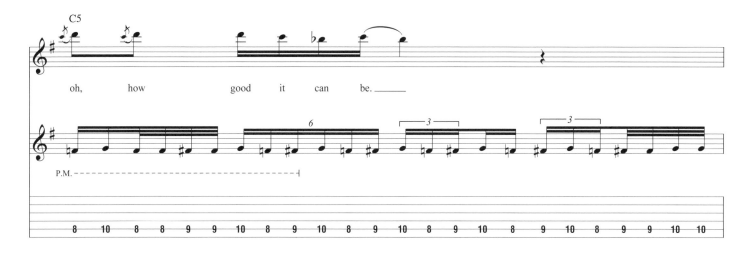

oh, how good it can be. _____

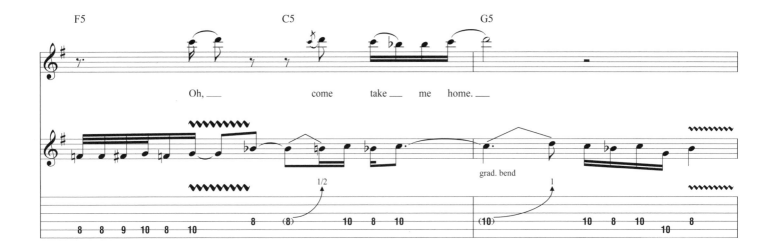

Oh, ___ come take ___ me home. ___

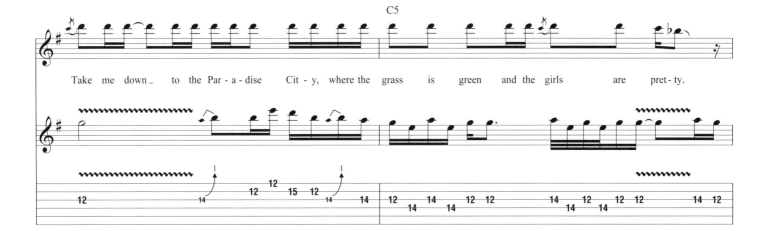

Take me down ___ to the Par - a - dise Cit - y, where the grass is green and the girls are pret - ty.

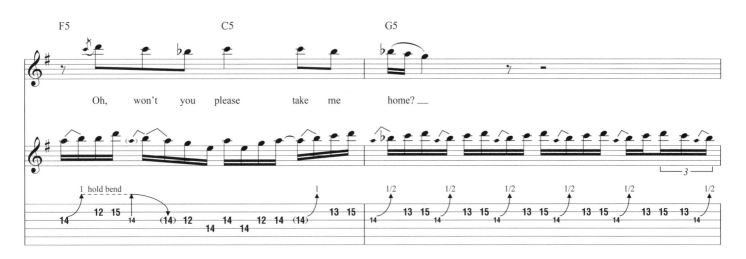

Oh, won't you please take me home? ___

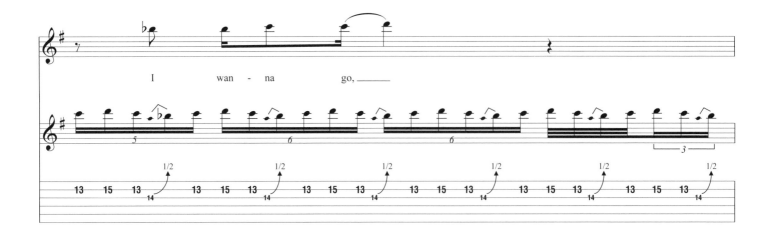

I wan - na go, ___

I wan - na go. _____

Oh, won't you please take me home? _____

Yeah,   ba - by.

Rebel Yell

Words and Music by Billy Idol and Steve Stevens

Verse

2nd time, Gtr. 3 tacet

1. Last night __ a lit - tle danc - er came danc - in' to my door. __
2. She don't __ like slav - 'ry, she won't sit and beg. _____

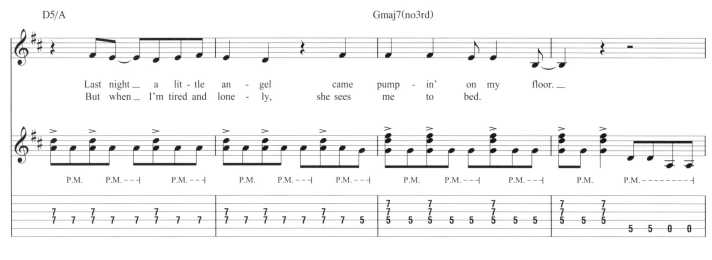

Last night __ a lit - tle an - gel came pump - in' on my floor. __
But when __ I'm tired and lone - ly, she sees me to bed.

Gtr. 2: w/ Rhy. Fig. 1

She said, __ "Uh, come, ba - by. _____ You got a li - cense for __ love,
What set you free __ and brought you to me, _____ babe?

and if ___ it ex - pires ___ pray help from a - bove." ___ Be - cause ___
What set you free? I need you here by me.

P.M. P.M. - - ┤ P.M. - - ┤ P.M. P.M. - - ┤ P.M. - - ┤ P.M. P.M. - - ┤ P.M. - - ┤ P.M.

𝄋 Chorus

3rd time, Gtr. 4 tacet

in the mid-night hour, ___ she cried, "More, more, more." ___

Rhy. Fig. 2

With a reb - el yell, ___ she cried, "More, more, more." ___ Ow! ___

End Rhy. Fig. 2

Gtr. 2: w/ Rhy. Fig. 2
2nd time, Gtr. 2: w/ Rhy. Fig. 2 (1st 6 meas.)

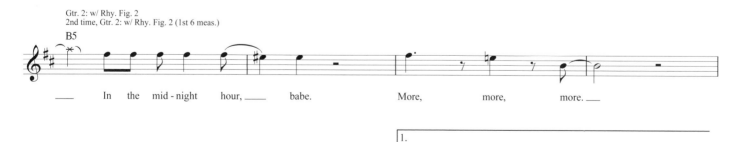

___ In the mid-night hour, ___ babe. More, more, more. ___

1.

To Coda ✪

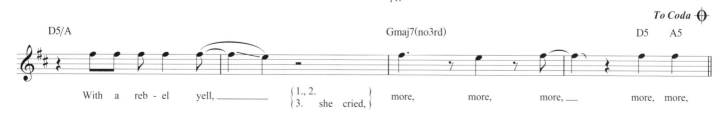

With a reb - el yell, ___ { 1., 2.   } more, more, more, ___ more, more,
{ 3. she cried, }

Just so long, __ just so long it don't mess up his hair. __

Interlude

Wow!   Ow!

Guitar Solo
Gtr. 1 tacet
Gtr. 2: w/ Rhy. Fig. 2 (2 times)

slight P.H. *w/ "ray gun"--
sound effect

*Lexicon PCM 41
digital delay

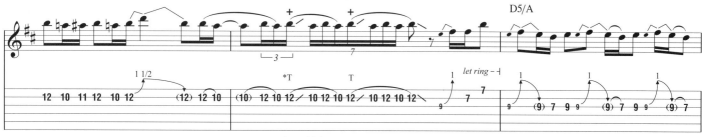

*T = Pick-hand tapped slide

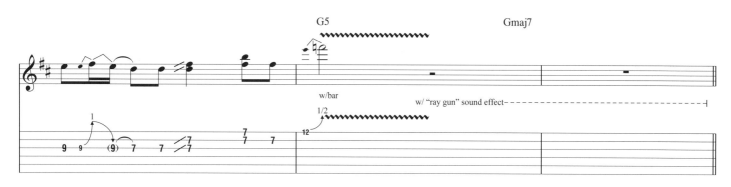

Interlude

Gtr. 3 tacet

Verse

*Vol. swell
**Publison harmonizer
***Chord symbols reflect implied harmony.

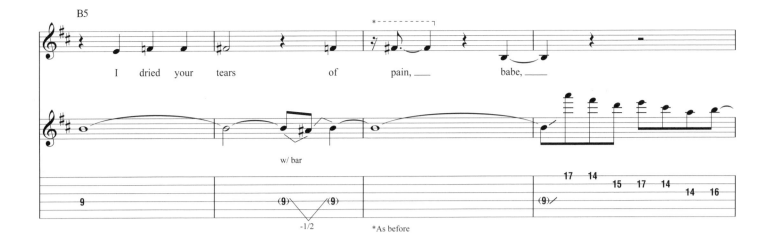

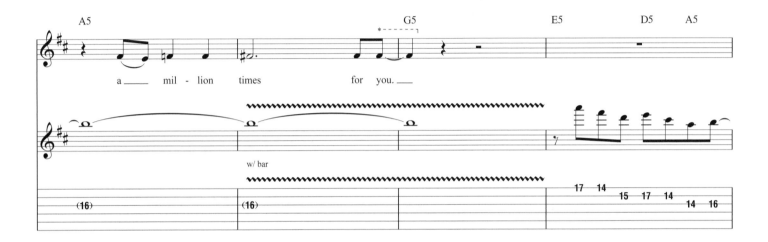

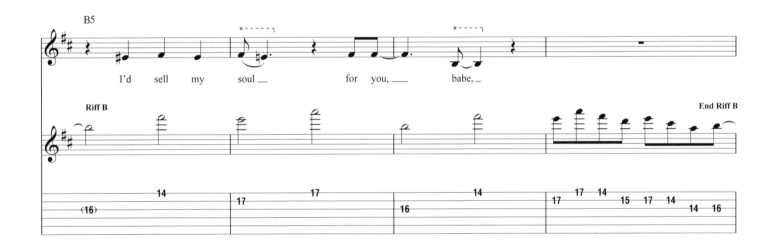

*w/ echo set for whole-note regeneration w/ 1 repeat.

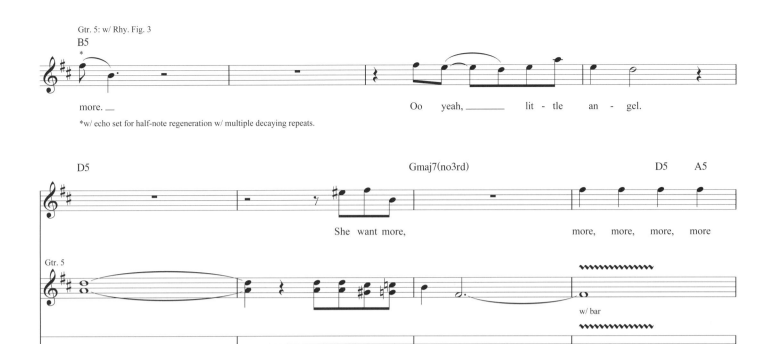

Gtr. 5: w/ Rhy. Fig. 3

*w/ echo set for half-note regeneration w/ multiple decaying repeats.

more. ___

Oo yeah, _____ lit - tle an - gel.

She want more, ___

more, more, more, more

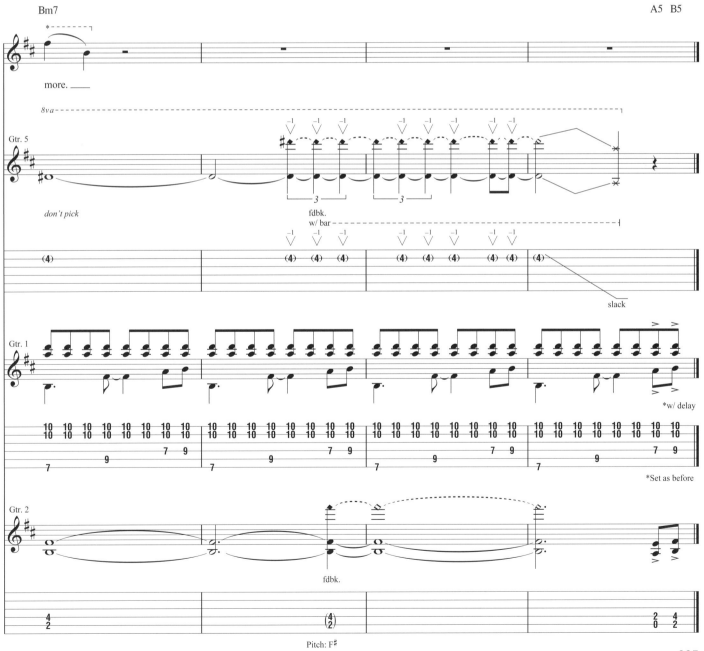

more. ___

Pitch: F#

Renegade

Words and Music by Tommy Shaw

Intro
Moderately slow ♩ = 96

N.C.(Gm)

Oh, __ ma-ma, I'm in fear for my life from the long __ arm __ of the law. __

Law-man has put an end to my run-ning and I'm so far __ from my home. __

Oh, ma-ma, I can hear you a cry-ing, you're so scared and all a-lone. __

Hang-man is com-ing down from the gal-lows and I don't have ver-y long. __

𝄋 Chorus

*Gm7 C/G Gm7 C/G Gm7 C/G Gm7

__ The jig is up, the news is out, __ they've fi-nal-ly __ found __ me, the
(Yeah!) __

Rhy. Fill 1 **End Rhy. Fill 1** **Riff A**

Gtrs. 1 & 2 (dist.)

*Chord symbols reflect basic harmony.

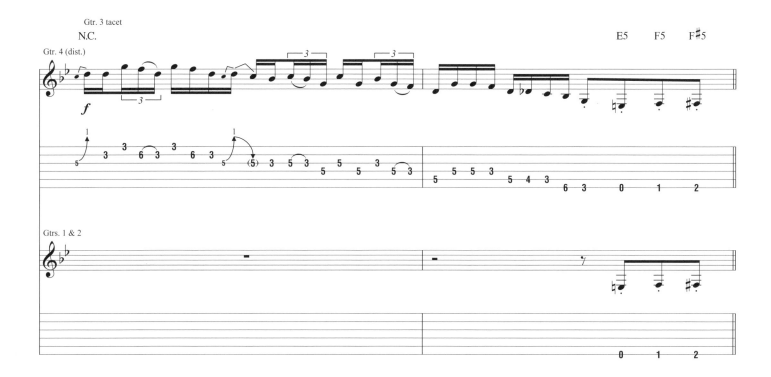

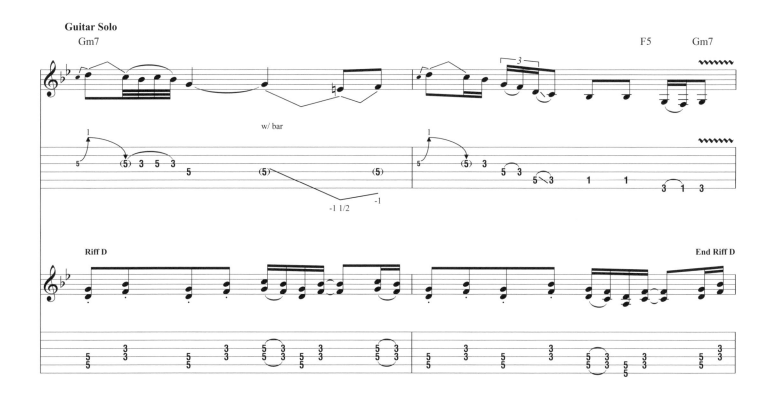

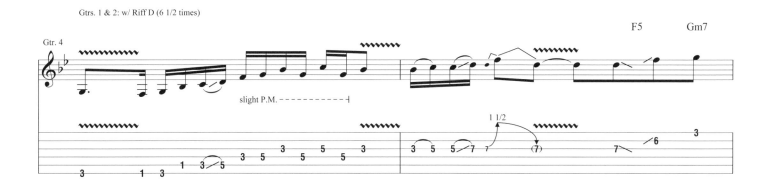

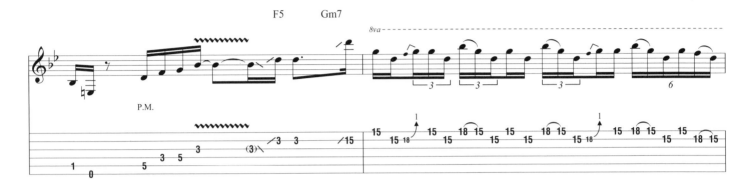

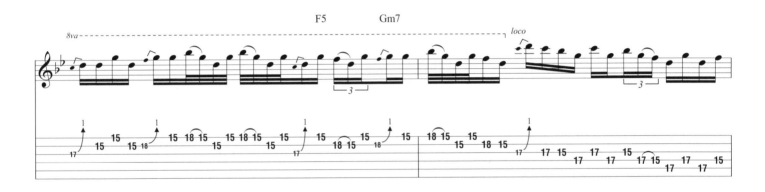

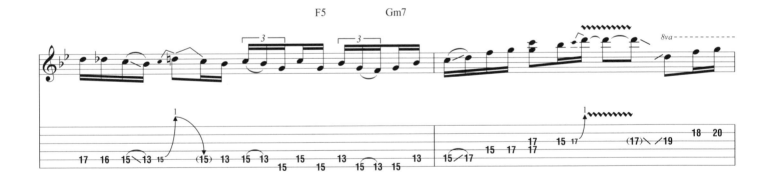

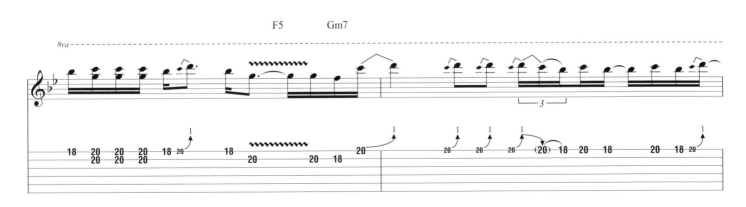

Interlude

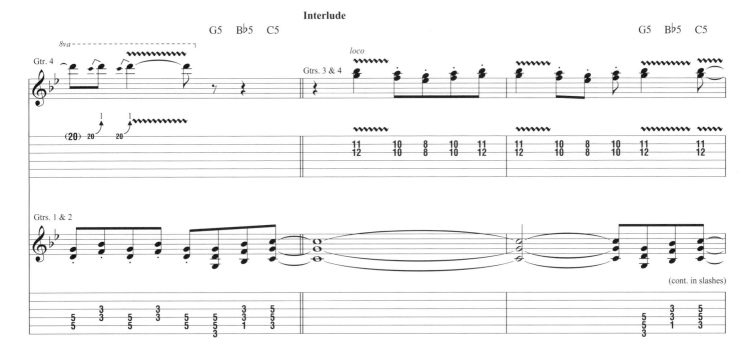

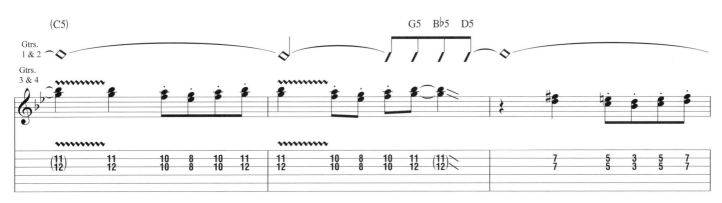

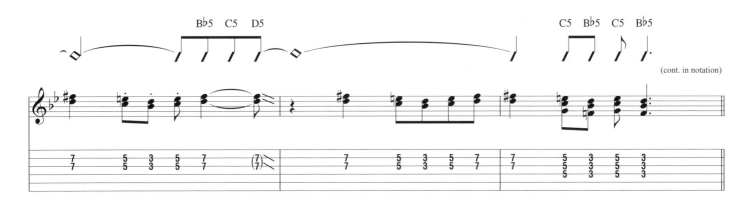

Interlude

Oh ma - ma, I'm in fear for my life from the long___ arm___ of the law.___

Outro-Guitar Solo

Gtrs. 1 & 2: w/ Riff D (till fade)
Gtr. 3 tacet

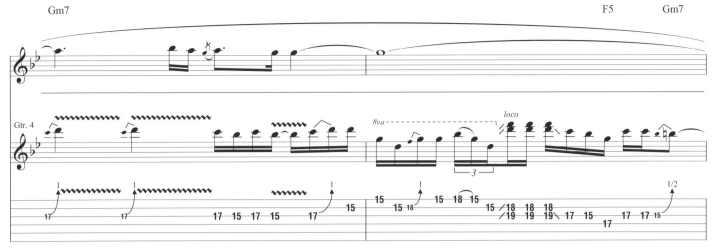

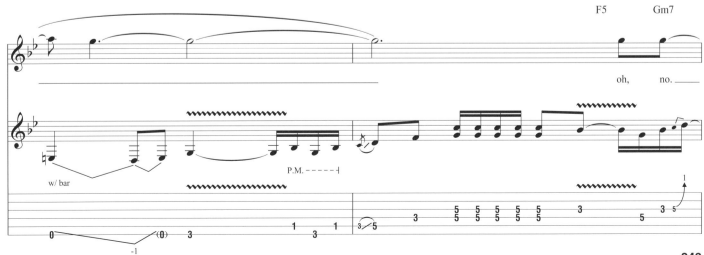

243

F5   Gm7

w/ Voc. ad lib. (next 5 meas.)

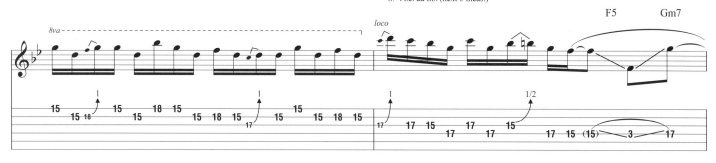

F5   Gm7

Begin fade

F5   Gm7

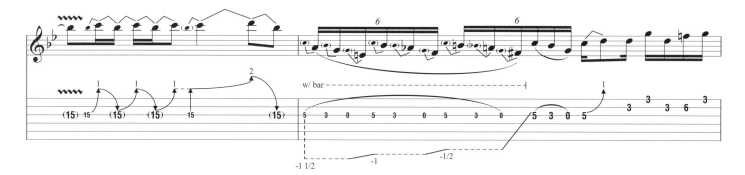

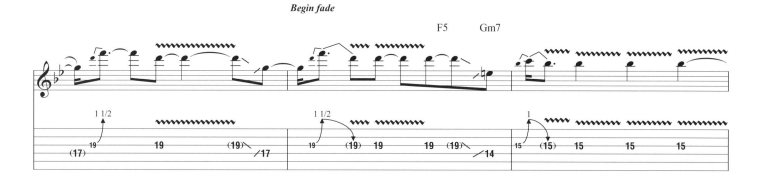

Fade out

F5   Gm7   F5 Gm7

Yeah,   yeah,   yeah.   I can't go.

w/ bar

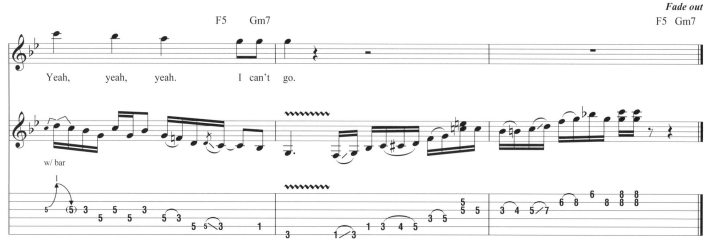

from Journey - *Frontiers*

Separate Ways
(Worlds Apart)

Words and Music by Steve Perry and Jonathan Cain

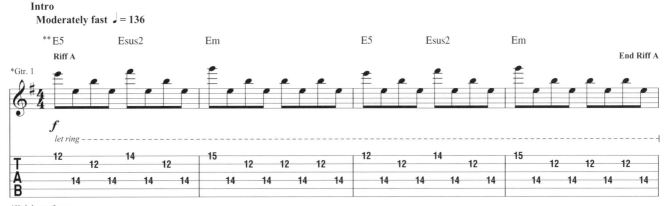

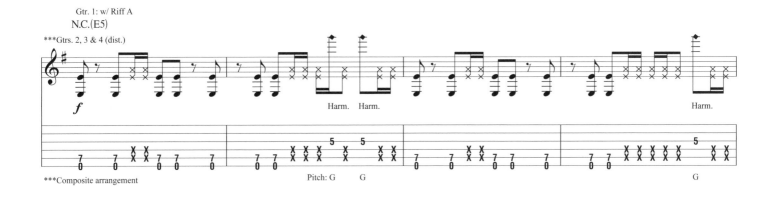

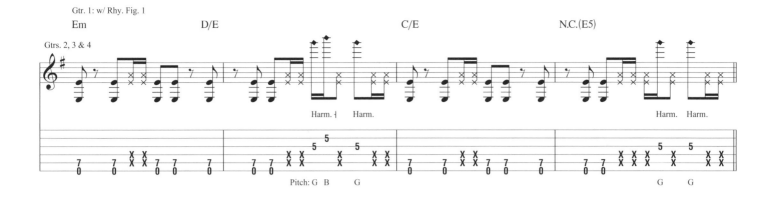

Verse

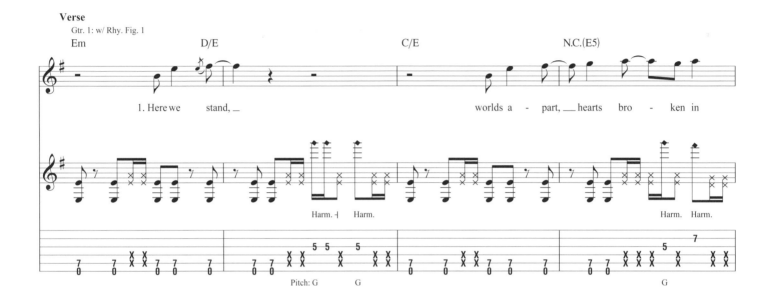

1. Here we stand, __ worlds a - part, __ hearts bro - ken in two, two, __ two. __

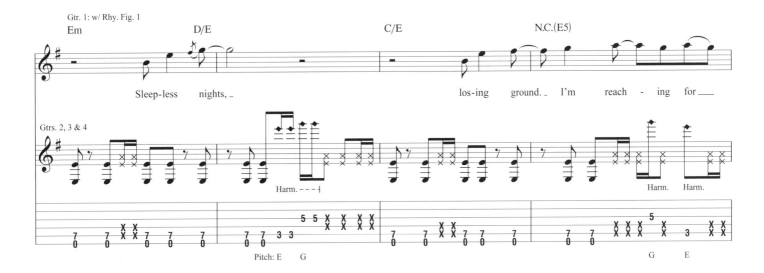

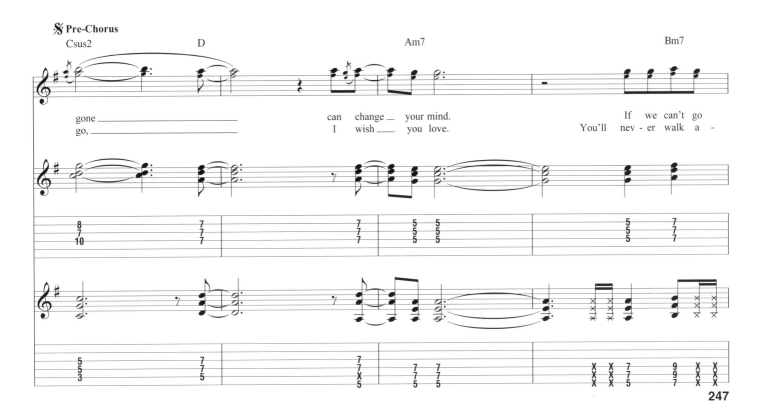

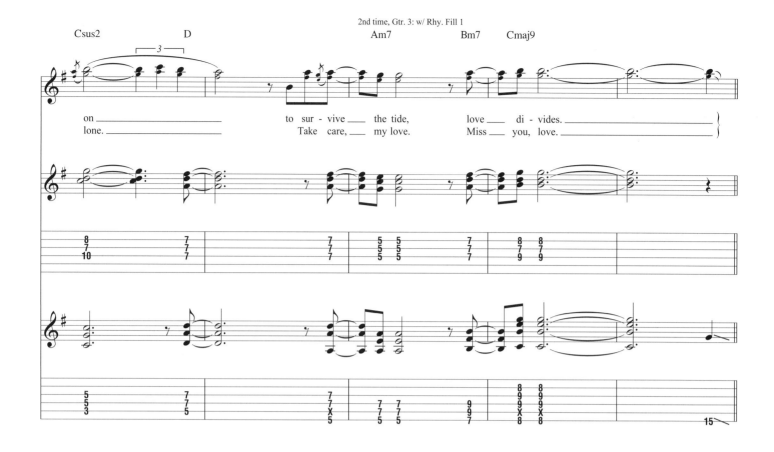

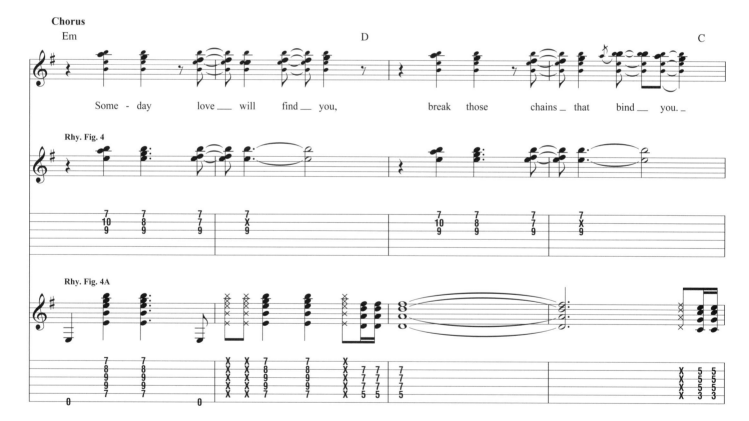

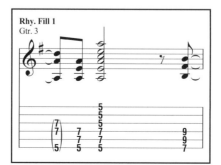

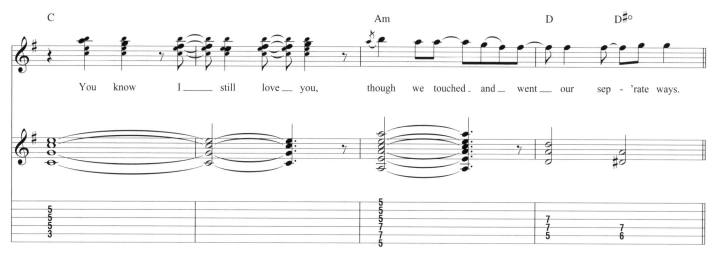

Guitar Solo

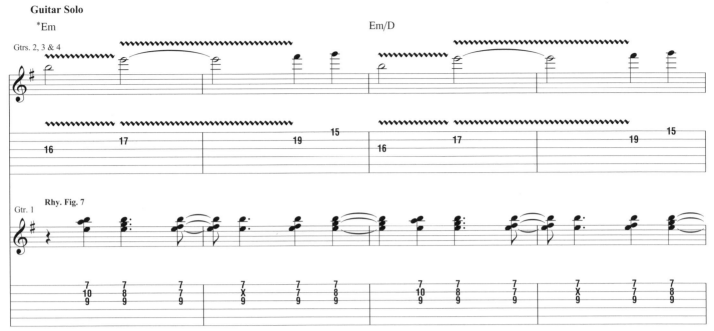

*Chord symbols reflect basic harmony.

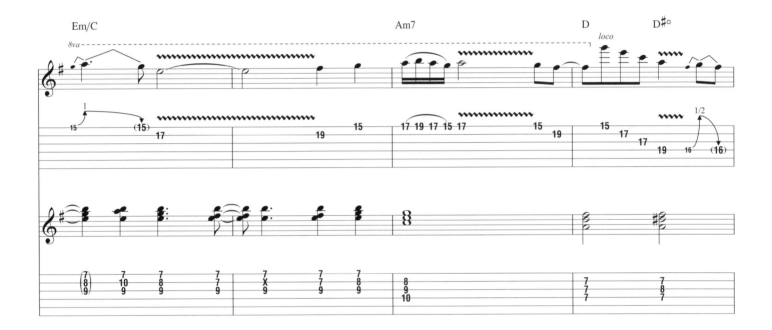

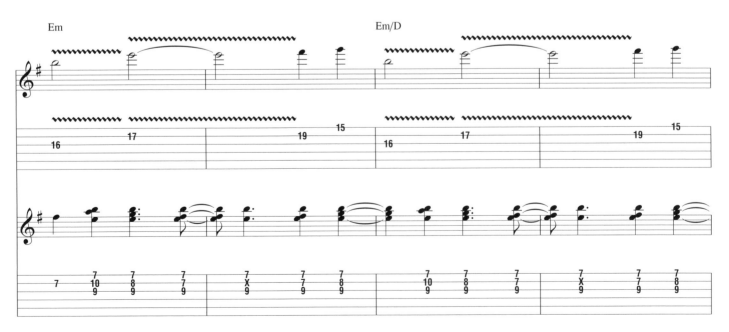

Em/C

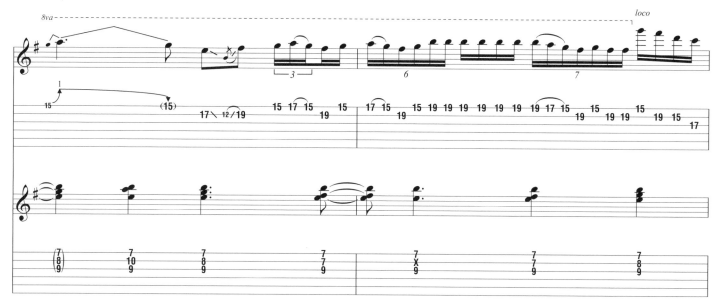

Am7   D   D#°

End Rhy. Fig. 7

Interlude
Gtr. 1: w/ Riff A (3 times)

E5   G5

Gtrs. 2, 3 & 4

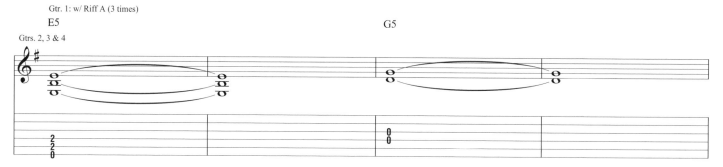

C5   A5   N.C.

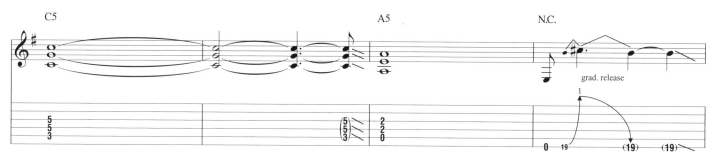

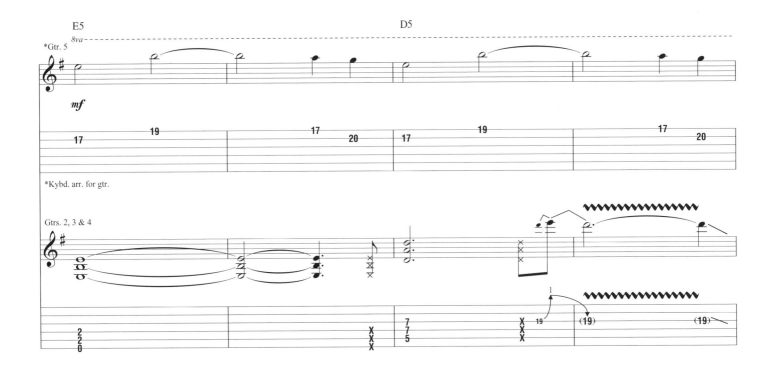

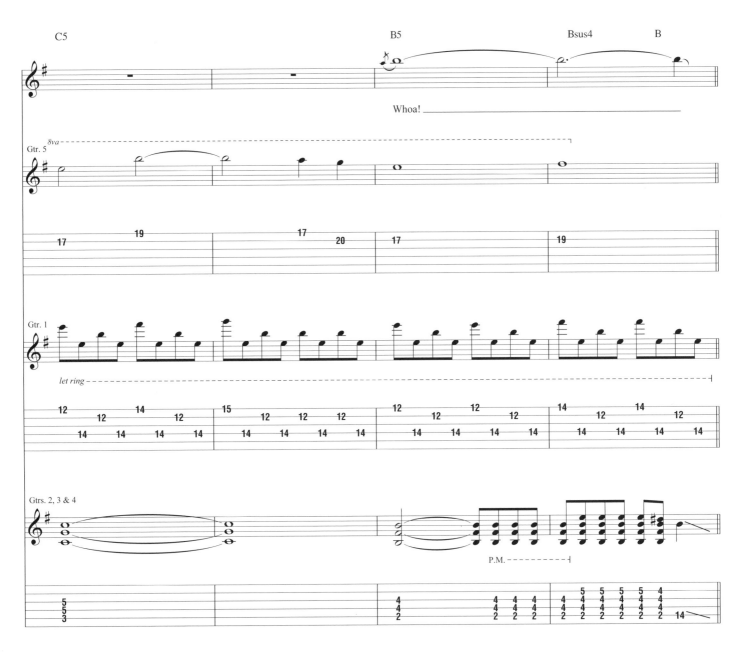

Chorus

Gtr. 1: w/ Rhy. Fig. 4
Gtrs. 2, 3 & 4: w/ Rhy. Fig. 4A (1 1/2 times)
Gtr. 5 tacet

Some - day   love ___ will   find ___ you,   break those   chains ___ that   bind ___ you. ___

One   night   will ___ re - mind ___ you.

Gtr. 1: w/ Rhy. Fig. 6

If   he   ev - er   hurts ___ you,   true   love   won't ___ de - sert ___ you. ___

You   know   I ___ still   love ___ you.

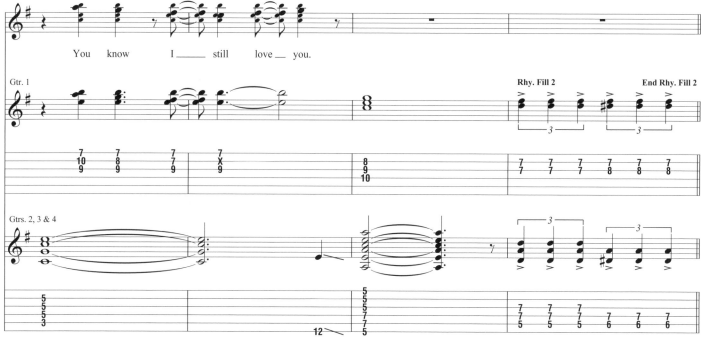

Gtr. 1

Rhy. Fill 2   End Rhy. Fill 2

Gtrs. 2, 3 & 4

Guitar Solo

Gtr. 1: w/ Rhy. Fig. 7

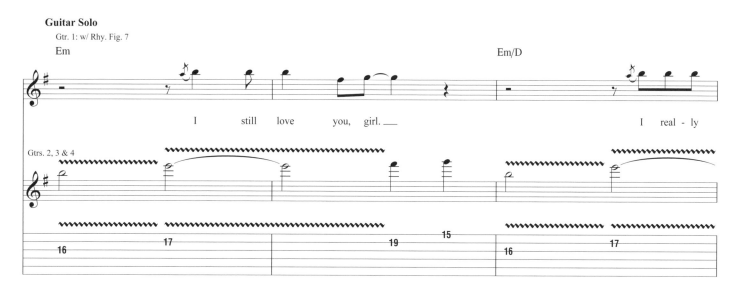

I   still   love   you, girl. ___   I   real - ly

Gtrs. 2, 3 & 4

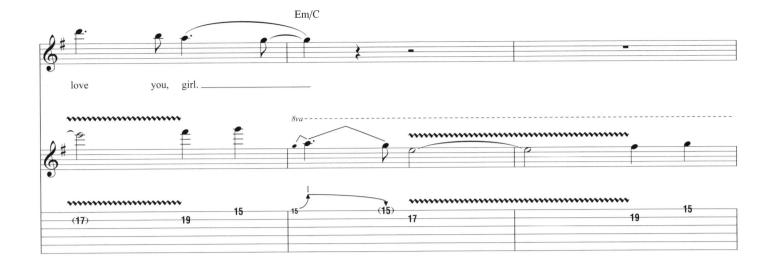

love   you, girl. ____

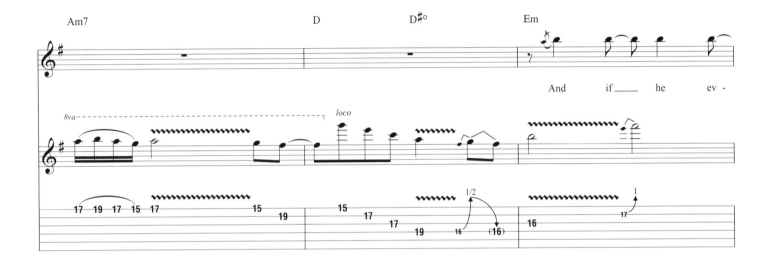

And   if ___ he   ev -

- er   hurts ___ you,   true ___ love   won't ___ de - sert ___ you.

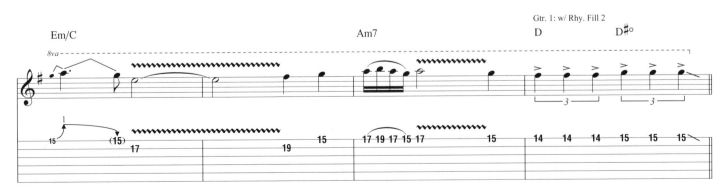

Outro

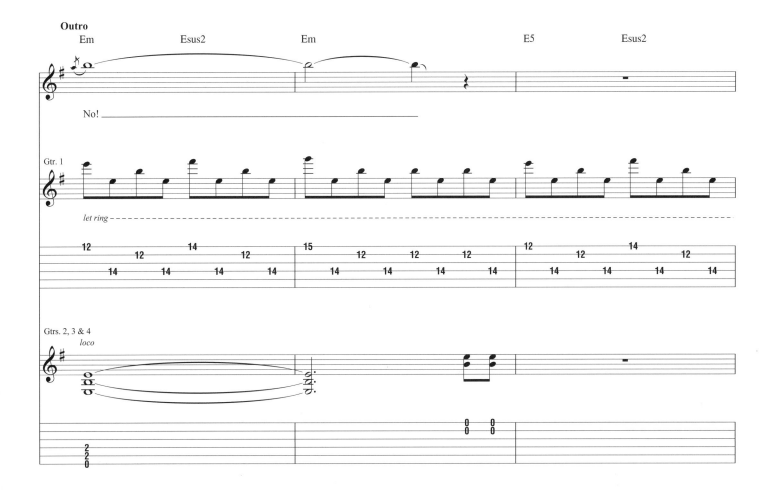

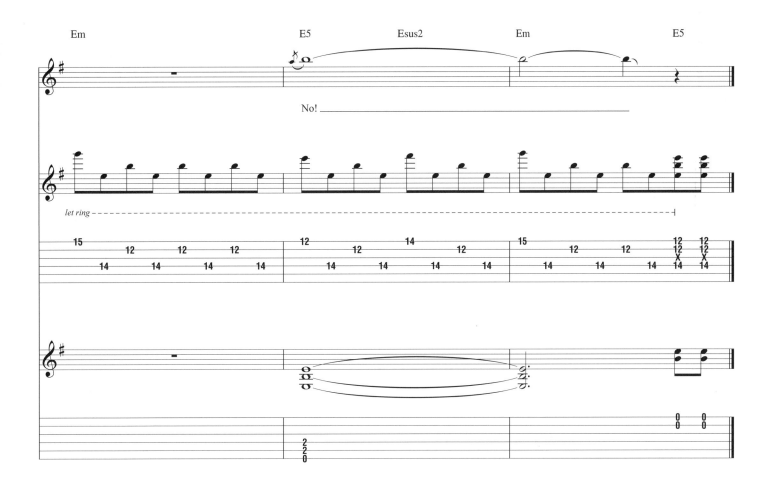

from Robert Plant - *Now and Zen*

Ship of Fools

Words and Music by Robert Plant and Philip Johnstone

Intro
Moderately slow ♩ = 93

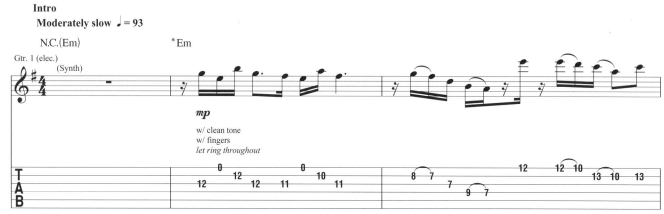

*Chord symbols reflect overall harmony.

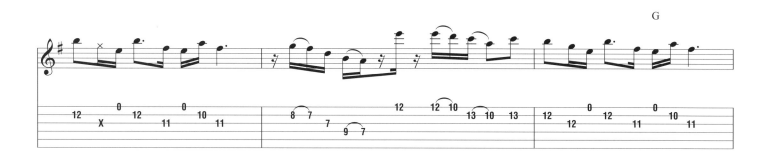

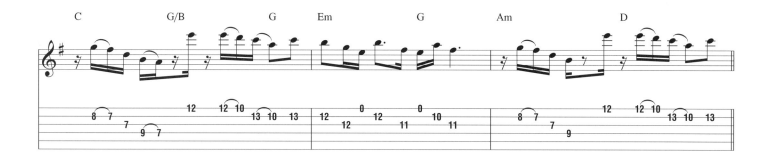

Verse

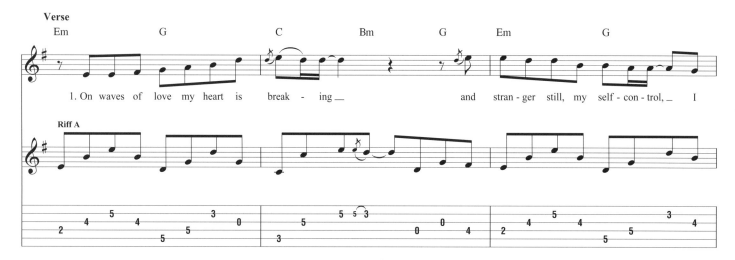

1. On waves of love my heart is break - ing __ and stran - ger still, my self - con - trol, __ I

Riff A

can't re - ly ___ on ___ an - y - more. ___ New tides sur - prise ___ my world, it's chang - ing, with - in ___

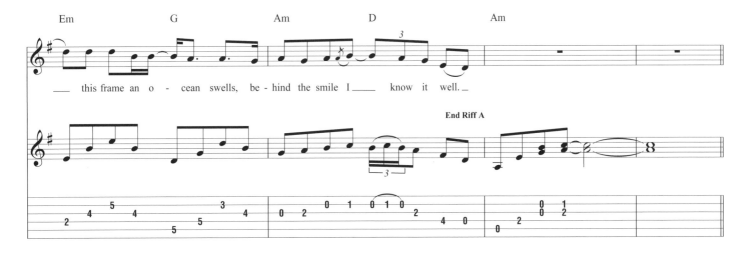

___ this frame an o - cean swells, be - hind the smile I ___ know it well. ___

End Riff A

Verse

Gtr. 1: w/ Riff A

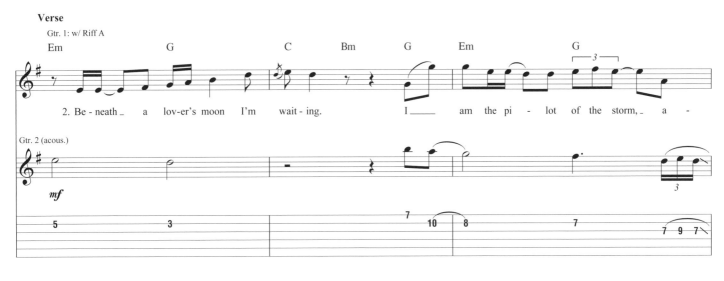

2. Be - neath ___ a lov-er's moon I'm wait - ing. I ___ am the pi - lot of the storm, a -

Gtr. 2 (acous.)

mf

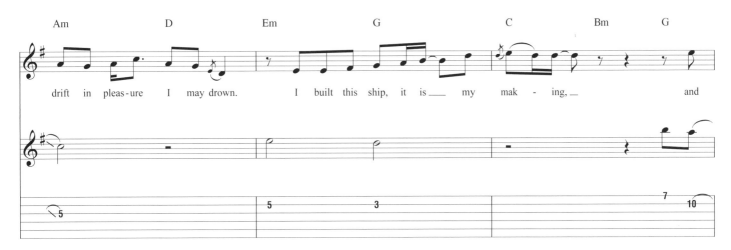

drift in pleas - ure I may drown. I built this ship, it is ___ my mak - ing, ___ and

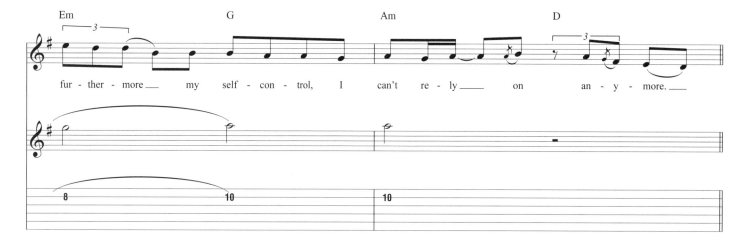

fur - ther - more ___ my self - con - trol, I can't re - ly ___ on an - y - more. ___

Pre-Chorus

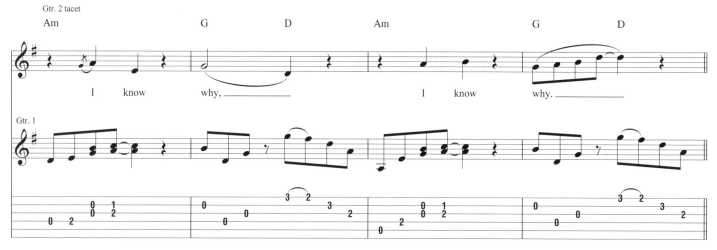

Gtr. 2 tacet

I know why, ___ I know why. ___

Gtr. 1

Chorus

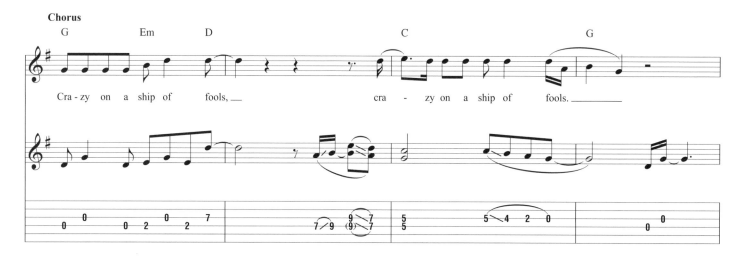

Cra - zy on a ship of fools, ___ cra - zy on a ship of fools. ___

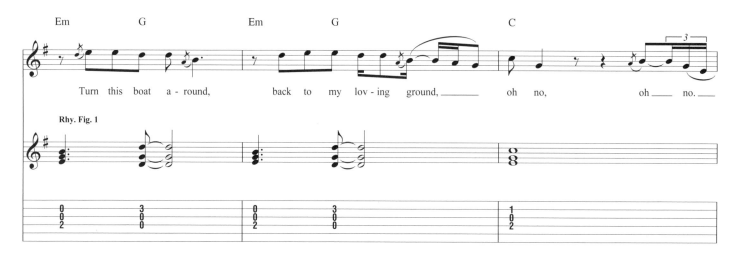

Turn this boat a - round, back to my lov - ing ground, ___ oh no, oh ___ no. ___

Rhy. Fig. 1

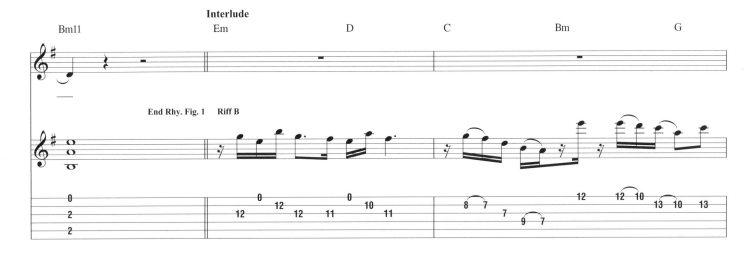

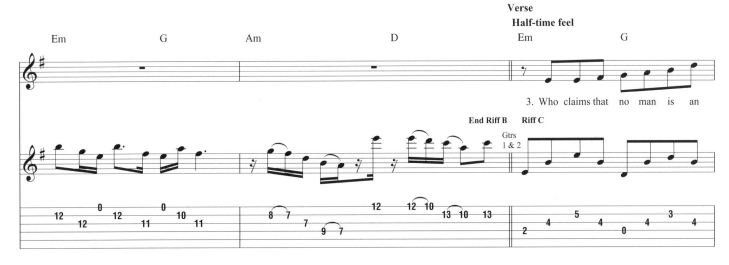

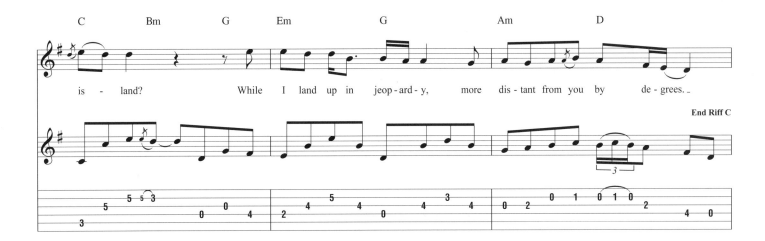

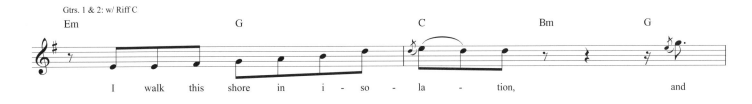

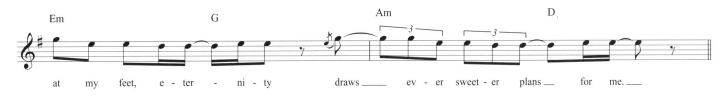

Pre-Chorus

I know why, ___ I know ___ why.

Chorus

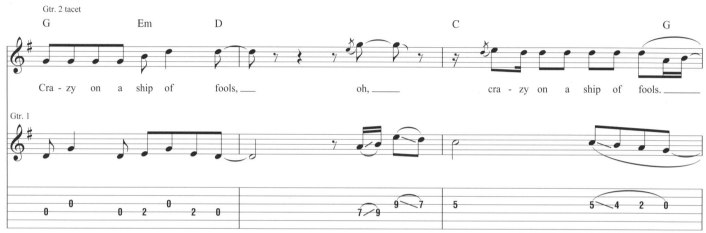

Cra-zy on a ship of fools, ___ oh, ___ cra-zy on a ship of fools. ___

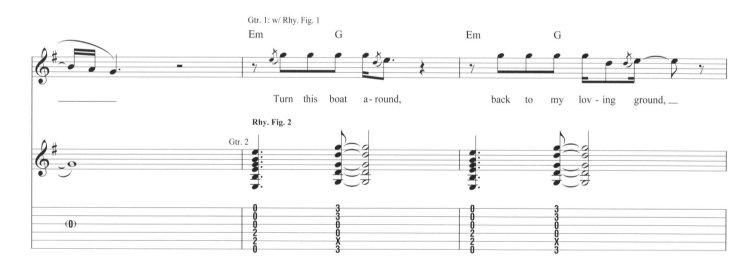

Turn this boat a-round, back to my lov-ing ground, ___

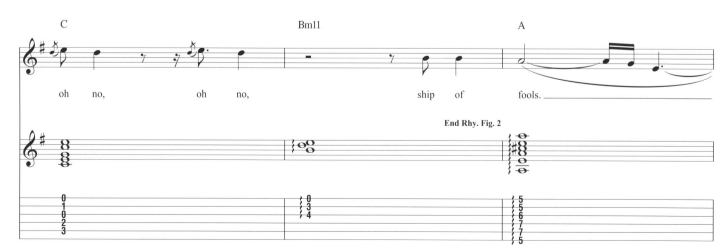

oh no, oh no, ship of fools. ___

Guitar Solo

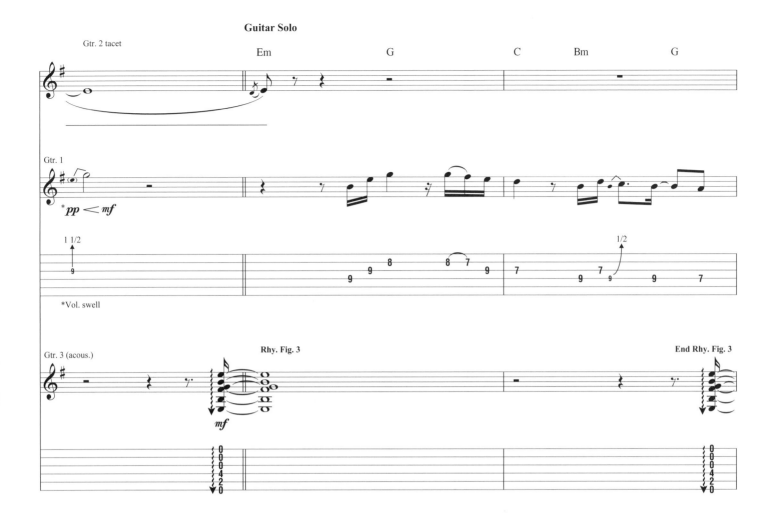

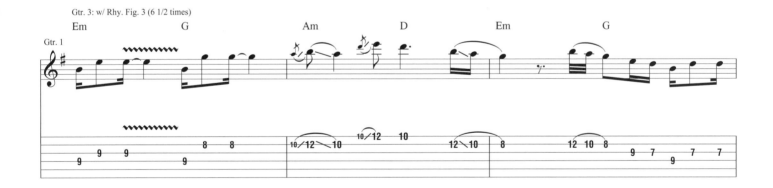

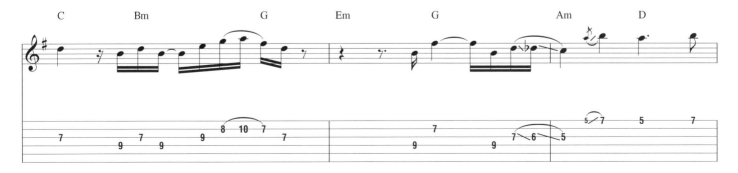

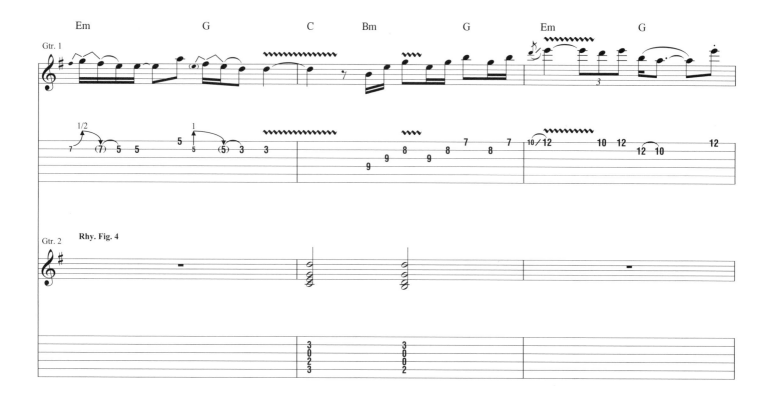

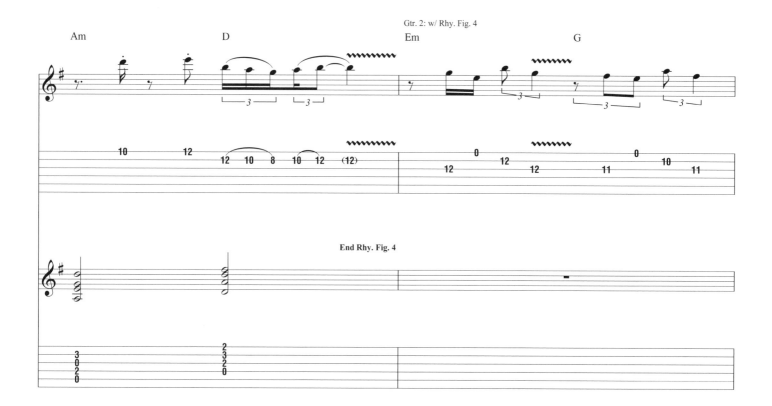

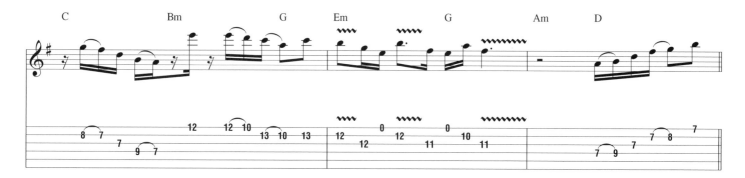

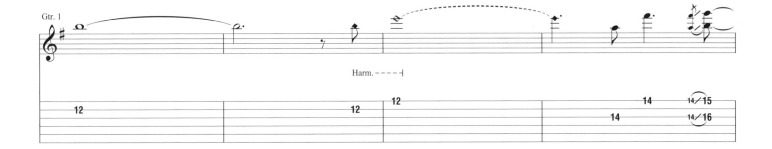

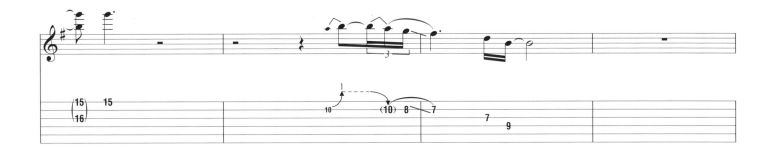

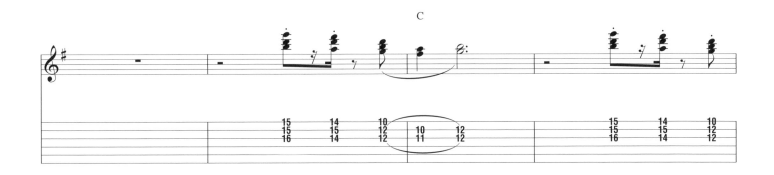

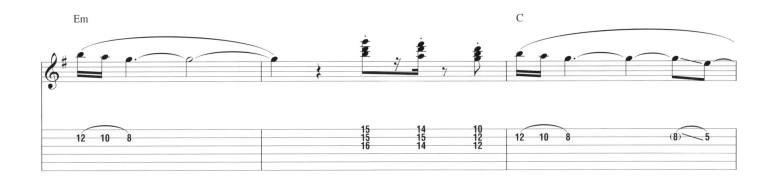

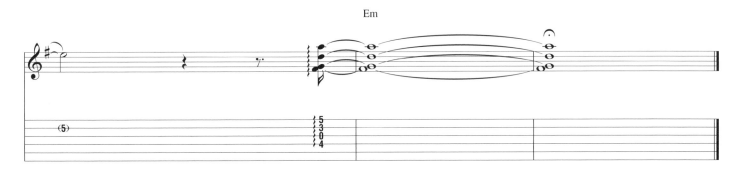

from Lynyrd Skynyrd - *The Essential*

Simple Man

Words and Music by Ronnie Van Zant and Gary Rossington

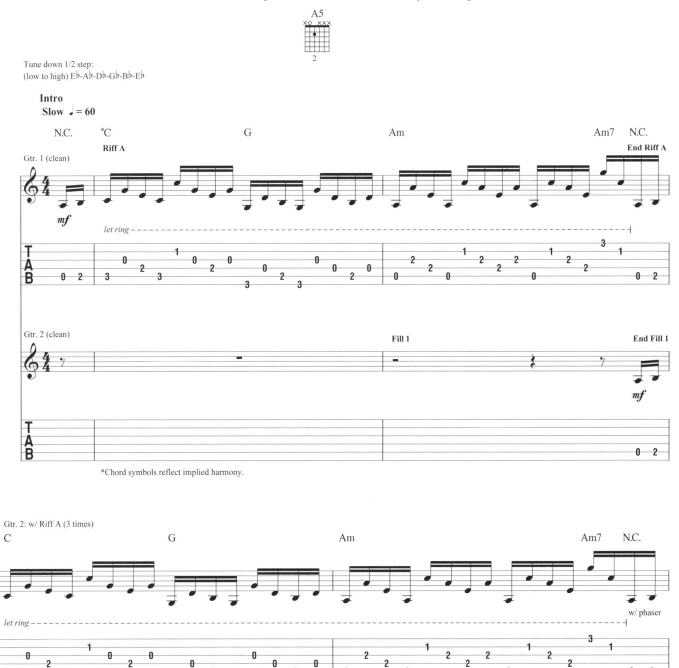

Tune down 1/2 step:
(low to high) Eb-Ab-Db-Gb-Bb-Eb

*Chord symbols reflect implied harmony.

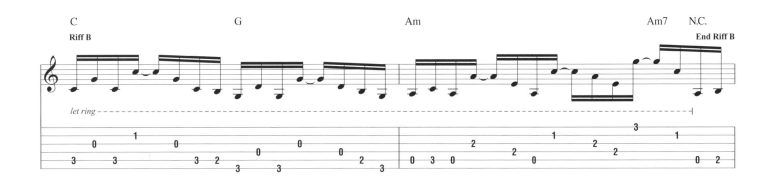

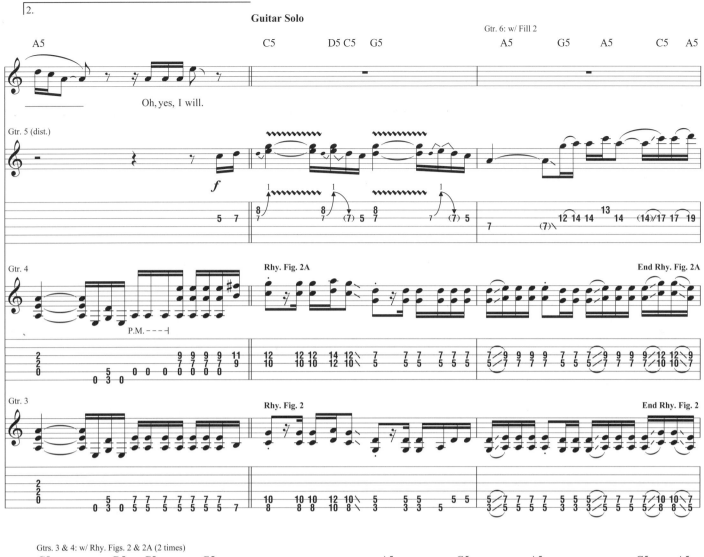

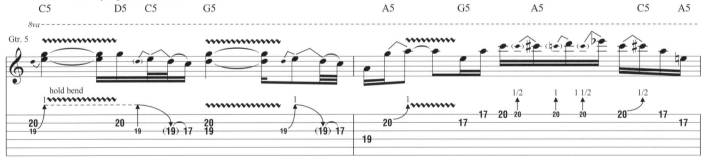

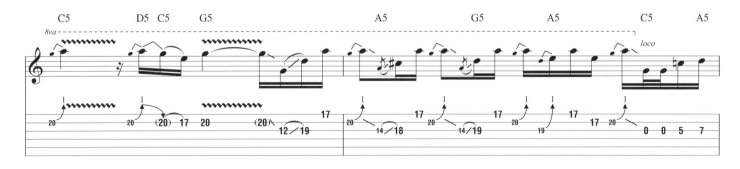

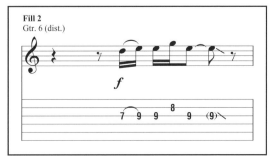

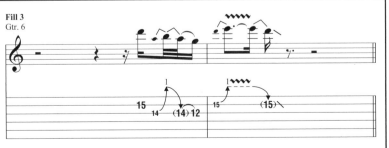

Interlude

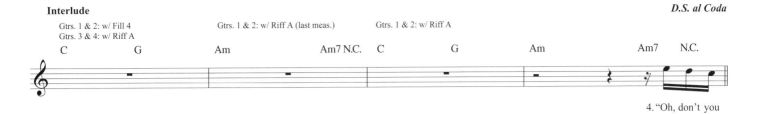

4. "Oh, don't you

And, ba - by, be a sim - ple, _____ be a sim - ple man. __

Begin fade   *Fade out*

Or be _ some - thin' __ you love and un - der - stand. ____ Ba - by, be a

from Rush - *Permanent Waves*

Spirit of Radio

Words and Music by Geddy Lee, Alex Lifeson and Neil Peart

Intro
Moderately fast ♩ = 136

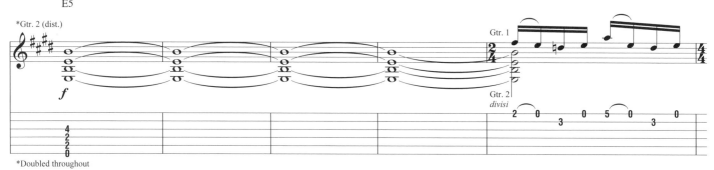

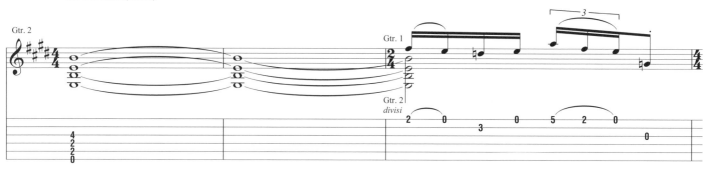

Faster ♩ = 183

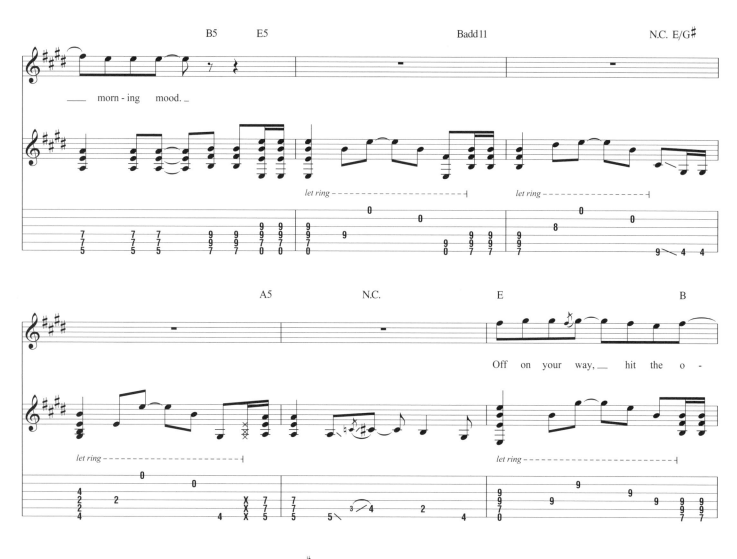

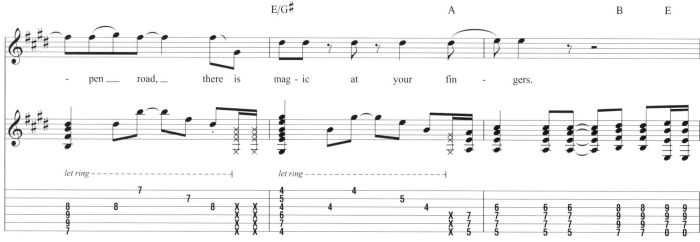

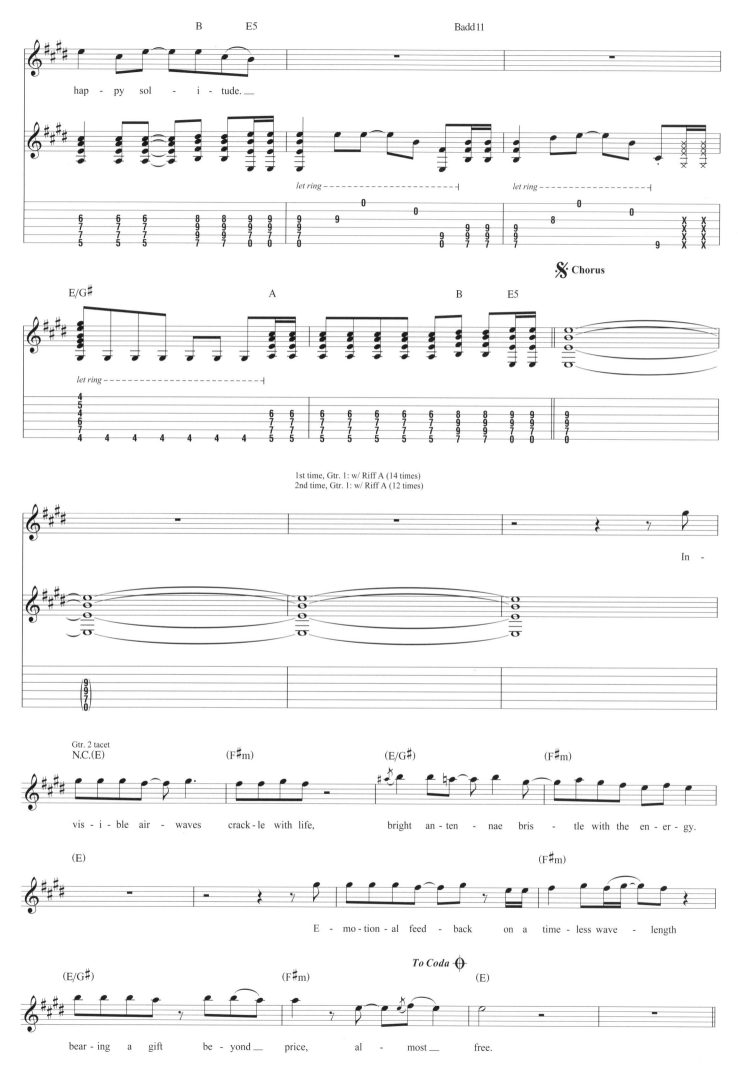

Verse

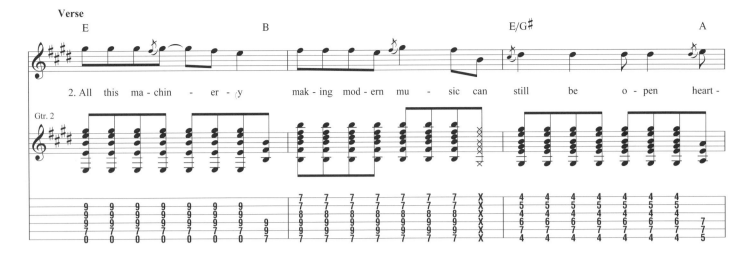

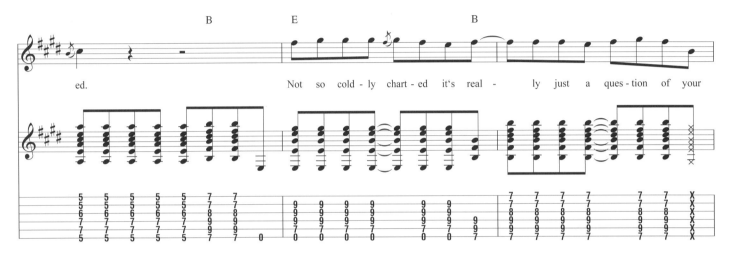

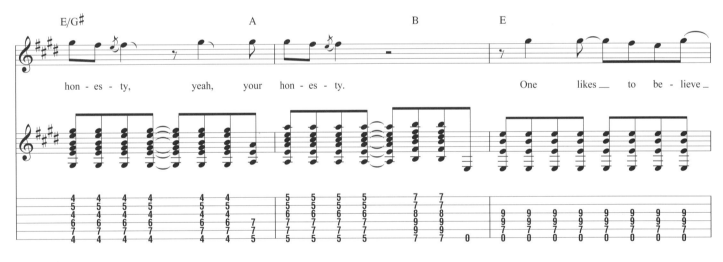

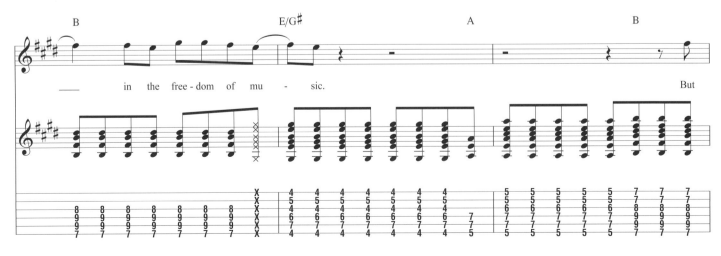

glit - ter - ing priz - es and end - less com - pro - mis - es shat - ter the il - lu - sion of in -

teg - ri - ty, ___ yeah.

D.S. al Coda

Coda
Interlude

free.

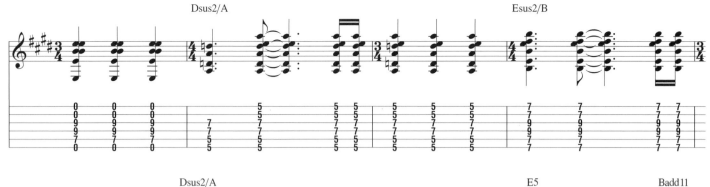

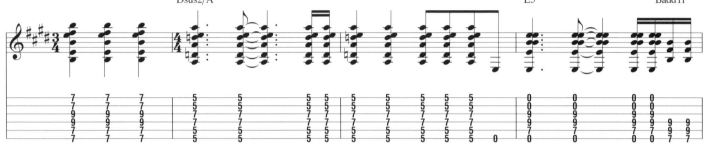

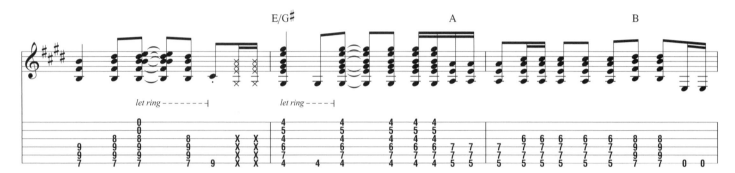

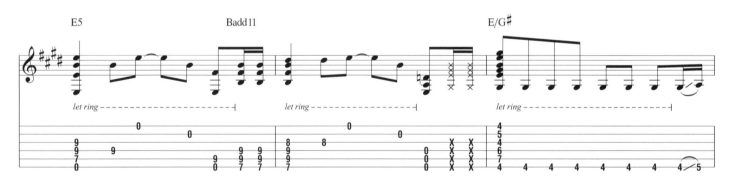

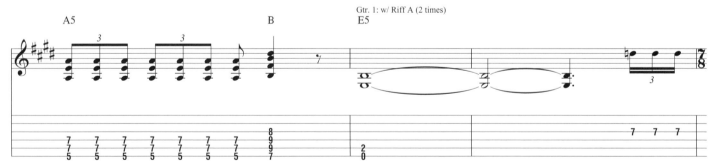

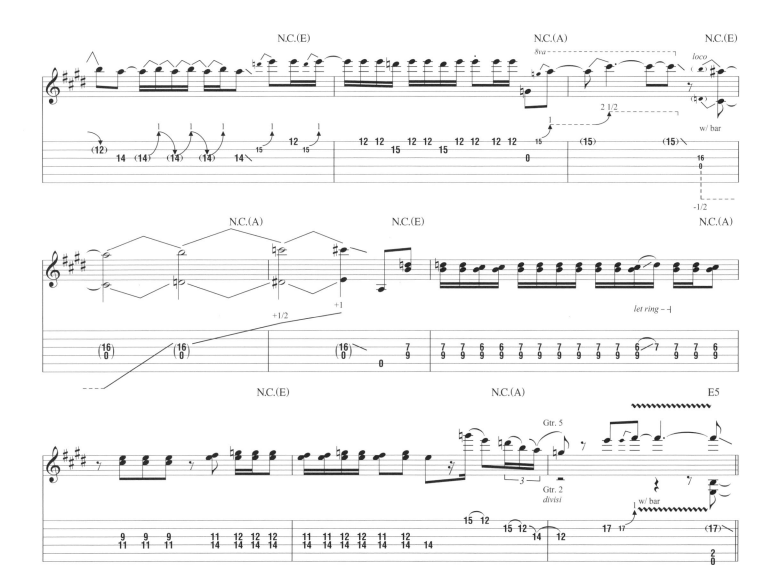

Outro

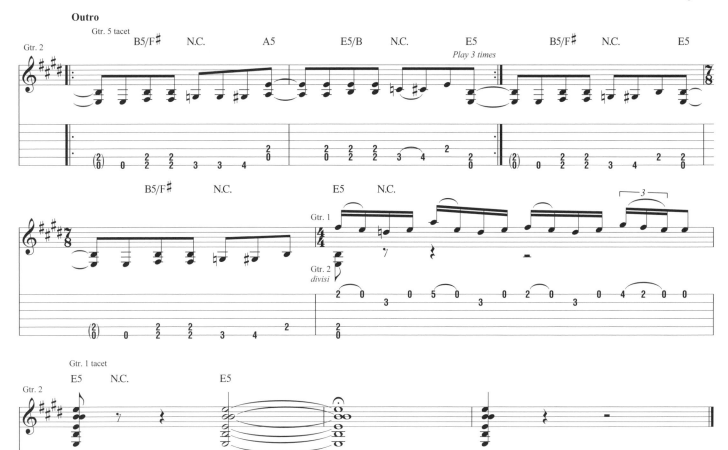

Sultans of Swing

Words and Music by Mark Knopfler

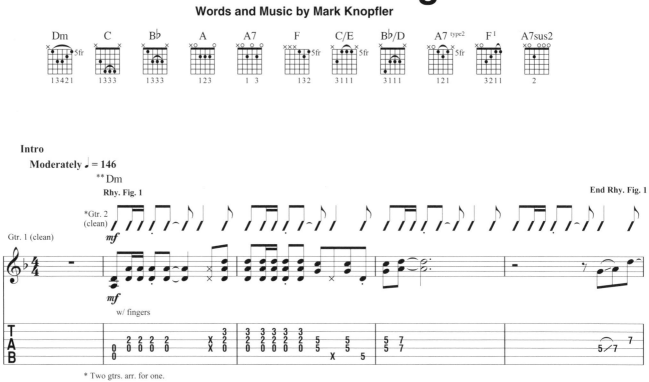

Intro

Moderately ♩ = 146

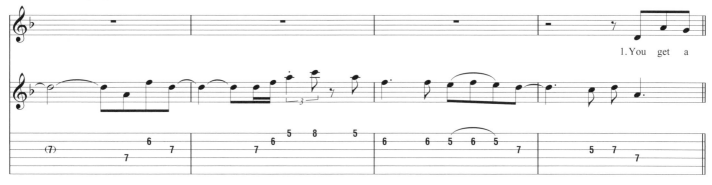

* Two gtrs. arr. for one.

** See top of page for chord diagrams pertaining to rhythm slashes.

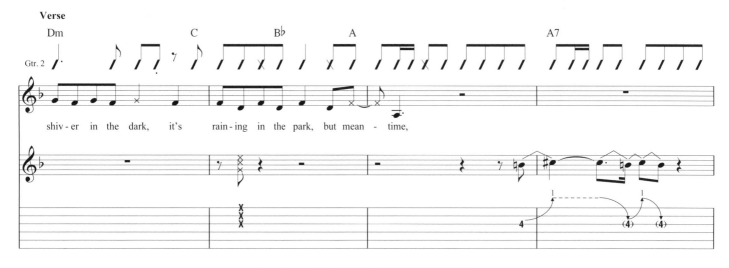

south of the riv-er you stop, and you hold ____ ev-'ry-thing.

A band is blow-ing Dix - ie dou-ble four ___ time,

you feel al - right when you hear the mu-sic ___ ring.

let ring -------------------

(cont. in notation)

(cont. in slash)

Verse

2. Well, now you step in - side, __ but you don't see too man - y fac-

-es, coming in out of the rain __

they hear the jazz __ go down.

Com - pe - ti - tion in oth - er plac - es, _____

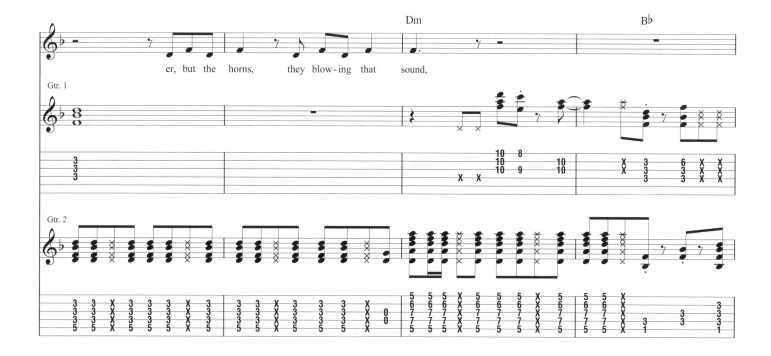

er, but the horns, they blow - ing that sound,

Gtr. 1

Gtr. 2

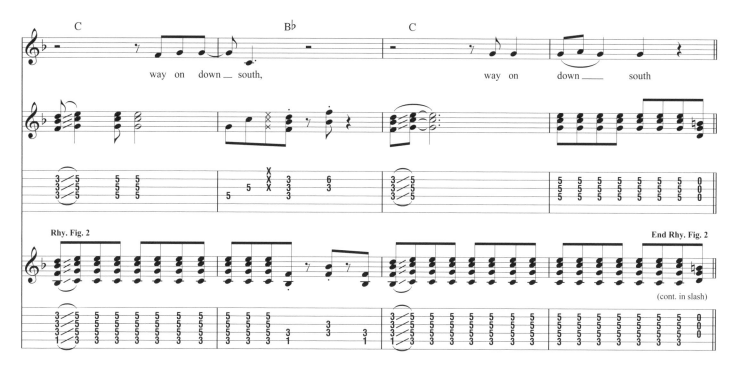

way on down __ south, _____ way on down ____ south

Rhy. Fig. 2

End Rhy. Fig. 2

(cont. in slash)

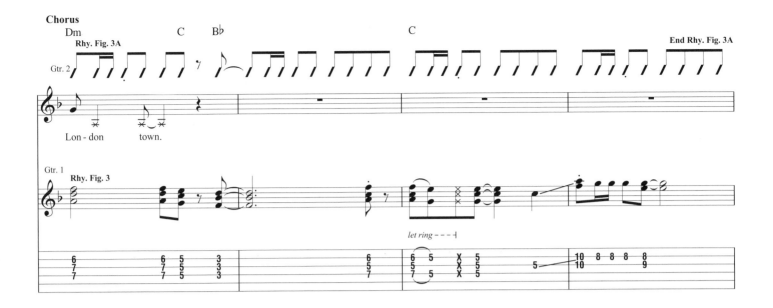

London town.

3. You check out Gui-tar George,

he knows all the chords, ____

mind, he's strict-ly rhy-thm, he

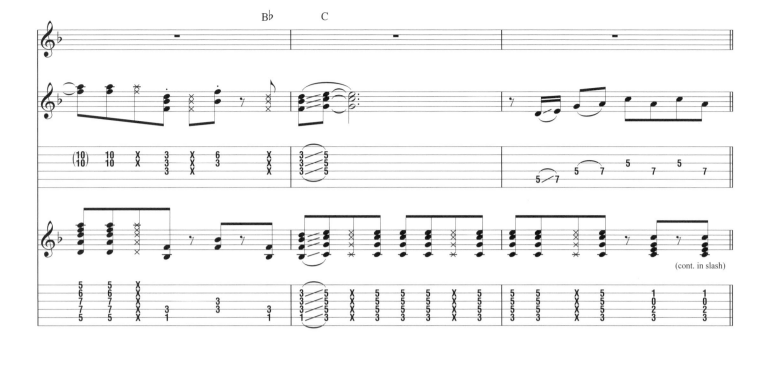

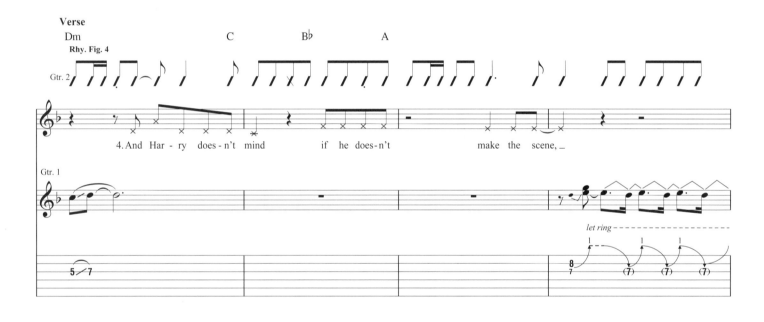

Verse

4. And Har-ry does-n't mind if he does-n't make the scene, _

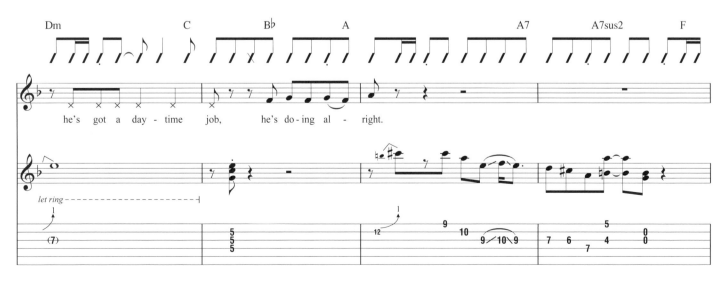

he's got a day-time job, he's do-ing al - right.

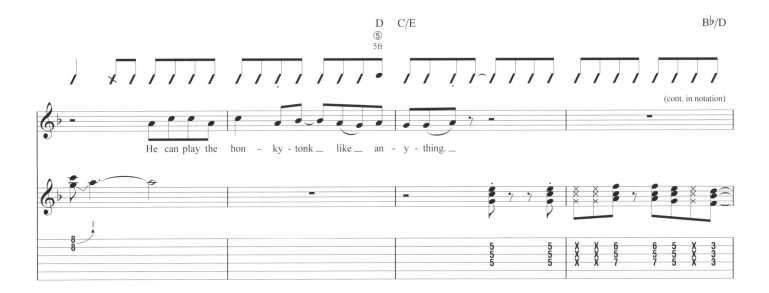

He can play the hon - ky - tonk __ like __ an - y - thing. __

(cont. in notation)

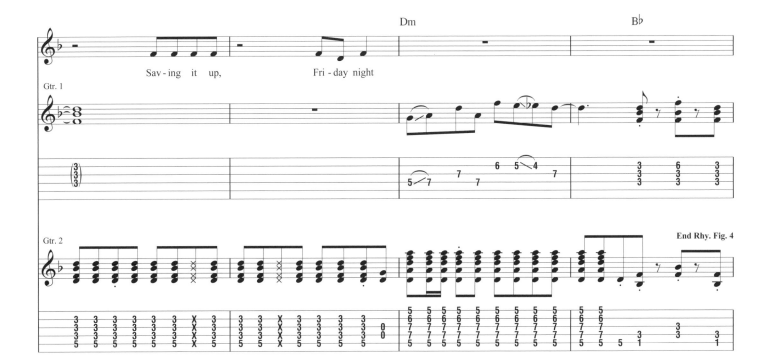

Sav - ing it up,   Fri - day night

Gtr. 1

Gtr. 2

End Rhy. Fig. 4

Gtr. 2: w/ Rhy. Fig. 2

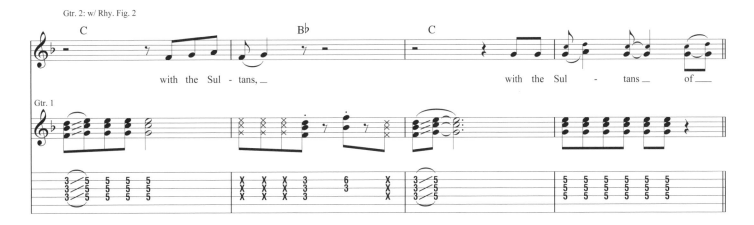

with the Sul - tans, __   with the Sul - tans __ of __

Gtr. 1

Chorus

Gtr. 1: w/ Rhy. Fig. 3
Gtr. 2: w/ Rhy. Fig. 3A, 2 times

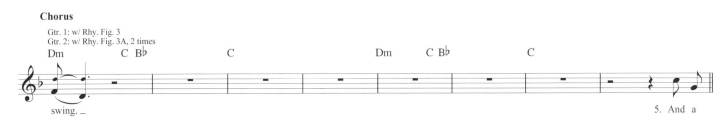

Dm   C Bb   C   Dm   C Bb   C

swing. __

5. And a

Verse

crowd of young boys, __ they're fool-ing a -round __ in the cor - ner,

drunk and dressed in their best brown bag - gies, and __ their plat - form __ soles.

They don't give a damn a - bout an - y trum-pet play-ing band, __

it ain't what they call rock and roll. __

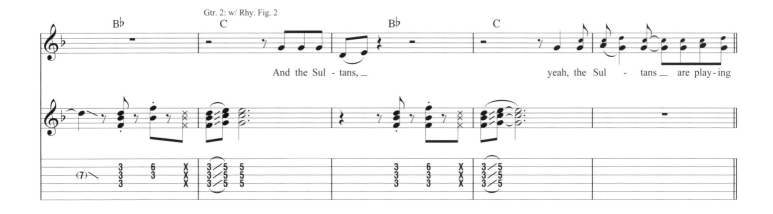

And the Sul - tans, __ yeah, the Sul - tans __ are play-ing

Chorus

Gtr. 1: w/ Rhy. Fig. 3
Gtr. 2: w/ Rhy. Fig. 3A (2 times)

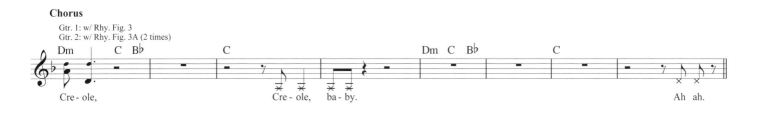

Cre - ole, Cre - ole, ba - by. Ah ah.

Guitar Solo

Gtr. 2: w/ Rhy. Fig. 4

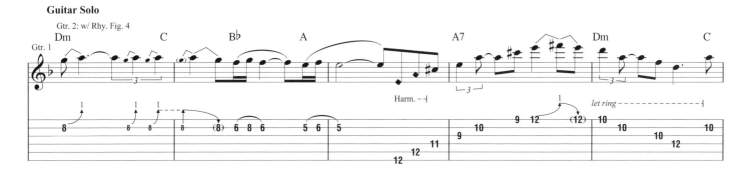

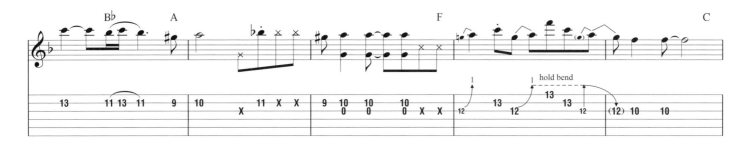

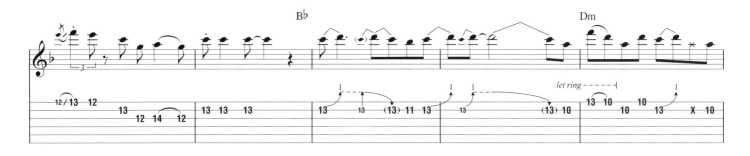

Gtr. 2: w/ Rhy. Fig. 2

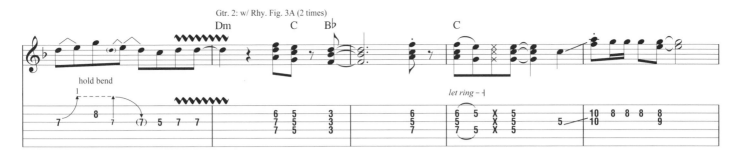

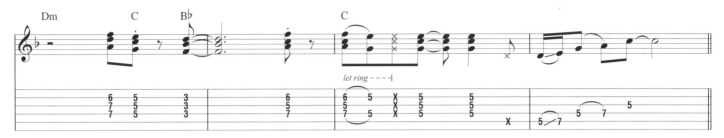

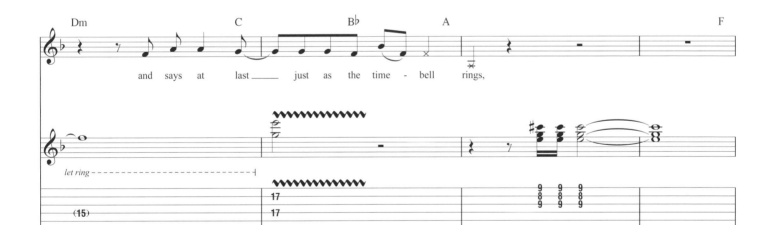

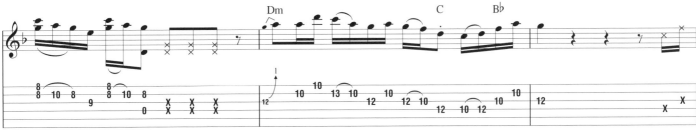

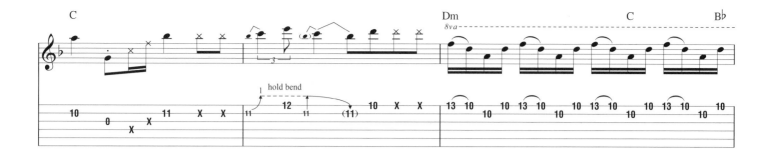

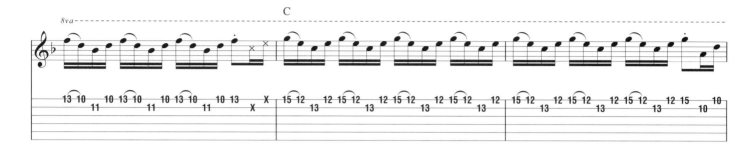

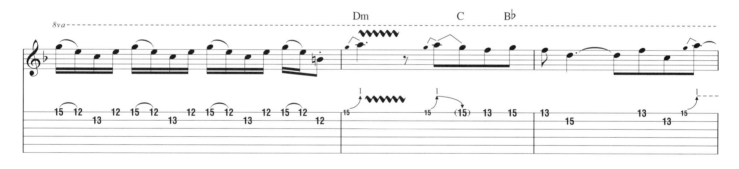

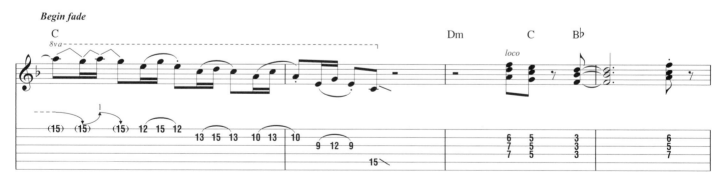

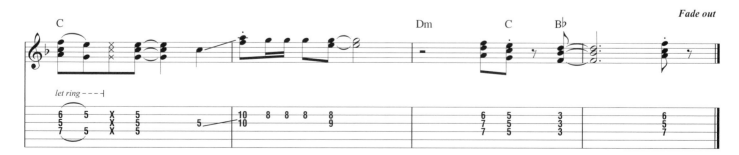

from U2 - *War*

Sunday Bloody Sunday

Words and Music by U2

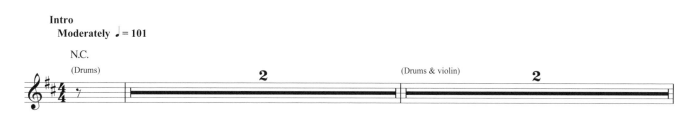

Tune down 1/2 step:
(low to high) E♭-A♭-D♭-G♭-B♭-E♭

Intro
Moderately ♩ = 101

Yeah. ___

Hm, _____ hm. ____

Riff A
Gtr. 1 (elec.)

End Riff A

mf

w/ clean tone

let ring - - - - - - - - - - - - - - - -

Riff A1
Gtr. 2 (acous.)

End Riff A1

mf

let ring - - - - - - - - - - - - - - - -

*Chord symbols reflect implied harmony.

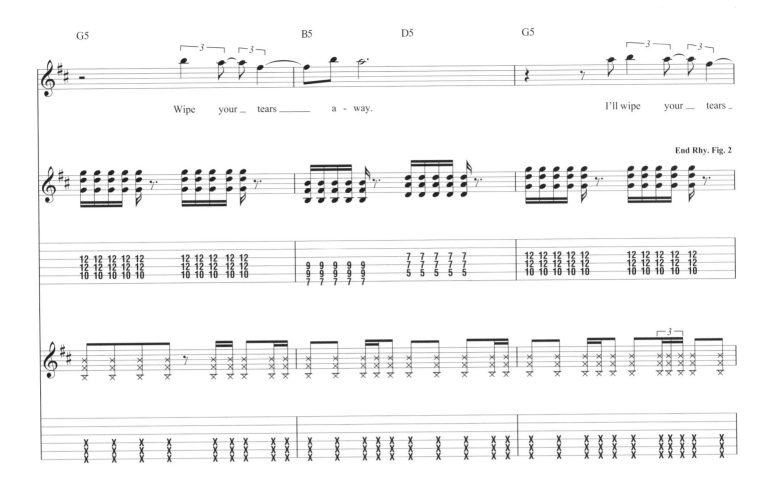

Wipe your tears ___ a - way. I'll wipe your ___ tears ___

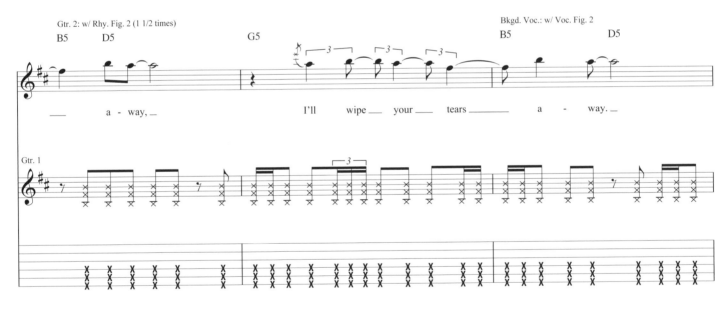

Gtr. 2: w/ Rhy. Fig. 2 (1 1/2 times)

Bkgd. Voc.: w/ Voc. Fig. 2

___ a - way, ___ I'll wipe ___ your ___ tears ___ a - way. ___

Gtr. 1

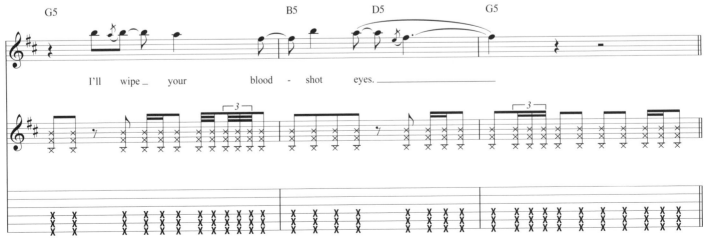

I'll wipe ___ your blood - shot eyes. ___

GUITAR NOTATION LEGEND

Guitar music can be notated three different ways: on a *musical staff*, in *tablature*, and in *rhythm slashes*.

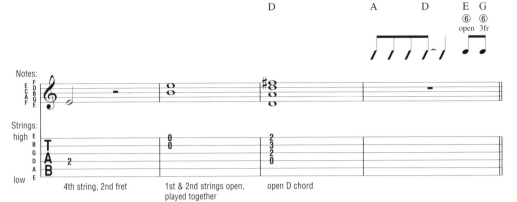

RHYTHM SLASHES are written above the staff. Strum chords in the rhythm indicated. Use the chord diagrams found at the top of the first page of the transcription for the appropriate chord voicings. Round noteheads indicate single notes.

THE MUSICAL STAFF shows pitches and rhythms and is divided by bar lines into measures. Pitches are named after the first seven letters of the alphabet.

TABLATURE graphically represents the guitar fingerboard. Each horizontal line represents a string, and each number represents a fret.

4th string, 2nd fret   1st & 2nd strings open, played together   open D chord

---

HALF-STEP BEND: Strike the note and bend up 1/2 step.

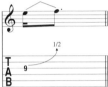

WHOLE-STEP BEND: Strike the note and bend up one step.

GRACE NOTE BEND: Strike the note and immediately bend up as indicated.

SLIGHT (MICROTONE) BEND: Strike the note and bend up 1/4 step.

BEND AND RELEASE: Strike the note and bend up as indicated, then release back to the original note. Only the first note is struck.

PRE-BEND: Bend the note as indicated, then strike it.

VIBRATO: The string is vibrated by rapidly bending and releasing the note with the fretting hand.

WIDE VIBRATO: The pitch is varied to a greater degree by vibrating with the fretting hand.

HAMMER-ON: Strike the first (lower) note with one finger, then sound the higher note (on the same string) with another finger by fretting it without picking.

PULL-OFF: Place both fingers on the notes to be sounded. Strike the first note and without picking, pull the finger off to sound the second (lower) note.

LEGATO SLIDE: Strike the first note and then slide the same fret-hand finger up or down to the second note. The second note is not struck.

SHIFT SLIDE: Same as legato slide, except the second note is struck.

TRILL: Very rapidly alternate between the notes indicated by continuously hammering on and pulling off.

TAPPING: Hammer ("tap") the fret indicated with the pick-hand index or middle finger and pull off to the note fretted by the fret hand.

NATURAL HARMONIC: Strike the note while the fret-hand lightly touches the string directly over the fret indicated.

PINCH HARMONIC: The note is fretted normally and a harmonic is produced by adding the edge of the thumb or the tip of the index finger of the pick hand to the normal pick attack.

PICK SCRAPE: The edge of the pick is rubbed down (or up) the string, producing a scratchy sound.

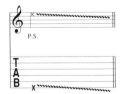

MUFFLED STRINGS: A percussive sound is produced by laying the fret hand across the string(s) without depressing, and striking them with the pick hand.

PALM MUTING: The note is partially muted by the pick hand lightly touching the string(s) just before the bridge.

RAKE: Drag the pick across the strings indicated with a single motion.

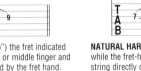

TREMOLO PICKING: The note is picked as rapidly and continuously as possible.

VIBRATO BAR DIVE AND RETURN: The pitch of the note or chord is dropped a specified number of steps (in rhythm), then returned to the original pitch.

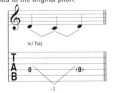

VIBRATO BAR SCOOP: Depress the bar just before striking the note, then quickly release the bar.

VIBRATO BAR DIP: Strike the note and then immediately drop a specified number of steps, then release back to the original pitch.